About th

CW01508625

Toby Howden grew up in Totnes in Devon and has been practising traditional martial arts since he was young. He spent several years working and studying in both Japan and China and holds a BA in Chinese and Religious Studies. He currently lives in Bath with his partner and three children. Instead of teaching self-defence to Special Forces and intelligence agencies, he works in a school. *Paper Tigers* is his first book.

PAPER TIGERS

PAPER TIGERS

TOBY HOWDEN

This edition first published in 2017

Unbound

6th Floor Mutual House, 70 Conduit Street, London W1S 2GF

www.unbound.com

ISBN (eBook): 978-1911586371
ISBN (Paperback): 978-1911586074

Design by Mecob

Cover image:
© Shutterstock.com

Printed by Clays Ltd, St Ives plc

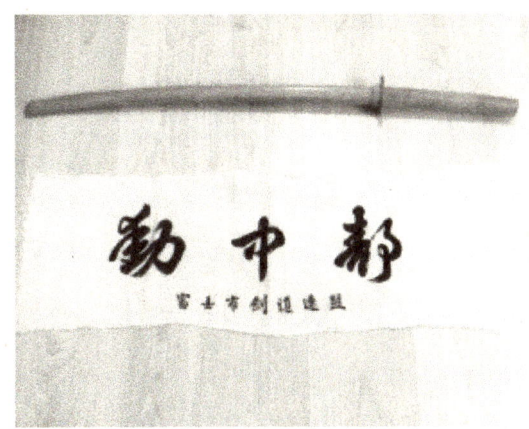

静 中 動
富士市剣道連盟

For all the Yoshiwara kendo teachers,
particularly Bryan Endacott (1974–2015)

Dear Reader,

The book you are holding came about in a rather different way to most others. It was funded directly by readers through a new website: Unbound.

Unbound is the creation of three writers. We started the company because we believed there had to be a better deal for both writers and readers. On the Unbound website, authors share the ideas for the books they want to write directly with readers. If enough of you support the book by pledging for it in advance, we produce a beautifully bound special subscribers' edition and distribute a regular edition and e-book wherever books are sold, in shops and online.

This new way of publishing is actually a very old idea (Samuel Johnson funded his dictionary this way). We're just using the internet to build each writer a network of patrons. Here, at the back of this book, you'll find the names of all the people who made it happen.

Publishing in this way means readers are no longer just passive consumers of the books they buy, and authors are free to write the books they really want. They get a much fairer return too – half the profits their books generate, rather than a tiny percentage of the cover price.

If you're not yet a subscriber, we hope that you'll want to join our publishing revolution and have your name listed in one of our books in the future. To get you started, here is a £5 discount on your first pledge. Just visit unbound.com, make your pledge and type KENDO17 in the promo code box when you check out.

Thank you for your support,

Dan, Justin and John
Founders, Unbound

Super Patrons

James & Kirsteen Atkinson Annear
Brian Balsdon
Bethany Blackmore
Nic Bouchard
Anthony Bristow
Daniel Brown
Marcus Butcher
Rita Chakraborty
Jo Cook
Sarah Dillingham
Fiona Duncan
Matt "Beard" Edwards
Hannah Ely
Andrew Endacott
Charlie Endacott
Rollen Flood
Jim & Jenny Furness
Robert Furness
Sue Furness
Oliver Gage
Jane Gower
Rachel Greene
Ed, Vie & Samuel Griffiths
Pat Hatchett
John & Helen Hatfield
Katrina & John Howden
Damian Howden
Dominic & Caroline Howden
Madeleine Howden
Will & Lottie Howden
Marcus Kielly
Dan Kieran
Tonia King
David Kiy
Diana Knight

Miranda Lovelock
Ric McDermott
Mike Mckeever
Andrew Miller
John Mitchinson
Brian Moss
Case Study Ninja
Duncan Noack-Cox
Liz Noel-Avis
Ed Norman
David Northmore
Tally Oliver
Katie Palmer
Sophia Pandit
Justin Pollard
Molly Povey
Sara Quiggin
Sandra Ryan
Kazue Shinoda
Dan Stevens
David Stewart
Jasper Sutcliffe
Maia Sutherland
Martin Wheeler
Lucas Whittaker

With grateful thanks to Sarah Dillingham who helped make this book happen.

Contents

	Prologue	xvii
1.	Slow Train to Yoshiwara	1
2.	The Old Ninja House	9
3.	Kendo by Candlelight	17
4.	A Factory of Dreams	25
5.	The Class	35
6.	*Senpai–Kohai*	43
7.	The New Boy	49
8.	The Heavy Sword	59
9.	Mount Odana	65
10.	Paper Tiger	73
11.	Doctors, Cockroaches and Temples	79
12.	The Dance of the Migrant Worker	89
13.	Runaway Holiday	97
14.	A Kicking in Kyoto	107
15.	The Night Train	117
16.	Buy Low, Sell High	125
17.	A Bowl of Ramen	133
18.	DJ Ladies Love and Blighty Four	141
19.	Merry *Christmasu*... Now Get Back to Work!	151
20.	Riding the Rollercoaster of Doom	159
21.	Kendo Dinner	173
22.	One Strike – One Kill	183
23.	All My Life's a Circle	191
24.	Fuji San	199
	Epilogue	209
	Author's Note	211
	Patrons	213

Prologue

On a freezing, wet January night, I sheltered beneath the neon lights of the Prince Charles Cinema in central London, just off Leicester Square, queuing up to see Jackie Chan's classic kung-fu movie *Drunken Master*.[1] The exotic secrets of Asian combat were still only accessible in the UK through two channels: by meeting an authentic living master or watching hilarious slapstick Hong Kong action flicks. Carefully, I counted my notes. The ticket would clean me out, but this was no mere film – this was research for my trip of a lifetime. While my friends were graduating from university, concentrating on their careers and relationships, or relaxing down the pub, I was attempting to turn myself into a deadly weapon at my local kung-fu class. I had never been career-driven – a belief conveniently reinforced by recreational drugs, raving and an almost total lack of qualifications. (My GCSE in Media Studies had so far failed to deliver any tangible rewards.) Instead, I devoured any books I could find on the fighting arts, while obsessing about the spiritual practices of long-dead scholar-warrior monks. I'd even taught myself how to count to 10 in Chinese. But although I respected my instructors, I craved a more authentic experience. Like many others before me, I assured myself that one day, when I was ready, I'd head East, return to the source, and find a genuine master to train with. Now my time had come. Watching a late-night showing of *Drunken Master* was all part of the plan.

The queue for the film was comprised of young, tense-looking guys like me, sporting headphones and hoodies, casually pretending not to be sizing each other up. We represented a small but dedicated subculture – Western martial-arts disciples, united by a love of Eastern philosophy and a yearning to relocate to a mist-shrouded mountain in the Middle Ages. But in marked contrast to the legendary masters of antiquity, we tended to be found hanging around the peripheries of house parties, failing to impress girls with phrases like, 'Of course in a street situation…' or dishing out unsolicited pseudo-medical advice to people with colds, such as, 'It's probably a deficiency of chi in your kidneys', all the while casually urging friends to grab our wrists and try to push us over. It's not that we were particularly obsessed with violence. Rather, it was the allure

---

1. *Drunken Master* (1978), Yuen Woo Ping, Seasonal Film Corporation.

of learning something special, mystical even – the possibility of self-mastery (which just happened to include the awesome ability to kick people's heads in).

The film was jaw-dropping, with Jackie Chan's physical dexterity smashing the boundaries of health and safety; the dubbing was, as ever, hilarious. It occurred to me that only a *real* man would have the balls to call himself 'Jackie'.

Once the rain had passed I ambled home through the streets of Chinatown. The sickly aroma of crispy roast duck hung in the night air. Red lanterns cast opium shadows across doorways. Rubbish and cardboard boxes littered adjacent alleyways. Pockets of late-night revellers swaying arm in arm drifted towards the Tube stations. Up ahead, a loud shout from some drunken lads barking challenges abruptly shocked me from my daydreams of imaginary scenarios in which I watched for invisible enemies. Instinctively, I crossed the road. Whatever their problem was, it was best not to get involved. Walk away: the first rule of martial arts. I clenched my fists and looked back over my shoulder. If they came at me, they were going to meet their maker.

Deep down though, I didn't really believe it anymore. Despite my years of training, the only conflict I was comfortable dealing with was still in my mind. Learning martial arts had enabled me to blissfully side-step the uncomfortable truth: that I was, essentially, a fairly timid person drifting between casual jobs who knew a hundred ways to put someone on the floor, but still hated confrontation. I needed something different, a new challenge, something authentic that could turn me into a real badass.

Bryan, one of my oldest friends and a fellow martial-arts obsessive, had met Suzuki Sensei[2] while hitchhiking across Japan. Although from radically different cultures, they shared a sense of humour and had become great, albeit highly unlikely, friends. Bryan always loved a challenge, and after Suzuki-san ('Mr Suzuki') introduced him to the joys of full-contact sword fighting, Bryan had taught himself Japanese and found a job in a traditional paper factory in order to study with him. In return, Bryan had promised to show his teacher the 'real' England. So, in the glorious summer of 1998, I found myself touring the country for a few weeks with my old school friend and a rather eccentric Japanese sword master in tow.

Suzuki-san came from a small town called Yoshiwara in the foothills of Mount Fuji, about a hundred miles outside Tokyo. Now in his mid-fifties, he

2. 'Sensei', meaning literally someone who has gone before another; it is generally used to mean 'teacher' or 'master'.

had a thin pencil moustache, and was going slightly grey, though he was deceptively fit. Although he worked long hours as a factory supervisor, he'd dedicated most of his spare time to kendo – the way of the sword. He held a seventh *dan* grade and passionately lived for teaching this art. Despite his role as an upstanding family man and pillar of the community, he was shockingly irreverent, very easy-going and loved nothing better than breaking out the *sake* – a proper drunken master! Weirdly, communicating wasn't a big problem. Of course, Bryan translated a lot, but Suzuki-san easily connected with people and exuded a rare energy and enthusiasm. He was quite unlike anyone I'd ever met before. His way of life stemmed directly from kendo, a discipline I knew nothing about and dismissively assumed to be an aggressive modern sport in which people in Darth Vader-like masks shouted a lot and whacked each other on the head with bamboo swords. Bryan proudly declared that this was pretty much an accurate view; however, Suzuki-san came from a very traditional *dojo* (martial-arts school) and it was clear to me that his art was much more than that. With Bryan translating, Suzuki-san told us that 'Kendo is a way of life, and that it is life itself that is the real challenge. The way of the sword is for defeating your personal demons, not for fighting other people.'

Yeah, I thought. But I bet it helps.

One evening, on the well-manicured lawn of a crumbling Devon castle, I watched open-mouthed as Suzuki-san demonstrated his skill with a sword. He was lightning fast and exuded martial power. His kendo style was old-school Japanese *bushido* (the way of the warrior), very different from modern sporting martial arts. This was pure, aggressive survival, full speed – do or die.

'Toby-san,' he warned me, 'kendo *kibishi*, Japan *kibishi*.' (Basically meaning, 'It's bloody difficult training over there.') I nodded seriously till he eventually declared with tongue-in-cheek concentration: 'Toby-san... *this* is a pen' – which, along with the words 'lucky' and 'ouchy' represented the extent of his English vocabulary (and pretty much encapsulated his philosophy in life). Suzuki-san sparred with Bryan wearing the body armour they'd brought with them, striking with controlled precision to show the vital points, dominating the ground and effortlessly taking him to the floor. It was a revelation. I felt as though everything I'd studied before was play-fighting. This wasn't like the long, drawn-out rehearsals I was used to ('If someone attacks you like this, you can grab them like that,' etc.). Suzuki-san's kendo was different. There weren't any 'what-ifs?' or 'buts'. This was the real deal – exactly what I'd been longing for, pure and simple: you think you can take me with a sword? Prove it.

Later, as we watched swallows expertly flitting across a deep-red sunset, my head swam with excitement in an early fog of wine and cigarettes. Suzuki-san talked about life and how lucky we were to be here. It seemed that, despite the cultural divide, he recognised a great deal of common ground; Britain and Japan were both islands with long and complex histories. Japan had its emperors and samurai[3] traditions, we had our royalty and knights in armour; they had martial arts, we had sport. Life was difficult, but we all had to persevere and, if we were lucky, we'd always find the time to get totally hammered with friends. It was a simple approach to life, but somehow profound.

He encouraged me to visit Japan and offered to teach me. He even had an old house we could stay in. In addition, Bryan seemed to think he could swing me a job in the paper factory. Well... what could be better? To have a real-life hard-drinking, sword-fighting, humorous version of Mr Miyagi (the wise old master from *The Karate Kid* films) turn up on your doorstep is surely every young man's dream? You definitely didn't get opportunities like that every day, and having already grown up on a diet of ninja films and kung-fu classes and lacking any other direction in life, I was fully primed for an oriental adventure.

*

3. 'Samurai' – the warrior nobility of ancient Japan.

There are no foreign lands. It is the traveller only who is foreign.

Robert Louis Stevenson

1

Slow Train to Yoshiwara

In sharp contrast to Suzuki-san's unshakable and easy-going confidence, I was prone to paralysing apprehension and disorganisation. I'd arrived in Tokyo's Narita Airport in the usual chaos – exhausted and almost penniless. Streams of happy, immaculately dressed Japanese tourists filed past me as I queued for immigration control. Suzuki-san had loaned me bamboo swords and body armour in the UK, and I was growing increasingly self-conscious about them as they disrespectfully protruded from my bags. I was also trying to tune in to some of the conversations around me, which, with their unfamiliar sounds, may as well have been birdsong. Mirroring the linguistic achievements of Suzuki-san, the extent of my Japanese vocabulary was, '*Kore wa pen desu*' ('This is a pen'). But much to my disappointment, as far as I could tell, no one appeared to be discussing pens.

An official motioned me forward.

'Reason for visit?' he said, studying my passport.

'Holiday,' I said quickly. 'And kendo… A kendo holiday.'

'How long do you intend on staying?'

'Oh, not long.'

He looked me up and down and then slowly slid a sword from my luggage, giving it an experimental swish in the air.

'Kendo *shinai*? *You*… study kendo?' he asked in disbelief, eyeing my out-of-shape physique.

'Yeah, totally,' I lied. 'Do you… study?'

'No, no,' interrupted another official. 'We judo,' he said, tapping his chest proudly. 'He second *dan*.'

'Oh great,' I said, grinning like a moron. For me, as a martial-arts enthusiast, this exchange seemed wonderfully fortuitous, but in reality all Japanese police and customs officers are required to hold a dan grade in kendo, judo or aikido. In fact, in Japan, it's probably like belonging to your local football or rugby club, rather than meaning you're some kind of double-hard ninja assassin. I resisted the urge to ask for a demonstration.

'Kendo very hard. Please enjoy your stay,' said the official, waving me through.

'... Thank you,' I blurted out, and gave them both the most outrageously low bow, which only a newly arrived Westerner is capable of. Their expressions remained totally impassive and, no doubt having seen it a hundred times before, they simply turned to examine the next disorientated foreigner. I gathered my stuff and walked resolutely towards the glittering daylight of the Arrivals lounge, intoning a solemn '*Kore wa pen desu*' to myself. Holy shit, I thought in disbelief. I'm actually in Japan.

Bryan picked me up at the airport with his petite girlfriend Kazue (pronounced Ka-zoo-eh). As we drove the 60 or so miles along the motorway into Tokyo, the sun-baked scenery flashed past. Bryan swigged from the bottle of angry-tramp-strength cider I'd brought with me, while Kazue, wearing a look of prac-tised determination, manoeuvred through the heavy traffic. Alongside the hard shoulder lay scattered houses and industrial units. Small, overgrown paddy fields were swiftly replaced with a solid wall of unhindered urbanisation sprawling in every direction: huge blocks of flats, shining metallic offices, colourful bill-boards and the steady throb of hot, crowded city life. It was early summer and the heat and humidity were intense.

Bryan looked leaner and stronger than I remembered him during his trip to the UK with Suzuki-san the previous summer. He was sunburnt, and had a bandana wrapped tightly around his head.

'This is the first weekend I've had free in months,' he announced. 'Been working my ass off in the factory and training in my spare time. It's the only way to relax over here... You're going to love it.' He laughed ominously, in a way that suggested I really wasn't going to love it. 'What do you fancy doing tonight?' he said, forcing the cider on me. I took a hesitant sip.

'Sleeping?'

'Sleeping? Sleep tomorrow. You're in Japan now. Right, that's settled. Let's hit the nearest bar.'

I caught Kazue's gaze in the mirror as an almost imperceptible ripple of eye rolling flickered across her face. She'd obviously got to know him fairly well already.

'Okay. Why not?' I said. I hadn't slept for nearly 30 hours and was starting to lose the plot. In contrast, Bryan continued swigging at the cider while tes-tifying to a now stoical-looking Kazue (who, I later discovered, didn't drink) about the unparalleled virtues of British alcohol. He put on some music and whacked the volume up. The pounding bass made the windows rattle. Kazue grimaced.

As Bryan and Kazue launched into a thunderous domestic, I suppressed a hysterical laugh. It was surreal watching my old friend and his partner bickering in Japanese, looking for all the world like a couple who had been married for 50 years. Bryan had always been fiercely independent; everything he ever did was on his terms. He'd been the first of my friends to leave home, get a ridiculous haircut, move to London and land a job DJing. He'd been fired for playing records backwards and, rather than do anything 'normal', he'd moved to Japan, learnt the language, found a job and become a ninja, just like that – bloody typical. I wondered how long he'd known Kazue (he'd never mentioned her), but it was obvious she could handle him and wasn't taking any shit. Eventually, Bryan reluctantly agreed to turn the music down to 'loud' and I resumed falling down my dark tunnel.

Tokyo was bright, vibrant and incredibly exciting. We turned off a giant motorway flyover, rushing through a maze of packed streets and colourful shops. I marvelled at how effortlessly Kazue navigated her way around (at least, I assumed she knew where she was going).

I was aware that I was running out of steam. Things were getting hazy. It was too much – partying would have to wait.

'Er, guys,' I said. 'Sorry to be a killjoy, but if I don't go to sleep soon, I'm actually going to die.' They stared at me for a few seconds, mulling over the potential inconvenience.

'Okay, okay... Chill out, no worries,' said Bryan. 'We'll get the train back to Yoshiwara where Suzuki-san lives and Kazue will head home and catch up with us in a few days. Sure you don't want to go clubbing?'

I shook my weary head. We drove on for a few more minutes, then entered the biggest intersection I'd ever seen. Huge video screens towered above us, streaming a hypnotic fog of advertising. Abruptly, Kazue pulled up on the kerb.

'I drop here – okay, Bryan?' she said through clenched teeth. It wasn't a question. Bryan leapt out into the seething crowds and began haphazardly hurling bags into a pile on the pavement. The outside heat and noise flooded in, cancelling out the air conditioning.

Kazue turned and smiled at me sweetly. 'This is Shinjuku,' she said, stiffly gesturing like a tour guide from the 1950s. 'You can get train to Suzuki-san's from here.'

I clambered out of the car, awestruck by the vibrating mass of heat, light, sound and movement. Even I'd heard of Shinjuku – one of the busiest crossings and train stations in the world and the inspiration for *Blade Runner*. As Kazue pulled away into the mass of dense traffic, I felt as if I'd been dropped off by my mum on the first day of school.

A vast tide of pedestrian life flowed around us. Smoking and sweating on the searing pavement, we discussed our options as thousands of legs flashed by in a strobing blur. People politely wove their way around us, the occasional one glancing down and doing a slight double take. With Bryan's bandana and my swords, we probably resembled a couple of insane shipwrecked pirates. But looking different felt kind of liberating. We seemed to be the only Westerners in an unending sea of Japanese commuters, and would have stood out regardless.

It was dusk by the time we finally stopped watching the crowds and got it together sufficiently to descend into the depths of Shinjuku Station. Bryan led the way through a bewildering maze of tunnels, turnstiles and subterranean shops. We bought tickets from a friendly talking vending machine and stopped outside a noodle bar. It was covered in blue flags inscribed with striking white calligraphy. Faded photographs of scary-looking meat delicacies were stuck to the windows. Inside, a few businessmen were slurping noodles and tapping away at laptops propped up a bar.

While Bryan staggered inside to order some food, I studied the unending flow of people – salarymen in smart, black identikit suits, shoppers, school kids, housewives, trendies and traditionalists. The Japanese, for their part, mercifully appeared to pay foreigners very little attention, or if they did have a peek, it seemed to take the form of a subtle sideways glance, rather than outright staring. Just as I was congratulating myself on being such an observant little amateur sociologist, I felt a sharp tap on my shoulder. A tiny old lady carrying a small bamboo cane and wearing a rather beautiful traditional kimono was standing behind me. She gazed down at the bamboo swords protruding from my bags and muttered something I couldn't understand (although I was pretty sure it was nothing to do with pens), then glided indignantly, yet gracefully away. I tried to look apologetic.

'Sorry,' I called after her in English. She reminded me of my grandma in Yorkshire, who, upon hearing that I was off to Japan, had given me a long lecture about the terrible things the Japanese had done during the Second World War. I was fairly sure she envisaged me being held captive, *Deer Hunter*-style, in a tiny bamboo cage, while being let out occasionally to build a railroad.[1] Still, I couldn't help suspecting that quite a lot of Japanese deeply resented clumsy Westerners like myself turning up and attempting to learn their most hallowed martial secrets. Judging by the old lady's tone, what she'd said was probably something along the lines of, 'How bloody disrespectful sitting on a kendo sword. People like you, blah blah blah grrr.' At least, I hoped it wasn't any worse than that. Of course, I may have got it all wrong and she could simply have been commenting that, 'Never have I seen the force so strong in one so young.'

Five minutes later, Bryan returned with two bowls of half-spilled steaming noodles and disposable wooden chopsticks. As we slurped away and I dropped food all over myself, I explained what had happened and asked if we were doing anything wrong or particularly taboo. He was genuinely surprised and dismissed the whole incident. I was beginning to suspect that he'd been here long enough to be experiencing a sort of allergic reaction to Japanese rules and politeness. On the other hand, despite being a fiery Westerner at heart, he understood and loved the place better than anyone else I knew, and there was little doubt he was devoted to studying kendo. He'd even managed to get his black belt the previous year. When Bryan got into something, he always became immersed to the point of total obsession. He once wrote me a letter stating that, 'If kendo was a pop song it would be number one for ever.' That was his approach to life, and it suited Japanese sword fighting perfectly: whatever you do, do it completely, with no hesitation, no regrets, or don't do it at all. Unless, of course, it involved dealing with authority, girlfriends or angry landlords, in which case, like me, he swiftly drowned in a tsunami of crippling self-doubt and indecision.

After eating, we set off on an especially hot and confusing half-hour mission to locate the correct platform for Yoshiwara[2] in Shizuoka province, where Suzuki-san lived, about 100 miles outside Tokyo. Due to my lack of money, we opted for the tortuously slow commuter train (as opposed to the 'Shinkansen' or superfast Bullet Train). It didn't matter though; it was way past rush hour and the train we jumped aboard was mellow and blissfully quiet. As our empty carriage hypnotically swayed from side to side, a fresh breeze blew in through the open windows. I was relieved, having imagined being rammed into a claustrophobic train by a white-gloved guard. I peered into the darkness as we passed sporadic lights and houses drifting past.

'So, what's the deal with you and Kazue? Are you guys a couple?'

'It's cool. We're just... friends,' he mumbled, looking shy. His erratic,

1. Incidentally, this isn't meant to offend anyone who has actually been held captive in a tiny bamboo cage and forced to build a railroad.
2. Not to be confused with the ancient red-light district of Yoshiwara in Tokyo itself.

manic behaviour belied a sensitive soul. We had a time-honoured routine of manfully ignoring each other's social anxieties and strange personality traits. Growing up in Devon, we'd spent a lot of time partying in my home town of Totnes, a small, picturesque, historic place with the unlikely reputation as the alternative capital of England. Hanging out somewhere where life moved at its own good pace, marijuana was considered part of your five a day and trust-fund hippies mingled with tourists and ruddy-faced farmers made for a confusing education in normality. It was little wonder we'd been drawn to martial arts. Discipline and hard work were a novelty for both of us.

Bryan stared catatonically into the near-empty bottle of cider and half-heartedly puffed away on a cigarette. I guessed it was around eight o'clock at night. We didn't really know what time we'd get to Suzuki-san's, but Bryan confidently declared that the journey would take approximately 'Fucking hours', so I slid down on to the sticky plastic seat, shut my eyes and passed out.

*

It's not good because it's old, it's old because it's good.
Anonymous

2

The Old Ninja House

I woke abruptly as Bryan yanked me from my seat.

'Quick, it's Yoshiwara. Wake up, we're here, we're here.'

We threw our belongings from the carriage, leapt out after them like a pair of deranged parachutists and collapsed in a pile on our bags. Nothing happened for about two minutes, then the doors unhurriedly closed behind us. We lay on the warm Tarmac of the deserted platform and took in our surroundings. Yoshiwara was no more than a very empty station with a small ticket office and a few black characters stencilled over a whitewashed pedestrian bridge. Other than the large insects above us, buzzing around flickering strip lighting, it was eerily quiet and smelled of damp vegetation. Cautiously, I peered down the tracks. The noise and frantic pace of Tokyo seemed like a distant memory. In fact, it was so peaceful we lay back and snoozed for an hour or so.

Eventually, I sat up to take stock.

'Okay… We've successfully made it to the middle of nowhere – what now?' I asked.

Bryan coughed, grimaced and dug out a black flip phone. He squinted at it through one bleary eye. While I gathered our bags, he stood on a bench to try to get a better signal, rattling away in Japanese to Mr Suzuki. I could just make out a few words: 'Blah blah blah, Suzuki-san. Blah blah bah, Toby-san. Hahahaha blah blah blah…'

I would need to learn Japanese if I was going to master kendo, but it all seemed impossibly complicated. I'd briefly tried to give it a go back home with my copy of *Japanese for Busy People*, but somehow I'd never been able to find the time. Previously, me and academia[1] had not got on. After four years of studying French at school I could barely ask how to buy alcohol and fags (actually quite useful, now I think about it), and I could tell that Japanese was going to be a nightmare to learn.

---

1. Or should that be 'academia and I'?

Still, I thought, Bryan appears to have managed it, and like me he spent his schooldays wasted and bunking off, so how hard could it be?

We crossed the platform and headed for the exit. The path led past several empty bicycle racks then came out on to a small winding road surrounded by tall wire railings. It was a cloudy, moonless night, but I could make out some traditional wooden houses silhouetted by distant street lighting. Apart from the steady chorus of chirping insects, the whole place was devoid of life. As we followed the white lines down the middle of the road, Bryan explained that Suzuki-san had finished work and was in a local bar, but he was going to come and find us. No sooner had he finished speaking than we heard a commotion in the distance. It was Suzuki-san jogging towards us, triumphantly shouting my name as though I were a returning war hero.

'TOBY-SAN, TOBY-SAN, *DOMO DOMO*, IN JAPAAAN, LUCKY, THIS IS A PEN!'

He looked as if he'd stepped straight out of a 1980s beach party, with mirrored aviator sunglasses, shorts, T-shirt and flip-flops, and a headscarf over his shoulders. I was worried we'd wake the entire neighbourhood as we bounded over to him and jumped up and down like idiots. For a brief moment, the stress of our epic journey evaporated.

Suzuki-san insisted we go and have a celebratory drink. We walked a few hundred yards further down the road and turned into an exceptionally narrow alleyway. It consisted of several tightly packed single-storey houses securely screened behind high stone walls and rows of ancient, twisted trees. At the end was an old, black wooden house with a curved roof and a dilapidated lean-to built on to one side. As we approached the spooky-looking building, Bryan, who had been animatedly chatting away in Japanese, announced: '*This* is Suzuki-san's old family home.'

'Wow. So... he really doesn't mind us staying here?' I turned to Suzuki-san, gesturing towards the house. 'Is it really okay?'

'Okay.' He laughed, giving me a double thumbs up and grinning beneath his mirrored shades, like an extra from *Top Gun*.

'He's got a modern place with his family just up over the hill,' said Bryan. 'His parents live round the corner and use the garden for growing veg, but they're happy for us to stay. I've been crashing here for a week or so. I was living in the office of the paper factory for a couple of years, but I've seriously had enough of that place. It was rent-free, but still, it wasn't anything like this! Okay, so it needs a bit of work, but it could be really cool once we clear some of the junk and rubbish out. No one's actually lived here for years and it's just been used as a dumping ground, but it's got character... A proper ninja house.'

We stood gazing at it in awe. It really did look like a place where a ninja assassin might dwell – weathered, dark and alarmingly sinister-looking.

'It's perfect,' I said. 'Er… does Suzuki-san know I can't afford to pay him rent yet?'

'Don't worry, he knows. And besides, you'll be earning some cash when you start work at the paper factory. We can give him something for the electricity and water we use. You brought some duty-free whisky as a present for him, right?'

'Yeah, yeah, don't worry.'

'Ninja house.' Suzuki-san laughed, mischievously rattling open the worn sliding door. We piled in and took off our shoes while Suzuki-san crashed and banged around in the dark trying to locate the light switch.

Inside the house, the air was hot and still. It felt as if we were breaking into a dusty old museum. The muted lights flickered into life and a thin, wood-panelled hallway piled with books, rolls of wire, furniture, tools and assorted debris came into view. I stepped up blinking from the lowered entrance hall and followed them in. The wooden floor was covered with large, faded grass *tatami* mats and ornate opaque windows ran along the length of the wall. Several metres to the right, another battered sliding screen led into a central living area. I tiptoed carefully past the junk and poked my head round the corner. It was a surprisingly large room, with faded white walls and wooden beams and rows of dark shutters on either side. Packing boxes and old paper screens were piled up randomly across the floor. Although it was dilapidated, it was also the first Japanese house I had ever been in, and I felt as if we had just stepped straight into ancient Japan. In my mind, a distant flute sounded a shrill dramatic note. It was hard to tell exactly how old the place was, but it was clearly built way before electricity had been invented. It resembled a kind of sepia Kurosawa set… It all seemed a little mysterious, but maybe that was just the lack of sleep.

We cleared some space in the centre of the dusty room and pulled over a knee-height wooden table. I rummaged through my bags and respectfully presented Suzuki-san with a large bottle of whisky, which he cradled in his arms. Bryan sifted through some boxes and located a few pottery cups. Several cough-inducing shots later, we were eagerly toasting each other with the incontestable Japanese equivalent of 'Cheers' – '*Kampai*' ('Down in one'). Gradually, our conversation became louder and more spirited as the whisky took hold. We enthused about me being in Japan, the challenge of studying kendo and the anticipation of turning the house into a fully functioning abode fit for ninjas in training. The single overhead light cast a curious yellow circle around us, edged with sinister black shadows, giving the impression that we were sitting under a cruel, hot sun aboard a raft floating out at sea. I gazed around the antiquated room, blinking from the thick cigarette smoke, as my head started to spin and the vertical hold of my vision began to drift. I'd totally lost count of how many hours I had been travelling, but finally, I fell back on the *tatami* and slept.

I awoke the next morning, breathtakingly dehydrated, with a strange static electric crackling in my ears. The last 48 hours ran through my mind like a faded film reel, shoddily spliced together. I crawled over Bryan and Suzuki-san, who were still sleeping, and past the whisky debris, heading instinctively towards the rays of sunshine pouring in through the shutters. I managed to slide a panel half open and poke my head outside. The daylight was blinding and the summer heat intense. Somewhere, birds were singing and the sky was a beautiful, crystal-clear blue. In the distance, a single Chernobyl-like red-and-white-striped chimney puffed out a thin trail of smoke. I was looking out on to a slightly unkempt square traditional courtyard garden full of vegetables and fruit trees. It backed on to a high stone wall, and on the opposite side was framed by a ramshackle collection of crumbling outbuildings and bushes. There was a small path running round Suzuki's elderly parents' vegetable plots and, directly to my left, an even more decrepit part of the house, as yet unexplored. I stumbled down into the garden towards a rusty tap protruding from the wall. I crouched on a stone plinth underneath and turned the water on. It was wonderfully cool and refreshing. I felt slightly rested, although my body clock and sense of direction were deeply confused. One thing continued to puzzle me: I could still hear the loud crackling and began to wonder if my hearing had been damaged during the flight. Suddenly, it dawned on me – the noise was emanating from the fruit trees. I wandered over to investigate and found a large gathering of gigantic black-winged beetles (they must have been a good two or three inches in length) swarming around the tree trunks. I resisted the urge to run screaming and beat a hasty retreat to the tap.

'Morning, Tobes,' announced Bryan weakly, poking his head out of the door. He stumbled outside to join me for a protracted coughing fit and squatted down under the tap for a fully-clothed shower. 'How you feeling?' he asked.

'Great. Er, whereabouts is the toilet?'

'Ah.'

'Ah… You mean there is no toilet?'

'Well, I think there might be a bath somewhere,' he said, giving me a look that seemed to say, there may be no toilet, but only a madman would move into a house without a bath. 'Look, it's fine. We can use the one in the local shop.'

'Hmm.'

'Oh… and there's no kitchen either,' he said in as casual way as he could muster, gazing round the garden and yawning nonchalantly.

'I see,' I said flatly, fully expecting him to announce that the house was also built on an ancient Indian burial ground. I could certainly see the potential, but still, I swallowed a familiar pang of frustration. It shouldn't have surprised me – Bryan rarely did anything the conventional way. 'Well, I guess it is free,' I went on. 'It's going to be a bit like camping, but we'll sort it out.'

'Yeah, don't worry,' said Bryan, grinning. 'It'll be great!'

Just to put this exchange into perspective, Bryan and I had a long and chequered history of unorthodox flat-sharing. Previously, we'd rented a tiny bedsit that smelled of cauliflowers, a gigantic warehouse apartment with a freestanding bath in the middle of the living room and – our pièce de résistance – a basement in east London with no windows, kitchen, toilet or doors. I'd thought we might be past roughing it, but Bryan's description of how much work the house was going to need clearly involved wearing rose-tinted spectacles, and it was a bit late to do anything about it now. It looked like this was simply going to be business as usual.

We draped some of our wet clothes on the edge of the roof and went back inside.

Suzuki-san appeared to be waking up. He was looking badly hung over. After a brief trip to the tap, he got Bryan to explain that he had to go to work, but would catch up with us later. He gathered together his briefcase and whisky and hobbled outside, rattling the front door and laughing painfully to himself while muttering 'Ouchy.'

It seemed that hard drinking was part of the deal if I wanted to become a fully fledged kendo master. I lay back against a packing box and gazed around. The house was like a bread oven and I found myself dripping with sweat again. In a far corner of the room lay a pile of bags and boxes that were obviously Bryan's. He'd moved his belongings in from the paper factory and piled them up like a nesting hamster. I was used to that from our previous flat-shares. There was a collection of kendo books, some swords, a laptop, a TV, beer cans and a large assortment of what looked like toy robots.

'We may have no toilet or kitchen,' said Bryan, 'but at least we've got the essentials.'

On the opposite side of the room was a small, neglected religious shrine: an ornate wooden box containing old candles and, in front of that, a thick piece of plaited rope with paper strips like lightning bolts hanging from it. Next to that sat a fist-sized papier-mâché doll's head painted bright red with fierce, staring eyes. It was slightly creepy and looked extremely pissed off.

'Man… check this out,' I said. 'Have we just moved into the house from *The Amityville Horror*, or what?'

'Oh yeah, it's an old shrine to the local deity – a good-luck charm or something. Everyone's got them round here. I'd have to ask Suzuki-san exactly what it's all about, but I'm sure we could get rid of it.'

'What? And risk angering the gods?' I said. 'No way.'

'Well, we're going to need all the help we can get to clear this place up.'

Bryan began chanting, rolling his eyes and flicking his tongue in and out like a demon. He added an enthusiastic little impromptu ritual dance for good measure. I laughed and threw myself on the floor to formally apologise to the shrine for our impudent behaviour, particularly Bryan's, both in the past and for what was inevitably to come.

After unpacking, we took a slow walk to the local shop to buy some food and so I could get a bit more orientated. As we strolled along the thin alleyway in the direction of the train station, Bryan explained that a kendo class was on tomorrow evening, but first he would take me down to the paper factory, or 'The Factory of Dreams' as he called it, to meet the boss.

'So what's it like working there?' I asked. I had a bizarre and naive image of the place resembling an efficient hi-tech secret laboratory – the employees all dressed in matching orange boiler suits doing early-morning exercises together and swearing undying allegiance to the company.

'Believe me,' he said, 'it's *fucking* hard work. Basically, the Japanese work ethic is a very long way away from how things get done (or rather, don't get done) at home. I'm not going to give you any more preconceptions, but let's just say you're really going to get to love paper.'

I honestly didn't know what to expect. I didn't particularly mind hard work, although I did my best to avoid it, and therefore usually ended up having to work harder because of it. And I'd dealt with difficult people before. But I was more concerned about how I was going to survive not speaking the language. 'Don't worry, you can shadow me at first,' said Bryan. 'Although I'm not going to translate for you all the time. Trust me, being around Japanese people is the only way to learn.'

'*Kore wa pen desu*,' I said confidently.

'Exactly.'

We rounded the corner on to the main road. To our right was a small 7-Eleven convenience store. It sat in stark contrast to the traditional Japanese houses surrounding it, a bit like a white plastic alien spaceship had suddenly landed and set up a shop. As the automatic doors slid open, I savoured the cool transition into air-conditioned joy. We both looked pretty rough and the staff seemed rather taken aback. 'Irasshaimase,' (literally, 'Welcome' or 'Come in') they cried in unison, turning and bowing towards us with military precision.

I was equally surprised, returning the compliment as formally as I could. They smiled apprehensively and resumed their work, standing to attention.

'It's just the Japanese way of welcoming customers.' Bryan laughed. 'And they don't expect you to formally bow back. Imagine popping into the local Co-op at home, curtsying and shouting, "Good day to you all!"'

He then disappeared for a long time into the toilets. I wandered up and down the bright, halogen-lit aisles, marvelling at the unfamiliar products and packaging and feeling a bit self-conscious. The abrupt transition between our medieval-style Japanese house and ubiquitous global culture left me feeling a bit hollow. It suddenly occurred to me that I was starving hungry, but as I could barely speak any Japanese, I would have to wait for Bryan's return. When he eventually reappeared, I was loitering at the newspaper section, thumbing through a surreal magazine called *Top Snipe*, which, as far as I could tell, was an alarmingly detailed children's guide to becoming a deadly urban sniper. It appeared that the spirit of the samurai was manifesting itself in surprising new ways. Bryan then gave me a swift tour of Japanese convenience food. Being vegetarian, I quickly saw that things weren't going to be easy. Everything appeared to be either meat or fish – or flavoured with meat or fish.

'Man, you're going to struggle here.' He chuckled. 'For the Japanese, not eating meat is like not eating food – it's unthinkable. Come on, try some. It'll make a man of you.'

In the end, I grabbed an odd assortment of rice cakes, seaweed and instant noodles, then headed back to our new home, munching on crisps that tasted suspiciously fishy.

*

Everyone has a plan, 'til they get hit.

Joe Louis

3

Kendo by Candlelight

That evening, we got down to the serious business of discussing kendo. The old wooden house was stifling, so we opened the shutters on to the garden in an attempt to cool the place down and get a breeze going. Japanese cicadas (*semi*) were chirping away in the trees and a few stars were visible through the yellowing twilight. We lit a few candles and mosquito coils, which seemed to have the opposite of the desired effect and actually attracted the insects instead, their high-pitched whining interrupting the tranquillity as we sporadically twitched and slapped at our arms and faces.

Bryan knelt behind the table, sipping beer thoughtfully and composing himself. He then gave me my first basic lesson in kendo. This initially involved some long, protracted silences and a great deal of emphasis on how hard, yet incredibly cool it all was.

'I can only describe what Suzuki-san and the other teachers have told me,' he said earnestly. 'Kendo is the way of the sword and evolved from the martial arts of the samurai…' He paused dramatically as if waiting for stunned applause.

I grunted serious agreement.

He continued: 'Over the centuries, the technique of fighting to the death with lethally sharp swords was refined to an advanced level of efficiency. The sword is at the very heart of traditional Japanese martial arts, but nowadays the practical uses of learning to wield an extremely dangerous weapon are a bit limited.' (Sad frown.) 'However, the discipline and control needed to effectively sword fight are key aspects of kendo that have endured to the present day.' He stared at me, as if searching for a sign that I had received his transmitted wisdom.

I nodded on cue. He was sitting up straighter now, looking more alive and energetic.

'Kendo initially works on a physical level, involving fitness, strength and speed. But, over time, you start to develop your own technique and mental focus, which ultimately, of course, results in a Zen-like, kick-ass fucking coolness.' (I suspected he was straying a little here from the classical explanation.)

He went on: 'Suzuki-san and everyone have been doing it all their lives, but man, they're really humble, y'know. With such a concentration of high-ranking teachers round here, I don't think they even realise how good they are. Any one of them could make a fortune teaching in the West, but they just get on with it; they live it. Shit, wait till you meet the head teacher, Takagi Sensei. He's in his eighties now, but he's still amazing. Suzuki-san is his number-one student, and if you think he's good, Takagi Sensei is the fucking *shogun*.[1] There are only a few people in Japan alive that have his ranking.'

I lit a cigarette and wafted the smoke around in an attempt to annoy the mosquitoes. I felt a twinge of apprehension about visiting the *dojo*. I'd checked out plenty of martial-arts classes in England, but unlike judo, karate and kung fu, kendo had never really been exported wholesale. Few Western martial artists ever seemed to actually go and study anything first-hand in Asia.

Suzuki-san and Bryan had tracked down a couple of small British kendo classes. Although they were warmly received and Suzuki-san was unfalteringly polite, I had sensed that he was a little underwhelmed by the British approach to kendo. Bryan, on the other hand, spoke – as ever – with the voice of unrestrained honesty.

'Man, it wasn't really even kendo,' he raged now. 'They just stood around discussing it. Great at intellectual theory, but none of them could actually do it. The teacher accused me of being too aggressive. ME!'

'Yeah…' I said, suppressing a laugh. 'Ridiculous. But don't the kendo teachers in Yoshiwara talk about kendo too?'

'Of course they do. But first kendo, then questions and discussion. It doesn't matter how much you know; if you don't actually *do it*, you never improve.'

I nodded my understanding. All too frequently in the UK, people expected to go to a class, pay their money, commit to a few years of having 'the secrets' revealed, without putting the necessary hard training in, until, hey presto, they got a black belt[2] and became a master – the end. My old kung-fu teacher used to joke that his entire system was written on the inside of his belt. He would peek inside it occasionally, pretending to check the accuracy of a technique. But the incontrovertible truth is that, regardless of how much you know intellectually, and whatever you have holding up your trousers, all martial arts require incred-

---

1. *Shogun* – a hereditary military dictator or commanding general.
2. The concept of black belts and grades is a relatively new idea first introduced through judo at the end of the 19th century. Previously, students would train with a master until he or she either died or had nothing left to teach. The association of a black belt with 'mastery' is a modern phenomenon. In fact, the Japanese term for a first-degree black belt, *shodan*, means 'beginning step'.

ible amounts of practice. You can teach anyone the theory of a move, but until it's been repeated thousands of times, tested and internalised, it remains pretty much mental and physical baggage. As the old Chinese proverb (roughly) goes: 'I don't fear the man who knows a thousand techniques; I fear the man who has practised a single technique a thousand times.'

Bryan was looking slightly flushed now. He had been in Japan on his own studying for years with no close English-speaking friends to talk to, and now it felt like he was having a bit of an emotional outpouring. It was clear from the expression on his face that it had been an intense and transformative experience.

We sat for a while just soaking up the atmosphere, listening to the various chirping, clicking and buzzing sounds around us. A beautiful quarter moon had risen above the soft, fading strip of light on the horizon. It seemed like a familiar old friend in such unusual surroundings, and if I'd known any haikus, it would have been hard to find a more fitting situation for a recital.

After a while, Bryan got up and disappeared into one of his boxes, re-emerging with a large, dubious-looking carton of drink and a couple of delicate china bowls. He poured out some of the clear liquid and offered it to me ceremoniously.

'Ever tried *sake*... rice wine?'

'No.'

'Well, meet its poor relation, *shochu*.[3] Enjoy.'

We sank a couple of fiery shots, *kampai*'d a few more times and continued with the lesson.

'Right then, etiquette...' He looked at me with a pained expression. 'Tomorrow, you'll only be watching. I'm sure you'll get the hang of it. Just bow a lot and do what everyone else does. Oh, and don't step over anyone's gear. It's considered really bad form.'

He then talked me through the names of the various bits of dark-blue kendo body armour (*bogu*) that he had laid out next to us on the *tatami*.

'Basically, it's compressed cotton, just thick enough to stop serious injury, but it still hurts like hell. First, the padded, metal-grilled helmet (*men*), the gloves (*kote*), the breastplate (*do*), the belt that hangs in front of your groin (*tare*) and the wide, skirt-like trousers (*hakama*).'

I repeated the unfamiliar names until they started to stick. It was getting complicated already and I began to see the fairly obvious practical reasons as to why it wasn't more widely studied outside of Japan.

---

3. *Shochu* is distilled from barley, sweet potatoes or rice, unlike the more widely known *sake*, which is brewed rice wine.

'Right, that's enough talking. Let's suit up.'

First we changed into *keikogi* (the embroidered robes that are worn underneath), then began donning the armour. I wrapped a cotton scarf round my head to absorb the sweat and slipped the helmet on. It was a strange, claustrophobic sensation and immediately prompted me to begin breathing like Darth Vader – no doubt a common reaction among first-time Western *kendoka* (kendo practitioners). After squeezing into the remaining equipment, I sat to attention with my hands on my hips, ready for battle. The thick cotton armour felt constricting and was absolutely boiling. Jesus, I thought – I might well be the first *kendoka* ever to drop dead simply from the exertion of getting changed.

Bryan picked up one of the swords and showed me roughly how to hold it. The kendo *shinai* is basically a non-lethal stand-in for both the *katana* (the traditional razor-sharp, steel-bladed samurai sword) and the *bokuto*, or wooden practice sword.[4] *Shinai* are usually made of four strips of bamboo lashed together by leather cord with a circular hand guard just above the hilt. They're slightly flexible and not as heavy as wooden swords, meaning that a skilful *kendoka* can deliver painful whipping strikes and thrusts with full force.

Bryan's eyes seemed to darken as he demonstrated some rapid practice swipes, the bamboo sword making a loud cracking sound with the force and speed of his blows. He looked at me slyly, raising an eyebrow and nodding with mock confidence. I raised my sword dramatically in response to the challenge and swished it as hard as I could through the air. The lame slowness and total absence of power surprised even me, as did the lack of any cool thwacking sound.

'Hmm, mine doesn't seem to work properly,' I cried, shaking it with feigned disappointment. 'But don't worry, I'll still kick your head in.'

'Okay.' Bryan smiled and poured another shot of *shochu*. 'Right now... in the garden. I'll take you to the fucking cleaners.'

'Bring it on, lady-boy,' I shouted happily, tripping over my *hakama* and falling into the table, sending the drinks and ashtray flying. Outside, the garden was luminous in the dusky candlelight. Bryan continued to warm up with vigorous practice strikes. He showed me some basic techniques and I tried, in vain, to co-ordinate swinging the sword in time with my footwork and to see where I was going through the mask. This proved almost impossible and I just looked as if I was having some kind of angry fit with a stick. There seemed to be only one sensible course of action.

---

4. *Bokuto* – more commonly known in the West as a *bokken* and used when performing *kata* – solo forms for developing technique and simulating combat scenarios.

'Okay,' I announced with mock bravado, 'I think I've got the hang of this now. Let's do it.' I growled, turning to face him in an aggressive en-garde stance.

Bryan raised both eyebrows, frozen for a moment in disbelief, then sighed, put his helmet on and turned to face me with a resigned look of cruelty. Letting out a couple of loud screams, he immediately rained down several blistering strikes on my wrists and head – so hard and fast they left me stunned, wincing at the pain.

'Owwwwwwww. *Shit*,' I cried, dropping the sword in the dirt and rubbing my wrist in agony.

'That's terrible, Tobes. You should *never* drop your sword – it's considered really shameful.'

I fumbled around in the half light and slowly picked it up again.

'Oh yeah, well how about… THIS?' I shouted, landing a blow so utterly weak that he just stood there with his sword to one side while I, on the other hand, lost my balance and went careering into the vegetable patch as the *shinai* glanced off his helmet. He swiftly fought back with more punishing head strikes. My scalp stung with pain and I briefly saw bright, flashing red lights dancing around my eyes. We went on like this for a little while until it all became too much. I simply couldn't help myself, and retaliated the only way I knew how – by punching him in the head.

'What the…? You, you… can't do that,' he said with a bizarre mixture of amusement and anger.

'Yes, I can,' I said, throwing away my sword and jabbing at him a few more times to prove my point. The kendo gear provided excellent protection for kung-fu sparring.

'Right, that's it,' he shouted, landing a succession of agonising sword strikes to my head. I howled with pain and laughter, and danced around him doing my best Bruce Lee impression as we exchanged blows and war cries. This went on for several minutes.

'Punch, thwack, crack'… 'Yaaaah'… 'Smack, punch, thwack, crack'… 'Owwww'.

I really hoped our neighbours in the adjacent houses were either open-minded or out.

Eventually, I collided forcefully with an old twin-tub washing machine by one of the dilapidated sheds and raised my hands in exhausted surrender. I could hardly breathe, and a mosquito had flown into my mask. It was so unbelievably hot we both dived straight for the cold tap. We were literally steaming.

I took off my padded gloves and examined the large red welts forming around my wrists. 'Ow, that hurts.' I winced, dabbing my injuries with the sopping wet headscarf.

'Wait till you have a go with the kendo teachers,' said Bryan proudly. 'Suzuki-san once hit me so hard my wrist turned black.'

As we stumbled back into the house and peeled off the rest of our armour, Bryan showed me how to properly pack it all away (a long and complex ritual). We changed back into T-shirts and shorts, poured another drink and knelt back round the table. As I tenderly rubbed my bruised head with throbbing hands, an embryonic doubt as to whether I possessed the determination to deal with the pain of mastering kendo was slowly forming.

'So what do you think?' asked Bryan. 'Cool, huh?'

'Yeah… definitely,' I said pensively. 'Surprisingly difficult though.'

It certainly seemed like kendo was going to be a million miles away from any of the martial arts I was familiar with. I had used swords plenty of times before when practising kung-fu forms, but I'd never done full-contact sparring with them, and I definitely wasn't used to being belted quite so hard. Most of my previous martial-arts training had involved trying to avoid being hit; in contrast, this felt like repeatedly running into a brick wall. The pain was simply unavoidable. I strongly suspected I possessed the kendo equivalent of what boxers refer to as a 'glass jaw' (one punch and you were out cold). The kendo en-garde position was difficult to attack, as the opponent's sword was aimed directly at throat level. This made it tricky to judge distance or find an opening to strike. Also, the speed with which the blows were delivered meant that any flashy defensive moves (of which I had many) would prove totally redundant. I began to get a sense of why the art of the Japanese sword was described as 'ruthlessly efficient'; it was a bit like gun slinging.

Meanwhile, the obligatory late-night drinking conversations that all young, glassy-eyed martial-arts enthusiasts are required to have continued – specifically, 'The technical merits of different forms of fighting'. It was something we were very experienced at, having both spent an inordinate amount of time boring our friends and families (and anyone else who would listen to our obsessive and frequently misinformed opinions about Eastern martial practices). We viewed learning martial arts as something exotic that represented the polar opposite of our education. At secondary school, I had never really been inspired by my teachers, who were stressed out by the daily drudgery and pressure of trying to educate disinterested kids like me. I remember soul-crushing phrases like: 'I know this is boring, but we all have to get through the syllabus', or, 'If you study hard and really apply yourself, you may be able to achieve a D in mathematics'. And, of course, who can forget the classic, 'It's your own time you're wasting'?

Relatively speaking, I didn't go to a bad school, or have an awful time there, it just lacked that seductive cocktail of danger, excitement and medieval weaponry that so many young boys crave. And it wasn't until I started studying martial arts and finally met teachers who genuinely believed in what they were doing, and, perhaps more importantly, actually seemed to enjoy their lives, that I really started wanting to learn anything.

'Damn straight,' said Bryan quietly and bitterly, listening to my anti-establishment rant and nodding in pained agreement. 'There was nothing in school about ninjas... Nothing.'

Candlelight danced across the polished wooden beams and the frame of the house creaked like an arthritic old man. Despite having been in Japan for barely 48 hours, I had never felt so incredibly far away from England. We talked and drank *shochu* till the candles burnt down, then lay back in the darkness, watching the blue smoke of the mosquito coils spiral out towards the garden and dissipate into the night. Eventually, after a protracted discussion about who would win in a fight between Bruce Lee and Jackie Chan, we fell asleep on the floor with the shutter doors wide open.

*

People travel to faraway places to watch, in fascination, the kind of people they ignore at home.

Dagobert D. Runes

4

A Factory of Dreams

The next morning was as bright and humid as ever. We woke early to the familiar and now slightly annoying chorus of chirping *semi*, washed at the rusty tap in the garden and changed into some respectable, fresh clothes. Much to Bryan's delight, the large red welts on my wrist were beginning to turn an angry yellowy-green colour. The unavoidable reality of sorting out work had finally arrived and I was nervous at the prospect of visiting the factory and having an interview. Bryan assured me, however, that it was just a formality, the boss having already almost told him I could work there. It took me a few seconds to pick up on his use of the word 'almost', but there was no time to brood over the implications.

As we left the house, Bryan revealed an old, steel-framed bike stashed beneath some bits of wood in one of the sheds. Rust and cobwebs aside, it looked roadworthy but the saddle had clearly been designed by a pervert and neither of us had attempted a 'backy' for years. After a couple of false starts, we went wobbling off down the alleyway. Keeping our balance required maintaining high speeds, otherwise steering became impossible. We shot past the 7-Eleven, narrowly avoided killing some startled pedestrians, then rattled across an open railway crossing. The tightly packed houses soon gave way to a hot, empty road surrounded by fenced-off scrubland. From the relative vantage point of this open ground, I got my first good look at our wider surroundings.

Yoshiwara lay sprawled out to one side. It was a heavily industrialised town, with large electrical pylons, smoking chimneys and ugly concrete structures crowded randomly together like some sort of feng-shui disaster zone. Yet in the distance, dark-green fields stretched up towards an impressive ridge of sombre, imposing mountains. Thick clouds enveloped the peaks, forming a swirling mass of silhouettes.

'You can see Mt Fuji from here,' cried Bryan, furiously pedalling away.

'Whereabouts?' I shouted back, through gritted teeth, knuckles white from the effort of clinging on.

'It's hidden behind the clouds at the moment, but it's usually just over there behind those other mountains.'

'Usually?'

I strained my eyes trying to penetrate the clouds but the view was totally obscured. Although I couldn't see it, it seemed rather odd to think that we were directly below an active volcano that could erupt at any time. The risk of earthquakes and tsunamis meant that, if it all kicked off at once, the results would be spectacular.

'So, is it safe?'

'Don't worry. It's hundreds of years since it last erupted.'

'Doesn't that make it overdue, then?'

Bryan laughed with glee at the thought. Or rather, at my discomfort at the thought.

Ahead, the parched tarmac road cut directly through the middle of a huge, post-apocalyptic-looking industrial compound – a mass of towering, rusty buildings, steel girders, steaming vents and flashing yellow warning lights.

'Oh… shit. Is that where you work?'

'No. Don't worry, it's not far though. That's one of the really big paper factories; this area is famous for them. Mad, huh? Wait till you see it at night. It looks like something out of *Star Wars*.'

We rode on, through the intimidating heat and metallic grinding sounds of the compound, then travelled for about another mile, passing several disused paddy fields and a few neglected tea plantations. Eventually, as we reached the outskirts of town, a single white industrial unit loomed into view.

'This is it,' Bryan announced.

We jumped off the bike and hobbled the last few hundred metres. I felt apprehensive and sore. The paper factory was a large, rectangular building made of breeze-blocks and steel, with a plastic, corrugated roof that glinted in the sun. Two giant, metal sliding doors were open and a couple of skips and a small, yellow forklift truck were parked to the side. A few Middle Eastern-looking guys and a thin Japanese man with a moustache sat smoking on wooden pallets, grinning at us. I noted with slight disappointment that no one appeared to be wearing matching boiler suits, nor did the place resemble a hi-tech secret laboratory in any way whatsoever.

'*Ohayo gozaimasu*,' they called out ('Good morning' or, literally, 'It is nice of you to be diligent in the early morning').

'*Ohayo*,' replied Bryan in a work-like tone, before breaking into free-flowing Japanese. Then he motioned me to come forward and began the introductions: 'Blah blah blah Toby-san blah blah.'

I nodded, smiled and casually tried to go with the flow, like the new boy in class. The Japanese guy jumped up first and held out his hand earnestly.

'Hel... lo.' He grinned, looking very pleased with himself. He'd obviously just been practising. He pointed at himself and said 'Shimizusan!' very slowly, like a children's TV presenter.

'Shemisooosan,' I repeated carefully, and everyone nodded their approval.

'Is this the boss?' I asked Bryan.

'Oh no, these guys just work here. The boss is probably inside, congratulating himself on being so rich and fat.'

Next, the Middle Eastern guys introduced themselves. Sami was about 40, dressed in tight combats and a vest that made him look immensely hairy and sweaty. Then came Toni, about 20 years old, tall, lanky and tanned in a tight red vest. It seemed as though he'd modelled his rather remarkable appearance on 'disco meets Rambo' (minus the physique) but it was his spectacular mullet haircut that really caught my eye. Jalal, who was quite a bit older, obviously considered himself to be in charge. He gave me a macho, bone-crushing hand-shake.

They offered us a smoke, sat back down and began chatting away in Arabic. Bryan gave me the lowdown.

'Those guys are from Iraq,' he whispered. 'Well, obviously apart from Shimizusan. They're illegal immigrants who came over during the Gulf War and now they can't go back, poor bastards. Toni and Sami are okay. Jalal reckons he was some kind of big-shot Special Forces soldier, but you'll find that he's basically just a gigantic prick. They spend their entire lives here making the boss rich. It's good money but they're not interested in Japan in the slightest. They just blam all their wages on prostitutes and terrible nightclubs, then have to come back and make paper all over again. What a life. Come on, I'll show you round.'

The shady warehouse felt a little cooler than outside, but the humidity was still severe and I was already starting to feel drained; I wondered if I would survive working here. Directly to the left was a small doorway leading through to an office. Opposite that were a long, waist-high table running the length of the entrance-way stacked with cardboard boxes and a couple of ineffective whirring fans. Stretching off into the distance were two 8-foot-tall rows of complex manufacturing equipment, which hummed and whirred loudly, rapidly coiling thin white strips of paper on to large spinning spools. It looked a bit like an archaic government computer from the 1960s. Further back, heaps of shrink-wrapped pallets were stacked up practically to the ceiling and gigantic rolls of paper lined the walls, ready to be cut and spun into smaller reels. We walked towards the back, where a few people were lethargically poking one of the machines.

'Okay,' whispered Bryan, 'this is Shachousan,[1] so act cool.'

Everyone stopped what they were doing and turned to greet us. A pear-shaped guy in his twenties, wearing jogging pants and flip-flops, stepped forward and patted Bryan on the shoulders like a dog. He didn't appear very boss-like and seemed totally lost for words. In fact, he reminded me of a bewildered tourist. I did my best, most sincere formal bow and smiled nervously. Bryan introduced me and they chatted for a while. I hoped he was delivering the 'He's-a-solid-team-player-yet-works-well-as-an-individual' speech. I found myself nodding, trying to act serious and professional, as though I could follow what they were saying. But something was clearly wrong – the introduction was taking too long. The boss was looking concerned and kept glancing at me doubtfully, as though Bryan were doing a bad job trying to sell him a dodgy second-hand car. They wandered into the office for a few minutes, Bryan looking anxious. My trip of a lifetime was clearly in jeopardy. I smiled at two workers who'd stopped poking at the machinery and were staring at me in thinly veiled disgust.

Just as I had convinced myself I was going home and that it was probably a good thing, Bryan and the boss returned, smiling. 'It's okay,' said Bryan. 'He's agreed to take you on. You can start in a few days once you've got acclimatised.'

The boss stepped forward.

'Ah... pleaseu... worku... hardu,' he said, shaking my hand and giving me a long, encouraging look.

'*Hai*,' I said determinedly (roughly meaning 'Correct'), bowing again.

The two workers loitering in the background came forward now and simultaneously bowed in crisp formation. They were wearing matching white overalls and shirts. One was tall and bony, and rather surprisingly appeared to have ginger hair; the other was stocky with buck teeth, thick glasses and a kamikaze-style headband. They said something formal, flashed Bryan a resentful nod, then withdrew to the back of the factory where they returned to prodding the machinery. I had an ominously bad feeling about them and got the distinct impression they were less than happy to have me aboard. The boss appeared blissfully oblivious to the tension and sauntered off to his office with a Cheshire cat-like grin.

'That was close,' said Bryan. 'He was worried that because you're on a

---

1. 'Shachousan' – 'Mr Boss'.

tourist visa, he could get into serious trouble, but I said we'd keep it under wraps. Besides, he's done it before, and, anyway, he doesn't really give a shit. It's all just money to him.'

'Thanks,' I said, feeling relieved and concerned in equal measure. 'So who were those other guys?'

'Don't worry about those two,' said Bryan, shaking his head. 'They're a couple of career fuckwits. The fat one's MC Squared because he's such a genius, and the ginger one's so ugly I named him the Puganought.'

'Yeah, I got the feeling they don't like us much.'

'They don't like anyone. The only reason they're here is because they know the boss and spend all their time kissing his arse. Basically, they're miserable because they're too stupid to do anything other than spend the rest of their lives working here. The boss is all right though. He means well. He took over this place a couple of years ago. His dad's got a larger factory in Numazu – the nearest big town. He's the real boss. Shachousan doesn't have a clue what he's doing; he's just a big kid, really. Come on, I'll show you the ropes.'

Bryan walked me round the factory, explaining how various machines worked and what we were expected to do. Basically, the place was set up as a kind of conveyer belt. Giant rolls of shiny white paper were slowly fed into one end and then cut into long unbroken strips, which were then subdivided into about ten thinner ribbons and automatically wound on to heavy reels. Once they were full, they were cut loose and carried over to the long table by the entrance, where they got packed into cardboard boxes. Finally, they were stacked on pallets, wrapped in giant rolls of cling film and sent off to America to be used as packaging for microchips in mobile phones. It all looked highly organised, back-breaking and catatonically boring. As we wandered among the machines, we bumped into a couple of other workers: a young baseball-capped Brazilian guy called Akio, who was shifting some pallets, and a very sweet, ancient Japanese woman making cardboard boxes. They were reassuringly friendly and we paused to chat for a while. Akio had grown up in Japan and worked in the factory mainly to pay for his expensive boy-racer, super-charged car habit. Bryan said he was a really good worker, although he apparently spent every waking second talking and fantasising about late-night motorway drag races – no doubt to an unrelenting mental theme tune of grungy rock and banging hip-hop. He had the slightly psycho look of someone who didn't get enough sleep, and I liked him immediately. The old woman had the contrasting appearance of an old sage. She seemed humble and softly spoken, and had beautiful warm, brown eyes and wrinkled skin like chamois leather. If there was a theme tune going on in her head, I figured it was probably from *The Sound of Music*. She seemed baffled that we had travelled here all the way from England and shyly confided that I was only the second foreigner she had ever met (Bryan being the first). Apparently, she was a legend in Yoshiwara – the grand old mistress of paper making – having worked in the local factories for decades.

'Imagine folding cardboard boxes for twelve hours every single day, all your life,' said Bryan sympathetically. 'It either results in madness or enlightenment. Actually, she's retiring soon and there's a vacancy going... Like I said, you're *really* going to get to love paper.'

I watched her, totally absorbed in concentration, and tried to imagine having that level of dedication to a menial task. I shivered; dear God, this kind of work was dangerous. Anyone could learn kendo, do a base jump or survive a cage fight, but to do this all day, every day without losing the plot required real guts. We stood for a while, enraptured by the speed and effortlessness of her movements: pick up cardboard, fold it, tape it, stack it, pick up cardboard, fold it, tape it, stack it... She looked so serene, her entire body working in one beautiful, fluid movement. Truly, she was a master. We respectfully bowed and waved goodbye. She giggled and went back to her work.

We emerged into the sunshine and Bryan had another impromptu cold shower under a tap around the corner. I sat smoking with the others in the shade of a skip while they laughed and mimed the universal crazy sign.

Shimizusan fanned himself with some cardboard. '*Ahhhhh atsui desu*,' he said, turning and directing the breeze at me. '*Atsui*,' he said more purposefully and pointed at the sun.

I nodded. '*Atsooey*, hot? Yeah, it's seriously *atsooey*.' We laughed.

Sami and Jalal threw me some sympathetic 'How-the-hell-did-we-end-up-here?' glances and Toni hummed a tune, eyes closed with his hand over his heart. He looked as though he was deeply involved in an imaginary slow jam at the disco.

A few minutes later, the machines ground to a stop and everyone promptly leapt up and went inside to pack the full rolls of paper. I lurked in the shadows, watching and trying not to get in the way. They were obviously aiming to get things done in as short a time as possible. The weighty paper reels were about the size of a car tyre and needed to be boxed up quickly but carefully. The slightest dent or mark would render them unusable and I imagined each one of them was worth quite a bit of money. They worked at a frenetic pace, sweating. I guessed I was witnessing the famous Japanese work ethic. It seemed like a far cry from the work culture at home, where, generally speaking – unless there was some kind of massive emergency – things tended to happen in their own good time. I imagined even the lowliest Japanese toilet cleaner probably woke up and said to themselves, 'Today I'm going to clean the most toilets in the world ever.' It was admirable, but also disturbing.

From the back of the factory, MC Squared and the Puganought were keeping a stern, watchful eye on things. They had scornful looks on their faces and appeared to be enjoying the spectacle immensely. I resigned myself to the fact that they were almost certainly going to be a great big pain in the arse. This whole operation went on for about 15 minutes, and when it was all done, everyone quietly assumed their previous positions, smoking and chatting as if nothing had happened.

I stood in the shade of the doorway trying to orientate myself. I was relieved to have a job, but I could see that it was going to be tough and I was going to have to learn to fit in very quickly.

The rest of the day was spent back at the Ninja House, shifting old broken screens, boxes and items of rubbish into piles in an effort to reclaim some long-lost floor space. An old vacuum cleaner sparked alarmingly, but nevertheless did a good job of dealing with the thick layers of dust covering the worn *tatami*. Gradually, we cleared out the main room, moving boxes and old furniture into the outbuildings, scrubbing the floor and polishing the woodwork. I even gave the shrine a quick wipe in as respectful a way as possible. We took a break for a while, admiring our handiwork. Bryan put his portable TV on top of a small wooden cabinet and switched it on. Having become accustomed to the dim, shaded room it was a shock to suddenly be confronted with bright moving pictures and sound again. The reception was pretty fuzzy, but good enough to see that Japanese TV was unfathomably weird. It seemed to be mainly composed of incomprehensible talk shows, samurai period dramas and cookery programmes featuring middle-aged housewives orgasmically proclaiming how delicious various items of raw fish tasted. I wondered if English TV, with its equally formulaic programmes and trashy celebrity game shows would seem as strange to a Japanese person. I guessed it might even be familiar. As we continued sorting out the junk, we discovered a small traditional fire pit under a panel of wood, complete with ancient white, powdery ash and a few charred metal utensils – a relic from the days before electricity. Although the idea of sitting around a hearty open fire during the winter was seductive, we were wise enough to realise that lighting a fire now would almost certainly result in immediate asphyxiation and death. We fearfully covered it back up and never spoke of it again. By late afternoon, the room appeared to be sparkling and looked twice the size. We used some of the less damaged screens to cordon off a couple of areas, and designated one side of the house as the kitchen/bar area. Finally, Bryan artfully arranged his swords and lit a candle in front of the shrine. We sat quietly looking out of the sliding doors on to the garden feeling proud. The Ninja House was ready for action.

*

You can only fight the way you practise.

Miyamoto Musashi

5

The Class

By the early evening, the damp heat had become intensely oppressive and I could feel the atmospheric pressure tightening the muscles in the back of my head. The syrupy air was nauseatingly still, storm clouds built on the horizon and low, ominous rumbles sporadically echoed down from the blackening mountains.

Around six o'clock, we took an unhurried walk up to Suzuki-san's house, which was five minutes away over the brow of a hill. I wondered if he'd recovered from the previous night's hangover. No cars were in the driveway and the place looked deserted. It was a large one-storey, tiled building surrounded by aromatic pine trees, with a few apathetic, long-eared cats sprawled out in the shadows. We pushed the door open and tentatively called out. There was no answer, so I peered inside. In the dim light of the hallway, I could just make out an impressive rack of assorted swords mounted on the wall above a chaotic pile of shoes and flip-flops. Bryan shouted a few more times, but there was nobody home, so we gave up and headed for the kendo school.

Yoshiwara was deserted. As we made our way through the empty streets, past secluded family houses and parked cars, the place felt eerily quiet. I began to wonder if anyone actually lived here.

'Is it always like this?' I asked.

'Yeah, pretty much,' said Bryan with a puzzled look that suggested he'd never really noticed before. 'I guess everyone's still at work.'

The kendo *dojo* was ten minutes from our house in the grounds of the local middle school, within a large, imposing sports hall. We were early, and sat outside on the steps waiting, watching the clouds continuing to gather. Bryan used the opportunity to attempt to teach me how to introduce myself. Etiquette required that on entering the *dojo* I go straight up to the head teacher, bow and say, '*Onegaishimasu*' (which roughly translates as, 'Please teach me/allow me to train with you'). Simple enough, but the rumbling thunder didn't help dispel my sense of foreboding, and my mind felt like a sieve. Bryan appeared to be having a hard time accepting that anyone could find memorising two words so difficult.

As the gloomy light faded, the humidity was unbelievably still increasing. I was dripping with sweat and developing an overwhelming urge to run away.

Gradually, other people finally began to arrive, bowing, waving and checking out the strange new Westerner with polite, small-town curiosity. Bryan introduced me to a few friends whose names passed me by. I nodded, bowed, shook hands and respectfully hovered in the background. Eventually, Suzuki-san pulled up in a large black, *A-Team*-style van, which Bryan described as the 'Suzuki-wagon'. He was shamelessly pumping out 1980s American rock anthems at full volume. He had been working some kind of crazy 24-hour shift in the paper factory, where he was employed as a supervisor, but seemed as relaxed as ever and in excellent humour.

The *dojo*, despite its size, was softly lit and stuffy. At the head of the hall hung a large draped banner bearing the calligraphy and emblem of the Yoshi-wara Kendo School. The place was rapidly filling up with people now. Around the edge of the room, along a thin, marked-off area, spectators and parents sat chatting and directing children to get changed, while the majority of the adults were stretching, carefully checking equipment and warming up with slow, purposeful sword swings. As we walked through the sliding doorway, I felt the eyes of the entire class look me up and down. I tried to act casual yet respectful, which doubtless just came across as alarmingly confused and self-conscious.

Suzuki-san marched us towards the head teacher, Takagi Sensei, who was standing quietly in the middle of the hall. Dressed in full battle gear, he was grey-haired, stern yet serene and appeared to be the living embodiment of a powerful ancient samurai master. As if to order, thunder rolled menacingly in the distance, and for a split second I felt as if I was being led to my execution. We all bowed in formation, then Suzuki-san introduced me. I willed every fibre of my body to appear self-effacing while I prematurely blurted out my embarrassing half-coughed attempt at '*Onegaishimasu*'. Takagi Sensei gave me a slightly bemused look. He turned to Suzuki-san and said a few words in a deep, gravelly voice (I guessed something along the lines of, 'Er, what did he just say?'), then motioned me to take a seat. Bryan escorted me to the edge of the class and explained that Takagi Sensei had said I was welcome at the *dojo* and to please train hard. He told me that I should sit in *seiza* (formal kneeling position; literally, 'proper sitting'), then he gave me an encouraging nod and disappeared to get changed.

I gazed around the hall, quietly watching more people arriving and warming up. It was a big class; there must have been at least 50 or 60 people. Near the entrance, beginners were being put through their paces with basic sword work, and at the far end, the senior teachers were starting to pair up and spar with each other. It was a noisy business, as shouts of attack rang out and the wincing crack and thud of bamboo hitting body armour reverberated across the hall.

Seiza isn't a position most Westerners are comfortable with, and although I was fairly supple, after about 15 minutes my knees felt as if they were on fire. I was struggling to maintain my posture and composure. Although no one had mentioned it, and certainly nobody was checking, I sensed there was a certain expectation that I endure this one simple task without complaining. It was turning into a matter of pride and, despite being an ignorant Westerner, I was determined to prove myself worthy... Well, at least worthy enough to watch. I sat quietly locked in a Herculean battle of self-control, attempting to mask my discomfort with an insane rigid expression of fake calm. A wave of panic rose as it occurred to me that I had absolutely no idea how long the class would last and that even 30 minutes or so of kneeling on the rock-hard floor meant I would probably never walk again.

Meanwhile, thunder boomed in the background, while flashes of lightning illuminated the hall in flickering bursts of intensity. My shirt was becoming embarrassingly soaked with dark patches of perspiration and my knees felt as if they were about to explode. I began to wonder if I would be the first person ever to collapse from the effort of simply watching a kendo class. But although I started to fidget with the pain, it was undeniably mesmerising and mildly distracting to watch so many people engaged in sword fighting.

The senior instructors were all giving captivating performances, but at the head of the hall Takagi Sensei stood out. The way he moved had a relaxed, natural power which reminded me of the old woman in the paper factory. His techniques looked graceful and effortless. It was fascinating to watch. Although he was fighting people half his age, he moved with a fast, calculated pace, occasionally letting out deep shouts that resounded loudly round the hall. His style of teaching appeared to consist of randomly picking students of all ages and testing their mettle. Each time he sparred, he seemed to be one step ahead, clinically delivering blows, keeping the pressure on, until the intimidated-looking students transcended their fear and pain and were consumed by a bruised determination – or, perhaps, a sense of revenge – and finally stopped holding back. It was as if they were thinking, Right, that's it, old man, now I'm determined to hit you, just once. Then Takagi Sensei would beam with encouragement; he seemed to be saying, 'Yes, that's it. Never give up. Go further than you thought was possible; now you're learning. *This* is it; *this* is kendo.'

Or else the guy just enjoyed beating the hell out of his students; I couldn't be sure.

Over the next few hours, the training continued with unrelenting intensity. Time condensed into a single point of never-ending discomfort. After what seemed like several lifetimes, very abruptly, a different shout rang out. Everyone immediately stopped what they were doing, laid their swords down, removed their helmets and hurriedly joined me in *seiza* in long, neat rows. Even the spectators by the doorway turned to face the front and assumed the position. Takagi Sensei and a couple of the most senior teachers, including Suzuki-san, sat to attention at the front. Their expressions were serious and focused, like ancient carved-stone Buddhas. It was certainly a side of Suzuki-san I had never witnessed before. The joking, easy-going person I knew was gone. Now he was a serious and powerful *sensei* who had spent his whole life in the *dojo* cultivating his skills.

The teachers examined everyone in the room, slowly, carefully, sizing us up like an old-fashioned military inspection. A minute later another fierce instruction was barked: '*Zazen*' (literally, 'seated meditation').[1] Before the echo had faded, the entire hall became deafeningly quiet and still. The sudden contrast with the previous few hours of chaotic noise and violence was astonishing. Everyone looked serene, eyes closed and utterly motionless. I could feel the blood pounding in my ears and my nervous fidgeting seemed to have reached an embarrassing level. Although the idea of Zen[2] in the West has come to represent an experiential state of enlightenment, the actual meaning and practice of Zen meditation is far less well known. Luckily, having once skimmed through a battered old copy of Paul Reps and Nyogen Senzaki's classic *Zen Flesh Zen Bones*[3] I figured I knew exactly what to do. I strained to empty my mind, count my breaths, contemplate the sound of one hand clapping, step though the gateless gate and awaken to the 'moment'.

As I tried in vain to experience the amazing interconnected oneness of everything, a more commanding mental image of my knees actually bursting into flames rudely crept in. My spiritual aspirations began to crumble before the growing and disappointing realisation that, despite my finest intentions, I couldn't wait for *zazen* to end and be free to wiggle my toes once again.

Obviously, spontaneous Zen awakenings required practice. I tried shifting my attention to something else. Outside, the first droplets of rain were almost

---

1. Technically referred to as mokuso in kendo practice.
2. 'Zen' is the Japanese pronunciation of the Chinese character *Chan* (禅), which is, in turn, a translation of the Pali word *Jhāna*, meaning 'concentrated meditation' or 'meditative stability'.
3. Reps, P. and Senzaki, N., *Zen Flesh, Zen Bones*, The Charles E. Tuttle Co., Inc. (1957).

imperceptibly beginning to fall. I opened my eyes and cautiously peered around. The entire class looked still and calm, bolt upright, their hands clasped serenely in their laps. The rain increased, beating down on the roof as the heavy pitter-patter developed into a roaring deluge. I shut my eyes again and resumed my efforts at meditating. Anyone who tells you that sitting quietly is easy and relaxing has definitely never tried it for three hours. Eventually, I gave up. I figured total enlightenment could probably wait till my second class and, instead, tuned my attention back to its default setting of 'randomly distracted', losing myself to the soothing pounding of the rain.

After an indefinable period of time, another sharp cry rang out and *zazen* came to an end as abruptly as it began. The hall was reanimated, throats were cleared and brows were mopped. A few groups of students went to kneel in front of the teachers for individual feedback and instructions. Takagi Sensei gestured in my direction and said a few words, as the whole room seemed to turn to stare at me and a few of the children giggled. I nodded, smiled courteously and felt acutely on show and out of place. Suzuki-san also spoke for a few minutes, and although I couldn't understand a word, his tone sounded reassuring and profound. With that, we all did a slow, formal kneeling bow and the class was over. Everybody stood up and began chatting, bowing to each other and getting changed. I leant back on the floor and very, very slowly attempted to unbend my legs. The swift flow of blood back into my feet was startlingly painful, the endorphin rush making me giddy, and it took a full five minutes before I could speak, let alone move. People around me laughed and consoled me with the now familiar word '*Atsui*'; I guessed they'd all been in my position once and knew how it felt.

Bryan appeared again, having got changed. 'Right, let's get out of here,' he announced. 'We're going to a bar just round the corner from our place; we're going to meet the teachers there. I've got to introduce you properly.'

'Okay, okay, slowly,' I whimpered feebly, pulling myself up by his legs. 'Hey, what did Takagi Sensei say to me at the end of the class?'

'Oh, he asked everyone to make you welcome, and he said that if Westerners like us have the dedication to travel all the way to Japan to study kendo, then they should all be inspired and train even harder.'

'Ah... right,' I said, half to myself, quietly chewing the words over with wonder and disbelief. 'Train... harder?'

We staggered out of the *dojo* straight into the pitch-black, mercifully cool downpour. I held my arms wide open to the rumbling, crackling sky. I could feel my toes. I could breathe again.

And I had survived my first-ever kendo class.

*

Wherever you are, it is your friends who make your world.

William James

6

Senpai–Kohai

We moved quickly, splashing along the uneven pavements in the dark, leaping over large puddles and bubbling drains. As we jogged back through the sleepy suburbs, the roads were steaming with a misty, surreal quality. We passed the futuristic, shimmering brightness of the 7-Eleven, then stopped outside a wooden house where a soft glow emanated from behind a silver-frosted screen.

'It's a private tavern the kendo teachers use,' announced Bryan, rapping on the window as I tried to shelter under the eaves. The sliding door opened and a frail, grey-haired man who had obviously been expecting us handed me a clean white towel and ushered us inside. He led us through a family living room, past an old lady wrapped in blankets, obliviously watching TV and kneeling on bare *tatami*. He shuffled along a dark adjoining corridor, switched some lights on, motioned us into what looked like a small backroom bar, then bowed and left us to it.

The room had a rough concrete floor and a sink where we quickly began wringing our clothes out. I noted with embarrassment the soggy trail of footprints that followed us incriminatingly through the house. A couple of metal tables were pushed together in the centre of the room and a glass-fronted fridge loaded with bottles of beer stood to one side. In the far corner, a ragged green parrot was asleep on a perch, looking old and forlorn. I sat on a stool and wearily failed to light a damp cigarette with a wet lighter.

'Give us a hand,' said Bryan, who had begun setting out the table with bottles and glasses. 'You're a student now, so you have to help serve. Y'know, pour the drinks – it's called *senpai–kohai*, teacher–student, or elder–younger. It's this unwritten Japanese rule where the youngest or the newest has to look after the seniors (and, theoretically, vice versa). It's just the way it works out here. You'll see. Hey,' he said, his face suddenly lighting up with glee, 'I've just realised – I'm your *senpai* now, so you have to do everything I tell you.'

I laughed, keeping it light. 'I'm sure that's not how it works,' I said. 'And, anyway, I'm a month older than you. Therefore, if anyone's the *shogun* around here, it's me.'

We opened some peanuts and crisps and offered a few to the parrot, who grabbed a beakful and turned his back to feast in silence. In the distance, I could hear other people arriving and the now-familiar upbeat cries of *'Domo, domo'*[1] from Suzuki-san, drifting down the corridor. The teachers entered jubilantly, taking their places around the table as we weaved between them, filling glasses and generally acting like dutiful *kohai*. After they had all settled down and got comfortable, Suzuki-san gave me a nod of approval, then motioned for me to go away – or so I thought. It took a few seconds for me to realise he was actually waving for me to come and sit down (in Japan, the beckoning hand signal is reversed). Someone poured me a drink and everyone let out a tired but jubilant *'Kampai'*, as if they had just returned from battle, which, in a way, they had.

The next ten minutes were spent vigorously toasting each other. There was definitely no shying away from the revelry. It seemed that Japanese drinking culture was a strict team activity, where you were honour-bound to match everyone drink for drink. But just as my head started to spin, the pace mellowed a little and people began to relax and talk. Gradually, I got to know the gang. Sitting next to myself and Suzuki-san was Watanabe Sensei, or Nabi-chan, as everybody called him: a cool, laid-back guy, who chain-smoked and had the dark air of 1970s cop about him – a sort of Japan-meets-*Hawaii-Five-O* look. Next to him sat Bryan, who was loudly doing some comical impressions of the kendo teacher's various facial expressions mid-sword fight. Then Takahashi Sensei, a tall, balding, well-built man in his fifties. He was quietly spoken, with an upbeat, intelligent expression. He sat silently, observing the proceedings. Alongside him was Nori Sensei, who was equally reserved, but looked a little the worse for wear and was struggling to stay awake. Finally, there was Aono (pronounced 'Aw-know') Sensei, a large, bald-headed Zen Buddhist priest with a deep, intimidating voice and an extremely blunt command of English.

In fact, Aono Sensei appeared to have the unusual talent of being able to make the most innocuous question or statement come across as rude and deeply patronising. 'I think kendo VERY difficult for you,' he said with unassailable authority. I fidgeted nervously and tried to hide behind my cigarette. Although this was doubtless true, I still felt a strange urge to try to karate chop the table in half just to prove him wrong.

Aono Sensei sized me up like he was looking at a lame horse that needed to be shot. 'I am Zen priest,' he announced with exotic grandeur. 'I like drink, I like girl, I eat meat, but you come my temple and I will show you Buddha!' He

---

1. The meaning of *domo* is dependent on intonation, situation and status, but Suzuki-san used it as a mischievous way of saying hello.

burst out cackling and refilled my glass. There was something about the silky-smooth way he pronounced the words 'show you Buddha' that made me suspect he was planning on either seducing or killing me – or perhaps both.

It was hard not to feel mildly freaked out and irritated by everyone's constant insistence on how difficult everything was going to be for me, but I really wasn't quite sure what to make of Aono-san. He came across like a corrupt, drunken Catholic priest, and I couldn't tell if he was a Zen master or a total charlatan.

'Toby-san,' Suzuki-san playfully inquired, 'kendo ouchy?'

I nodded and pointed at my knees: 'Kendo very ouchy; very cool, but very ouchy.' I added a rather lame double thumbs up for good measure.

'Ahh, *ganbatte*,' he said ('Try your best', 'endure', 'persevere'). 'Japan hardo.'

Everyone toasted me and appeared to approve of my response. Apparently having a bloody hard time was the first essential step in my kendo initiation. The drinks continued to flow and I tried to follow the conversation as best I could. As incomprehensible Japanese words flew past my numb ears, I focused on people's body language, expressions and tone of voice, heartily laughing and nodding away while listening to half-translated anecdotes and heated exchanges.

The teachers had, it seemed, all grown up together. They had spent their time in the sleepy suburb of Yoshiwara working hard, towing the strict Japanese line: marriage, kids, mortgages, social duties, kendo and personal sacrifice. Although they were all expert *sensei* in their own right, it was clear they looked to Suzuki-san as the real authority. He was the one who had really dedicated his life to martial arts. I felt as though I was being drawn into a secret fraternity of middle-aged Japanese kendo masters engaged in an illicit drinking session – a chance to finally let loose and taste some of the teenage kicks they missed out on, which seemed more than a little ironic as this was an area in which Bryan and I were consummate masters.

Everyone was now fairly drunk and having a hard time remembering that I didn't speak Japanese. Nabi-chan kept trying to rephrase slurred questions across the smoky table. Bryan stepped in to help: 'He wants to know what job you do. What's your career?'

'Oh right... Er, well, y'know... haven't really got one,' I said truthfully.

'They won't understand that.'

'Well... I was doing some mental-health work before I came over here – tell them my job is a bit like being a nurse.'

'Okay, I'll try to explain it.'

The teachers leant in expectantly, murmured, then looked surprised and confused. I wondered what Bryan had told them. Aono-san laughed with derision and waved a dismissive hand. Bryan reiterated his point to more serious murmurs of disbelief.

'Hmm… they don't understand,' said Bryan. 'They genuinely think I'm joking. You don't really get male nurses in Japan.'

'What the hell's wrong with nursing? Well, okay… tell them I'm a cowboy or something. I don't know… What do Japanese people do? A lumberjack, an oil rig worker – something macho.'

'Do you want me to tell them you were in the Village People?'

'Oh, forget it… *Kampai!*'

By the early hours of the morning, we were all looking fairly ruined. Bryan had jogged home to retrieve some jazz CDs and the whisky, Nori Sensei was snoring away on Takahashi Sensei's shoulder, Nabi-chan was still chain-smoking, in a trance, eyes shut, and the room was thick with smoke. Small piles of pistachio shells, crisps and overflowing ashtrays littered the table.

Aono Sensei was explaining to me with all the airs of a Jesuit missionary that, despite my futile objections, all Westerners were Christian and therefore couldn't possibly understand anything about Buddhism – and, by default, certainly could never become good at kendo either. Bryan and Suzuki-san appeared to be re-enacting kendo fights with their index fingers. The old shopkeeper eventually wandered in and began sweeping up wearily. It was time to go home. Everyone took the hint and started helping.

When we finally stumbled outside, the night air was fresh and sweet smelling. The storm had long since passed and, in the distance, cicadas had resumed their steady chirping. It took a few seconds for my eyes to adjust; the sleepy narrow streets were silhouetted by houses and an impenetrably black sky. A profound, aching tiredness washed over me. Suzuki-san and Takahashi Sensei located the Suzuki-wagon, climbed in, giggling hysterically like children, then rumbled off at an inebriated snail's pace, blasting out their loud rock anthems. It seemed highly unlikely they would make it home without getting arrested or lost, or crashing – or a combination of all three.

The remaining teachers said an emotional good night, bowed, hugged us, fell over, bowed again, then slipped away into the darkness in high spirits. We could hear them fading into the distance, singing and shouting like a crowd of kendo hooligans. And in a few moments, we were back at the Ninja House, laid flat out on the *tatami* and snoring for England.

*

Boredom is rage spread thin.

Paul Tillich

7

The New Boy

To my utter amazement, Bryan got up early the next day and went to work at the factory. I barely heard him go and slept my hangover off till around lunchtime. I woke in the usual pool of sweat and lay on my back for some time, staring at the ceiling, dozing and drifting in and out of jolting dreams.

Eventually, I opened the shutters. It was another steamingly hot day and the garden looked green and revitalised from the previous night's rain. I sipped water and spent a long time sitting, staring outside. Then, in the absence of anything else to do ahead of starting work at the paper factory the next day, I figured it was time to explore. At the end of the entrance hall, hidden behind some black lacquered screens, lay the inaccessible room piled ceiling high with every kind of debris imaginable. It had been used as a dumping ground for decades and seemed beyond any realistic chance of renovation, but I was intrigued to find out what lay beyond it. I took a deep breath and forced my way in, pushing bags, furniture, boxes, books and rubbish out of the way to create a path towards a doorway on the other side. I trod cautiously in bare feet, wary of mice and creepy crawlies. Almost immediately, I came across several alarming, gigantic, spindly red spiders. They appeared to be having a party underneath a packing crate and seemed to defy gravity as they scuttled off in different directions towards darker nooks and crannies. I froze with arachnophobic trepidation, let out a trembling sigh and continued moving towards the far side of the room. Once through the doorway, I found a blackened wooden porch with a desiccated panelled door at the top of some steps. The hinges protested with age as I eased it ajar. Inside, was a beautiful miniature tiled bathroom (minus an actual toilet) with a copper tap and traditional square sunken bath, just big enough to sit down in. Black mould and moss were growing in the corners and the whole place needed a serious deep clean. Still, I did a quick check for vengeful spiders, then clambered inside, slammed my head into a low beam and sat down in the empty bath. To my right, frosted windows faced the garden. I forced one open and, probably for the first time in many years, the fierce summer light and birdsong flooded in.

Not bad, I thought, gazing around with Indiana Jones-style satisfaction. I gritted my teeth, turned the tap on and, after some comical plumbing sounds, had my first breathtakingly cold traditional Japanese bath. Once I had adjusted to the temperature, I began to unwind a bit and take stock. My knees and feet were bruised from the previous night's *seiza*, my wrist was a jaundiced yellow colour from the kendo and angry, swollen mosquito bites ran along the veins in my arms and calves like track marks.

I lay back in the water, shut my eyes and attempted to distract myself by absentmindedly practising the few Japanese phrases I had so far managed to pick up... '*Atsui desu*' ('It's hot'), '*Ganbatte*' ('Persevere'), '*Hai*' ('Correct'), '*Ichi, ni, san, shi*' ('One, two, three, four'), '*Konichiwa*' ('Good day')... I rolled the words around my mouth, playing with their unfamiliar sounds, then tried them out in animated conversations: 'Aha, correct, it *is* hot, hmm, persevere, one two three four, why yes, this *is* a pen.'

I passed the afternoon twirling kendo swords around the garden like an angry majorette and loitering in the cool of the 7-Eleven, pretending to read newspapers and magazines – which, on reflection, considering the staff were already aware I didn't speak Japanese, must have confused the hell out of them.

Bryan returned home after dark, beer in hand, looking tired and sullen. Work clearly had the opposite effect to kendo on his mood. Plus, he'd had a call from Kazue, saying she'd been delayed in Tokyo and wouldn't be coming to Yoshiwara for a while.

'Never mind, mate,' I said, trying to cheer him up with some classic male advice. 'You hungry?' I pointed to a couple of packs of noodles I'd bought for tea.

Bryan regarded them with mild amusement. 'No, no, no,' he tutted, shaking his head, before reaching into his belongings and producing a large canvas duffle bag stuffed to bursting with instant noodles. 'I've been collecting these for years,' he said, proudly pouring them into a gigantic pile and passing his hands through them.

'Jesus.' I marvelled at the sheer obsession of it all. Some people came to Japan and bought antique fans, calligraphy or silk kimonos; Bryan collected noodles. To his credit though, he'd been busy: there was a range of styles – wheat-based, clear, rice, buckwheat, all dressed in bright packaging with garish, indecipherable calligraphy. 'I had no idea you were so into... Pot Noodles?'

'Pot... *Noodles*?' He looked as though he was about to throw up with outrage. 'These are *ramen*. It's like the equivalent of British fish 'n' chips, the Italian pizza, the French... uh, snails, except this isn't just food – it's art.' Carefully, he separated about 20 packets and arranged them in an artful pyramid. 'These are collectors' items,' he whispered with deadly seriousness. 'We can't eat them... *ever*. Not even if we're starving to death, okay?'

I nodded and prayed to God that we would never find ourselves in such dire straits.

Later on, Suzuki-san put in a brief appearance on his way home. Bryan asked him about the spiders. It turned out I hadn't imagined them; they were very real and, apparently, quite poisonous.

Bryan managed to swallow his culinary pride and we ate a frugal meal of the noodles I'd bought and bitter oranges from the garden, then fell asleep watching a trashy Kevin Costner film. Poor old Kevin had been dubbed and sounded like a Japanese Barry White.

The next day, we set off early on the bike and made quick headway across the train tracks, through the giant, steaming industrial compound, back towards the paper factory. The scene that greeted me was almost identical to my previous visit: the sun was beating down, the paper machines were humming and people were lolling around by the skips, smoking like it was going out of fashion. Inside, the old lady was still making cardboard boxes and the Puganought and MC Squared lurked in the shadows, looking gormless and generally dissatisfied with life.

Convention dictated that the first thing we needed to do was locate every employee, formally bow and say good morning. When this was done, Bryan went into the office to find some cigarettes, while I loitered in the entrance.

The boss wandered round the corner. I bowed and stood in excruciating silence, lost for words.

'*Atsui*,' he said, sniffing the air like an old farmer.

'*Hai, atsui*,' I replied too quickly, nodding like the village idiot. He laughed awkwardly and backtracked into the office, as though he'd conveniently forgotten to do something important.

Shadowing Bryan was easier said than done. The walkways between the rows of equipment were narrow and I was either in the way or conspicuously standing in the background doing nothing.

I hovered behind him and watched the spinning reels slowly grind to a halt. Everyone stood in lines then stepped forward and began pressing red and green switches to unclip them. I tried (and failed) to memorise the sequence. It seemed inevitable that sooner or later I would manage to press them in the exact order that would cause the entire conveyer belt to explode. It was anxiety-provoking.

Bryan cut the thin feed-line of paper, taped the loose end up and passed me a full reel. I staggered sideways and wobbled precariously over to the packing tables with it. Unsurprisingly, it weighed a ton. Next came the boxing up. I was tagged on to the end of the packing tables and followed everyone else's lead. The reels kept coming thick and fast. No one talked. They worked with a startling sense of urgency. It looked deceptively easy: taking four strips of cardboard, folding them into triangles, then poking them into the corners of a box to cushion the paper. Mind-bogglingly simple. Yet, despite all my best efforts, my triangles came out wonky and I couldn't match the pace. I got tied up with the packing tape, I failed to stick the boxes together properly, I bumped into people and generally interrupted the smooth flow of work. No one spoke, but I could feel a tense undercurrent of frustration. I was slowing the team down. This was serious. Notwithstanding the simple nature of the work, paper making required dexterity and concentration – neither of which I seemed to possess. There was very little recognition that it was my first day. Everyone was far too preoccupied by their own efforts (with the irritating exception of Jalal, who kept coming over and miming how to fold the cardboard properly). It was exasperating. Eventually, MC Squared unsympathetically escorted me out of the way to a large pile of flat cardboard and got me making boxes instead.

For the rest of the day, I worked on my own. It felt like a demotion, but at least I couldn't get in anyone's way, and I was actually slightly relieved. I sang along to myself in a robotic Stephen Hawking-style voice: 'Pick up cardboard, fold it, tape it, stack it.'

I figured I could become the old woman's disciple. She could teach me all her skills and I would become the young cardboard box apprentice. I gazed over at her magnificent pile of perfectly shaped masterpieces, then back to my own small, misshapen stack. The old lady threw me a benign grandmotherly smile from afar, as if she was looking at a baby sitting in a pile of its own shit.

My first day was passing very, very slowly. In the absence of a watch or any wall clocks, the changing of the paper reels was the only tangible measure of time. Every fifteen minutes or so, the frantic packing was repeated. From my lonely exile, I watched the other workers' (relatively) more varied routine with a growing sense of envy. Their rapid pace was depressing and I doubted if I would ever be able to keep up. This was actually a terrifying realisation, as the only job for an illegal, non-Japanese-speaking labourer here was making boxes. Most Westerners in Japan taught English or worked in business, but for that you needed working visas and qualifications – neither of which I had. This was the only thing that was going to enable me to stay in the country and study kendo. There was no getting round it. I was just going to have to suck it up.

Bryan occasionally passed by and we exchanged a few words, but after a while, the absence of conversation – or, indeed, any kind of stimulation whatsoever – resulted in a drowsy retreat into my own head. Authentic boredom takes time to develop, and I was still at the comparatively exciting 'Holy-shit-this-is-boring' phase. It wasn't until I'd been going at it for about four hours straight that I began to get an inkling of the previously unimagined levels of dullness I was destined for. I thought about Brian Keenan's book, *An Evil Cradling*,[1] and how, after being taken hostage in Beirut and kept blindfolded in isolation, he had gradually begun to replay his memories, reliving his entire life many times over. I cursed myself for having led such a dull existence. Reliving my own life was going to involve a great deal of watching myself sitting around staring at the telly. Actually, to be fair, there had been plenty of fun times, particularly getting wasted with friends and going to all-night raves, but although it had been brilliant at the time, it now seemed remote and surprisingly drab in retrospect. Here, thousands of miles away from home, in a stiflingly hot sweatshop, my memories seemed unreal, too distant; they just didn't really fit into any kind of entertaining narrative.

Back in England, I'd been really into DJing. Well, at least in theory. (I'd failed to get the money together to actually buy some decks, but I figured being a DJ was more of a state of mind, and I'd often mix tunes in my head.) Perhaps now it was the heat, or the physically repetitive nature of the work, but fragments of old tunes kept spinning round and round in my mind – surreal snippets of scratched '80s rap lyrics endlessly repeating.

At around four o'clock – or, perhaps more accurately, 'paper-reel-change number 32' – I suddenly realised that I'd been humming the same tune like a looped mantra for about three hours.

I sighed. If kendo had been a rollercoaster of emotion, then working in the factory was definitely going to be a merry-go-round of monotony. The steady whirr of the machines gradually drowned my thoughts out and seemed to add a tragic poignancy to the whole situation.

Jalal walked past me, stopped, pointed and brusquely motioned for me to make boxes for the umpteenth time. I bowed respectfully, thanking him for his insight and guidance, while simultaneously daydreaming about slamming his head into one of the spinning machines. He's such a jobsworth, I thought.

---

1. Keenan, B., *An Evil Cradling*, Hutchinson (1992).

Hey... that's it – that's his new name. Jobsworth wandered off looking self-important and pleased with himself.

At dusk, we all sat outside on pallets, taking a break. The sky was a rich gold colour and the setting sun lit up the distant foothills. We were weary and damp with sweat. The Iraqis chatted among themselves quietly and Shimizusan lay on his back, stroking his moustache, stretching and yawning. Akio just stared into space, jiggling his legs with nervous energy. MC Squared and the Puganought were sitting further away on their own, sneering sarcastically at the rest of us like a couple of school bullies. Bryan threw me a pack of Japanese cigarettes called Mild Seven. I lit one up, exhaled slowly and stared at the box.

'Strange,' I said. 'They're not mild and there aren't seven of them.'

He gave me a mystified look and opened his mouth as if to say something, then seemed to change his mind.

'So... what time do we finish?' I asked, my voice cracking slightly with desperation.

'Soon, probably. Basically, we stay until it's done... It... It's not so bad?' It sounded like a question – as if he was reassuring himself as much as me.

'Man, Jobsworth is doing my fucking head in,' I said, lowering my voice a little. 'He keeps ordering me around and telling me to do things I'm already doing.'

'Jobsworth?'

'Jalal,' I whispered. 'He's such a mini-boss.'

'Hahaha, yeah, true. He genuinely believes he's in charge.'

'You know I wouldn't mind if I was handling dangerous radioactive material or something, but I'm making cardboard boxes, for Christ's sake. I think even I can manage that.'

'Just ignore him; he'll get bored sooner or later. He does it to everyone, even me – and I've been here longer than he has. The guy's a lazy fucker. Just watch how he speeds up whenever Shachousan's around.'

I peered at the Iraqis out of the corner of my eye; they were huddled in a tight circle, no doubt having a similar conversation about us. Sami and Jobsworth looked tense and paranoid, as if they were in the middle of a massive drug deal. Their status as illegal immigrants made them virtual prisoners here. Deep down, behind the smiles and the bowing I suspected they loathed this job, despised Japan and were, no doubt, desperately missing their families and wishing things had turned out differently. I could sense their unhappiness.

'How did they end up here?'

'I'm not exactly sure,' said Bryan, lowering his voice to a whisper. 'All I know is some seriously bad shit happened to them. Sami's wife was killed or something. I think Jalal had a relative over here and somehow managed to get them out of Iraq, but it must have cost a lot of cash, and they sure as hell can't go back. Still, better than staying, I guess. They'd be out of here and back to Iraq in a shot if they could.'

It was tragic. I watched Toni sitting quietly, blinking and smiling at nothing in particular and felt immensely sad for him. However bad things got, at least I could leave if I had to.

To a certain extent, the entire factory seemed to be unfolding as an uneasy collection of power struggles and frustrations. Bryan and I represented the newly formed disgruntled British contingent. Bryan hated Jobsworth and Jobsworth hated Bryan. The Iraqis appeared to hate the Japanese and the Japanese, in turn, hated the Iraqis. Everyone was united in hating MC Squared and the Puganought, and they clearly hated everyone and everything. Akio, representing Brazil and wearing a constant rigid expression of 'Dude-what-fucking-ever', was too young and cool to get involved.

The deep, ironic weirdness of the situation was that this international quagmire of discontent was being played out beneath traditional Japanese work etiquette. As the newly arrived Westerner, I was used to being able to speak my mind to some extent. Here, it felt as if everyone was wearing a mask. In between the bowing and the hard work, fake smiles belied dark, resentful eyes, making the general tension seem all the more acute. Anywhere else, arguments and fights would almost certainly have erupted. Here though, the pretence of respect and politeness was religiously adhered to. When the boss was nearby, everyone offered round cigarettes, smiled and laughed, but as soon as he was out of sight, they returned to their separate groups and glowering bad moods (with the sole exception of the old lady, who I was beginning to suspect was actually some kind of divine being).

As the light finally faded, the machines ground to a halt again. Everyone wearily dragged themselves back to the packing tables. It took all the self-control I possessed to make myself go back inside and face the mountain of cardboard boxes for a last push. At 7.30, Bryan appeared and announced that we were done. He led me around the factory, where we said goodbye to everyone with the time-honoured phrase, '*Osaki ni shitsurei shimasu*' ('Please forgive my rudeness for leaving work early'), to which they all dutifully replied, '*Otsukaresama deshita*' ('We worked hard today'). I noticed Bryan seemed to have to hype himself up every time he had to say it, as if it caused him actual physical pain. He'd been working here for several years and had actually helped the boss set the place up when he'd first inherited the factory from his father. Bryan had worked like a dog, but now the boss was getting rich, while Bryan was left packing boxes. Shachousan clearly felt indebted to Bryan and treated him like an equal, but he'd promoted MC Squared and the Puganought to supervisors ahead of him. Bryan's resentment had been steadily building for some time. However bad things got though, formal etiquette still applied.

'Oh, please forgive my rudeness for daring to leave work... *please.*'

It was an exchange I would come to know all too well.

We rode home and had an early night. I slept soundly, and if I did dream, it almost certainly involved cardboard boxes.

*

It is more important to not fail than to succeed.

Japanese proverb

8

The Heavy Sword

'*Ichi, ni, san…*' Suzuki-san counted slowly and hypnotically, as he patiently watched me practising sword strikes. I was barely aware of the rest of the kendo class happening around me with the usual cacophony of screams and cracking, thudding noises. For now, I was still practising without a helmet, so it seemed unlikely anyone would try to hit me just yet – hopefully.

Suzuki-san's metronomic chanting had a faintly optimistic tone; perhaps it was an appeal to the gods that through sheer bloody-minded repetition my basic technique might improve. I raised the sword above my head and sliced through the hot, stuffy air, over and over, giving it my all. He watched me intently, as if searching for some incredibly well-hidden, vital fighting attribute. I was resigned to the relentless striking, content to execute basic techniques, for ever if necessary, but also savouring the fact that I could at least understand what Suzuki-san was actually saying for a change.

'*Ichi, ni, san. Ichi, ni, san…* Toby-san, ouchy?'

'Okay,' I said, smiling weakly, shaking my head.

He began counting with more urgency: '*Ichi, ni, san, ichi, ni, san, ichi, ni, san.*' As I struck faster, it occurred to me that I resembled one of those slightly speeded up black-and-white movie reels of Buster Keaton or Harold Lloyd. We carried on like this until I was soaked with sweat and struggling to lift my arms. It was tantamount to torture, but this was what I'd wanted, right? This was why I had come to Japan. What else had I expected? It was never going to be easy, after all. Finally, he motioned for me to take a break. I knelt at the edge of the class rubbing my arms discreetly, so as not to draw attention to myself.

The head teacher, Takagi Sensei, was prowling like a dangerous beast among the shadows at the end of the *dojo*. His presence alone made me feel as though I was under intense scrutiny; I imagined everyone else felt the same. I could easily pick him out, even with his helmet on, as I'd memorised the colour and style of his body armour, but he was mostly recognisable by the terrifying aura of sheer *fighto* – a permanent samurai-like aura of combat-readiness that seemed to surround him. I could never quite tell who anyone else was in the seething rows of sparring bodies though. Only when someone got really close could I peer into their helmet and see them smiling back at me, or hear an encouraging, 'Toby-san, okay? *Atsui desu!*'

Suzuki-san returned a few minutes later with Bryan, carrying a large wooden sword. He presented it to me with a formal bow. It was made from solid hardwood, thicker at the blade than on the handle and weighing considerably more than the bamboo *shinai* we normally used.

'*Suburito*,'[1] Suzuki-san said. 'Good ouchy.'

'He says you've got to take it home and practise at least one hundred strikes a day,' said Bryan, 'and that will help you improve. Although personally, I doubt it.'

'Thank you,' I said, laughing. 'I'd better take two.'

Back at the Ninja House, the kendo teachers knelt round the table drinking and reviewing the evening's battles. I kept my arms tucked in close to my body to stop them trembling with muscle fatigue as I poured the drinks. I wondered what these men's wives made of their hobbies: 'I'm off drinking and fighting again honey – don't wait up!' Perhaps it was a cultural thing? As ever, most of the conversations were completely incomprehensible or selectively translated by Bryan. The sheer complexities of the Japanese language were infuriating. As my attention tuned in and out, I felt punch-drunk and deeply frustrated that I wasn't able to speak my mind. Aono-san sidled up to me to speak a bit of English. I explained that Suzuki-san had lent me a *suburito*, and that he thought it might help me get faster at striking.

'Faster?' said Aono-san with surprise, as if I'd suggested the most ridiculous thing in the world. 'Hahaha, faster, yes, maybe,' he said, clearly meaning, 'No chance.' 'You know, you and Bryan are very young and...' – he licked his lips, searching for the correct word, then smiled – '... naive. I think you do not understand kendo. This is Japan, very hard for you,' he said, reiterating the obvious once more. I nodded, resigning myself to his point of view. Of course, he was technically correct – I didn't understand kendo yet, and Japan was certainly hard – but the way he said it incensed me. Still, there seemed little point in arguing, and I was fairly sure it would have been frowned on if I had. There it was again, *senpai–kohai* – and it was really starting to grate.

Aono-san studied me carefully, searching for the slightest flicker of irritation to pounce on. Bryan, who was eavesdropping, flashed me a brief eye roll towards the ceiling.

---

1. *Suburito* – a wooden *bokuto* practice sword, used for strengthening and conditioning.

'Why you come to Japan?' continued Aono-san in a matter-of-fact way. 'You think maybe kendo easy?'

'No,' I said, defensively. 'No, not because it's easy. It's because it's hard… and…'

I could see that Aono-san was revelling in my discomfort again. He knew exactly which of my buttons to press. He leant back, mopping his bald head and looking stern. Was this some kind of Zen test of my temperament or was he just trying to wind me up so much that my kendo would become awesome out of sheer vengeance?

Nabi-chan came over to save me. 'Toby-san, kendo okay,' he said, giving me a thumbs up and chiding Aono-san in a friendly way. Then they exchanged a few words in Japanese, and Aono-san laughed at me with such a mighty convulsion it shocked me. He scared me and he knew it. I caught Bryan's eye again. He subtly nodded slowly with a reassuring look. I turned back to Aono-san, laughed heartily and poured him another drink.

Practising every day with the heavy *suburito* was quite a workout. At first, it required breaking my daily hundred sword swings into manageable chunks. The last few sets always hurt, and it didn't help that the more I sweated, the more the mosquitoes seemed to bite me, but at least I had something concrete that I could understand and throw my energies into. My arms were getting stronger, and my sword strikes had definitely become faster – at least they felt faster to me. After a session with the *suburito*, in comparison the bamboo *shinai* felt like a toothpick.

My God, I thought one evening at the Ninja House, standing in the garden counting strikes to myself in Japanese. I really think this actually might be working.

'Toby-san, fighto.' Suzuki-san led me to a quiet corner of the *dojo* and helped squeeze me into Bryan's old worn set of body armour. It was late in the evening and we had been drilling moves and strikes until I felt numb. But now the time had finally come to test my fighting spirit.

My breathing resonated loudly in my ears as I peered at Suzuki-san nervously through the chrome grill of my mask. He bowed and took the kendo en-garde position (kamae), looking completely unassailable. I felt claustrophobic and slightly disorientated.

'*Hajime*,' ('Begin'), he shouted, motioning for me to attack. I picked up my *shinai*, bowed, adopted a fighting stance opposite him and took a deep breath.

This is it, I mused. I'm going to get killed. I paused for a few seconds, hoping to get the feel of things, trying to centre myself and find a way past Suzuki-san's impossible guard. He didn't move. He was very kindly giving me as much time as I needed, but I was completely at his mercy. It felt as though his every angle of attack was covered, while, in contrast, every one of mine felt wide open.

I gripped my sword tightly, rigidly, a novice's mistake. I took another deep breath. 'Come on then.' I was hyping myself up for the fight. This was it. There could be no holding back. 'Don't think – feel.' Oh my God, was I actually quoting Bruce Lee films to myself? I raised my sword and lunged at him. To my great surprise, I actually connected with the top of his helmet, only gently though. Even if we'd been using real swords it would have been annoying at best. Suzuki-san still didn't react. I sailed past him, then we both turned to face each other again. He made a few encouraging grunts that clearly meant, 'Come on, is that it?' and nodded for me to attack again.

I gritted my teeth, bounced up and down a little in my stance and went for it, this time surprising myself with the satisfying crack of the sword as it firmly made contact with his helmet. Now Suzuki-san struck back. It wasn't a devastating blow, and I knew he was just letting me know my vulnerable areas, but it stung. I struck again and he hit me back at such speed it took me a moment to register the strikes: one to the wrist and one to the top of the mask. *Kote, men.*

This went on for some time. I would try to belt him on the helmet with all the grace of an overweight parlour maid thwacking at a dusty carpet on wash day and, before I had even settled back into my stance, he would strike me back several times, wrist and head, thwack, crack. *Kote, men,* thud, smack. Not a fight exactly, but each time getting faster, more intense, the adrenaline kicking in, hitting and being hit slightly harder every time.

Despite the cotton headscarf I wore under my mask, my eyes ran with sweat. I tried my hardest to imitate Suzuki-san, but I was, of course, hopelessly outclassed. Although he took it easy on me, the sparring session hurt and seemed to last a very long time. The best I could do was try to keep up.

'So, you survived your first night of sparring, then?' said Bryan later with a smirk, as we got changed at the edge of the *dojo*.

'Yeah, sort of. It was… good? I think I can cope with the head strikes, although my wrists are really beginning to get sore. Actually, who am I kidding, my head seriously hurts as well.' I rubbed at the bruised patch on the crown of my head. 'In fact, I take it all back. I don't know if I can handle much more of this. Everything fucking hurts!'

'I was watching your "fight" with Suzuki-san. Remember, kendo masks have got the most amount of padding at the front. You need to look up more – stop worrying about getting hit so much. Keep your head up; don't watch your sword or your hands. If you do, the *shinai* will whip you on the back of your head – hurts like hell at first.'

'Now you tell me.'

'Also, you've got to keep your wrists in, or else they're a wide-open target. Anyone who knows what they're doing will get them every time. The teachers won't tell you about this; they'll just keep hitting you until you tuck them in. It's a pretty old-school way of getting the message across, but put it this way: it's a lesson you're never going to forget.'

'Ah. Yeah, I'm definitely beginning to get that, thanks.'

'You owe me one. Took me about a month to learn that. I remember I was so bruised I could hardly hold my bloody chopsticks at first.'

We sat for a while, lost in the silent wonder and contemplation of it all.

'So… I guess you should have probably used a fork,' I said.

Bryan just shook his head slowly.

*

No journey carries one far unless, as it extends into the world around us, it goes an equal distance into the world within.

Lillian Smith

9

Mount Odana

The weeks passed distressingly slowly, or at least the days did. Every night, it seemed as though I lay down on the soft *tatami* of the Ninja House for a couple of minutes and then BLAM – tomorrow was already happening. There I was: back in the airless factory, tired and irritable, standing in front of another colossal tower of unmade cardboard boxes with hours of drudgery to look forward to.

Sometimes, I felt utterly dissociated, as though I was in a barely conscious state, whereby my hands were working and I was just a casual observer. The mornings were always filled with self-pity. By the afternoon though, I had usually stopped fighting the boredom and entered into a far more comfortable world of weird daydreams and fantastic imaginary DJ sets.

Break times became very precious. Bryan and I chain-smoked, ate noodles, chatted about our lives back home and how ridiculously hot and difficult everything was here. Toni sang his Iraqi pop songs, Sami told me about the horrors of the Gulf War – mainly through disturbing mimes and his very convincing 'hundred-mile stare'. Shimizu-san taught me indispensable new phrases such as, '*Oni atsui*' ('Monster hot'),[1] '*Tsukareta*' ('Tired') and '*Taihen desu*' ('It's hard work'), and Jobsworth, MC Squared and the Puganought continued to be interfering and bossy – they were living proof that every country has its fair share of pricks.

One Friday evening, we returned home profoundly elated by the prospect of two whole days off. I was beginning to appreciate why Bryan had been so desperate to party when he'd picked me up from the airport.

This weekend, he was planning on going back to Tokyo and seeing Kazue. Since I didn't want to intrude, and plus I couldn't actually afford it, I had decided to explore some of the surrounding countryside. Bryan had lent me a book about the way of the samurai called *Hagakure*.[2] I was going to embark on a

---

1. As in: 'Christ, it's hot.' 'No, it's boiling.' 'Actually, it's *oni atsui*!'

journey into the heart of the ancient Japanese mountains, going back to nature where, like countless acolytes before me, I would train my body and mind and contemplate life and death (albeit only for two days). Bryan suggested that I take the bike and ride up Mount Odana, which stood just to the right of the still cloud-obscured Mount Fuji. Apparently, there was a small, winding road which turned into a snaking path leading up to a mist-shrouded shack where you could stay the night. It was definitely off the beaten track and occasionally visited by monks and adventurous walkers. It sounded perfect.

Bryan drew me a rough map showing me how to get to the shack, wished me luck then danced off to the train station in high spirits. As soon as he was gone, I began gathering equipment and making plans. I would take a small blanket (for the ludicrously unlikely eventuality that it turned cold), a wooden sword for practising kendo forms, candles, cigarettes, food, lots of water and some cooking equipment. I'd probably meet some ancient Zen hermit who would teach me sword moves that were so awesome he'd forbid me from ever using them, and I'd have to spend the rest of my life peacefully walking away from my attackers, secure in the knowledge that I secretly rocked. I thumbed through the *Hagakure*, looking for an inspirational sonnet to encapsulate the spirit of my adventure. It flipped open on a passage expounding the wisdom of drinking a tonic made from horse dung as a cure for bleeding – a surprising yet practical pearl of wisdom. I went outside and dutifully performed my obligatory 100 practise strikes with the heavy *suburito*. Halfway through, I noticed one of our neighbours peering over our fence watching me. '*Konbanwa*,' ('Good evening') I called out, smiling and waving without missing a beat. He looked startled that I could actually speak, nodded and waved back nervously and then, very slowly, sank down out of sight. As the only Westerners for miles around (or at least the only Westerners I'd seen since I'd been here), I figured we were a curiosity in suburban Yoshiwara. I wondered if that was the only way people here were comfortable relating to us. Later, I made noodles, smoked a few cigarettes and sat cooling off for a while in the empty silence of the house. The background drone from outside of a thousand insects came into focus. They sounded far more serious tonight, menacing even.

I left the house early the next morning and, after a brief stop for food, headed straight for Odana. I had borrowed a canvas rucksack from Bryan and tied a wooden sword to the bike's crossbar with some old shoelaces. The sun was just

---

2. Hagakure – meaning 'In the shadow of leaves', this is a 17th-century manual of *bushido*, 'the way of the warrior', written by Yamamoto Tsunetomo.

reaching its full strength and the sky was a perfect fairy-tale blue. After my initial reservations, I felt fantastic. I flew past a chessboard of sunken rice fields and withered brown haystacks. The road was totally empty of people and traffic, so I guided the rattling old bike through a series of death-defying stunts – swerving zigzags, a few attempted wheelies and, of course, letting go of the handlebars and pretending to fly. As I approached the foothills, wooden pylons and green tea bushes began to line the way. I pulled up at an isolated roadside vending machine for a break. Despite the remote location, it was well stocked – cans, coffee, hot chocolate, even beer – and I wondered who could possibly ever use it out there. For a brief second, an image popped into my head of me giving up on Odana and spending the entire weekend leant up against the machine, drunk out of my mind. I bought an ice-cold bottle of water and sat down.

The dark foliage of the surrounding tea bushes rustled in a warm breeze. They looked shiny and appealing. This was the first time I'd ever seen tea in its natural state at close quarters. I wasn't sure if you could make a cuppa from it, but as I got back on the bike I plucked a few leaves and pressed them inside my book just in case. Moving steadily upwards, the road started to wind its way through a parched alpine forest. Steep, reinforced concrete landslide defences and dense vegetation stretched upwards to dizzying heights. I began to feel dwarfed by the scale of the ascent and was soon drenched in sweat with the exertion of pedalling.

Odana had looked small in relation to its surroundings, but it was a mountain none the less and far higher than anything I was used to. It wasn't long before I found myself pushing the bike and gasping for breath. For several hours, I maintained a slow but steady pace, stopping only for water and to gaze back at an increasingly remote-looking Yoshiwara. By lunchtime, I had put a considerable amount of distance behind me. The road was starting to narrow and the air was also becoming noticeably less humid. My legs ached as I bent over the bike, head down, locked in the exertion and concentration of the climb, until I practically walked straight into the wooden fence which marked the end of the Tarmac road. A spindly footpath bordered by trees curled away into the distance.

This is it, I thought. *Sayonara* ('Farewell') civilisation. I stashed the bike in the undergrowth and headed off on foot with renewed vigour.

The terrain was slightly flatter now and the surrounding woods were carpeted in wispy yellow grasses. It was pleasantly warm and a few idle crows called out from the treetops. I strolled along, wooden sword and bag slung over my shoulder, brushing the tops of plants with my hands. Streams of tiny insects floated off into a gentle summer breeze and I felt lighter and more relaxed than I'd been for a long time. The stress and hard work of the paper factory were gradually beginning to evaporate. One way or another, communing with nature always seemed to sort me out. No one ever returned from watching a beautiful sunset or seeing the stars and thought, That was shit – what a waste of time.

Up ahead, a weathered timber building was set back among the trees. It resembled an old prairie cabin, with closed shuttered windows and sun-bleached knotted wood. I assumed this was the place Bryan had mentioned, and threw my stuff down and walked inside. There was a cold stone floor with a blackened fire pit, and rough benches lining the walls. It was dark and fairly unappealing (Bryan couldn't ever have stayed here, I thought), so I decided to press onwards towards the summit and sleep outside. It would be fine. I'd been a cub scout and was used to camping on Dartmoor. There was nothing to it. In fact, I was practically an expert. I could build a fire, whittle a spoon, tickle a trout, milk a badger, wrestle a bear… Actually, come to think of it…

The crows had stopped calling and everything had become very quiet and still. My breathing started to tighten and I could feel my heart pounding in my chest. I stared straight ahead along the path. Were there any dangerous wild animals in Japan? I had no idea. Surely Bryan would have mentioned it if there were. I pictured him, halfway through 'ladies' night' in Tokyo, beer in one hand, party poppers in the other, blissfully unaware of my plight.

I turned very slowly in a tight circle, peering into the trees. Was there any-thing out there? My hand instinctively reached for the handle of the *bokuto*. Could I beat an animal to death with a wooden sword? I seriously doubted it. I was a vegetarian, after all. Hell, I bet this was part of my kendo initiation. The teachers were probably all hiding in the trees right now, laughing at me – Aono Sensei slowly drawing his finger across his throat. I raised the sword above my head in my finest en-garde position and narrowed my eyes. The hairs on the back of my neck bristled with apprehension and a cold shiver shot down my spine. A long time passed.

Nothing happened.

Lowering the sword, I forced a weak, throaty laugh.

What would a real samurai warrior do? I hadn't read any more of the *Hagakure* yet, but I bet it a) didn't involve having an anxiety attack, and b) prob-ably did involve real swords and drinking potions made from horse shit.

'*Kore wa pen desu,*' I shouted with determination in my most macho samu-rai voice, twirling the sword around with sound effects and returning it to an imaginary scabbard. The echo took a long time to fade. I took a deep, heroic breath and set off again, berating myself for letting my imagination get the better of me.

The trail was becoming steeper again. In the distance, I could just make out some kind of giant white cliff. As I got closer, it dawned on me that I was actually looking at a dam spanning a gorge. There was no way around it and I soon found myself dwarfed in its shadow, gazing up at a rusty old metal ladder. It appeared to be about 50 feet high, but it was hard to judge as the top disappeared into a haze of fog. For some reason though, despite a strong aversion to falling to my death, I had an overwhelming urge to keep going. I felt strangely driven – like a true samurai. Adventure and mystery beckoned.

I tied the sword and bag together, gave the ladder a shake and pulled myself on to the lower rungs. It crossed my mind that I was about to do something spectacularly foolish. The structure seemed solid enough, but it still took a few minutes to persuade my legs that this was a good idea. My blood ran cold as I imagined what would happen if I fell.

Very, very cautiously, I began to climb. I stared straight ahead, holding on with white knuckles, forcing myself not to look down: hand over hand, stay calm, keep going. Before the sheer stupidity of the situation had had time to properly sink in, I was sliding over the top of the ladder and scrambling away from the edge on my belly. I lay there for a moment, breathless, marvelling at my recklessness, then knelt up and looked about. I was lying in the bed of a dry river scattered with giant sandy boulders. Twisted trees and tall bamboo branches were just visible between pockets of damp, drifting mist.

I leant over to look at the view and was immediately hit by a wave of vertigo. Immense, puffy white clouds glided past. Below, I could just make out occasional glimpses of the faraway Yoshiwaran plain. I eyed the ladder sheepishly. It was going to take some serious motivation to persuade myself to climb back down it again.

I spent some time scouting along the edge of the riverbed, jumping over fallen trees and exploring the prehistoric plateau. Gradually, I began to get my bearings. There was no path anymore, but steep, rocky ground led upwards away from the dam. I was determined to reach the summit, and strode on purposefully till I was immersed in a cool bank of wet fog. The higher I got, the more surreal everything became.

I found a sheltered flat ledge and decided to set up camp there. It was a good spot, shaded by ferns and gigantic overhanging bamboo shoots. Sticks and leaves were strewn about, and despite the damp atmosphere it proved easy to get a small fire going. I arranged my thin blanket and supplies and made myself comfortable. Rays of afternoon sunshine streamed through the campfire smoke and loud crackles reverberated across the valley. It was still warm, but the pockets of floating mist gave the place a dream-like atmosphere. Peering into the ghostly haze, I caught glimpses of ethereal tigers and dancing bears streaking through the dappled undergrowth. I lay back for a minute, shut my eyes and decided it was time for tea.

I boiled water and experimented with a few of the leaves I'd plucked from the foothills. They were intensely bitter and immediately turned the water into a putrid sludge. Perhaps they weren't from tea bushes, after all? Perhaps they were poisonous? I poured the liquid away, sipped a cup of plain hot water instead, and began thumbing through the *Hagakure*, searching for enlightenment. It wasn't exactly light reading.

As far as I could tell, being a samurai mainly involved serving your master and selflessly laying down your life. To be honest, it wasn't quite what I'd hoped for. Gradually though, as I sat by the fire trying to absorb the *Hagakure*'s authentic martial wisdom, some of the passages began to speak to me. I could see that it contained a poignant and powerful kind of logic. It stated that living with no concern for your own life was the true essence of the way of the warrior. This seemed to make perfect sense to me and I immediately resolved to live the rest of my life like a dead man. After all, someone who has given up on the constant self-obsessed efforts of trying to save their own neck would be fearless; they would be free to do the right thing – to be truly humble, to act without hesitation. Imagine trying to fight someone who literally didn't give a shit what happened to them. It was empowering stuff. I jumped up, gritting my teeth and feeling inspired. It was time to do some training…

I threw myself into practising sword strikes. My arms and legs were weak and stiff, but I ignored that – I pushed myself past my usual hundred repetitions, and kept going until my spirited attacks gradually degenerated into uncoordinated, exhausted swipes. I felt invigorated. Eventually, I placed the sword to one side and stood trembling, catching my breath and cooling down. After a while, I began tuning into the subtle sounds around me. The whole place felt alive. I could sense the ground and the air vibrating, insects and birds were singing and the trees swayed gently in the breeze. I was completely alone and way beyond the mad distractions and humdrum pettiness of civilisation. The isolation of Mount Odana was profound. Training alone out here in the elements was incredible.

'Why doesn't everyone do this?' I wondered out loud.

I felt sorry for all the people far below me slaving away in the heat, trying to get ahead, trying to save themselves. Didn't they realise it was all pointless? Life was an opportunity not to be missed, particularly not to be wasted making cardboard boxes. I spent the rest of the afternoon immersed in the simple joys of leaping from rock to rock, brandishing my sword like a lunatic and slaying imaginary demons in their thousands.

*

Dragon's head, snake's tail.

Ancient Japanese folk proverb

10

Paper Tiger

By about six o'clock, I was crouched close to the fire, wrapped in my blanket, staring fixedly at the top of the mountain. The shadows had lengthened and the evening drawn in. For the previous ten minutes, bizarre rustling sounds from the summit had begun to fill me with a sense of dread once more.

At first, there had been the distant snapping of twigs, but it was gradually starting to sound as though something large and possibly very menacing was heading my way. The euphoric training session had run out of steam and my new-found bravado was being sorely tested by the prospect of spending the night out here alone. I smoked nervously and gazed up through silhouetted bamboo leaves at the darkening sky. The glow of the campfire cast eerie rippling patterns across the trees, and the drifting sheets of mist looked impenetrable and full of danger. My imagination was working overtime.

Suddenly, a much closer sound alerted my attention. I sat bolt upright and gripped the sword tightly across my lap. I'd read somewhere that grizzlies can run as fast as racehorses and climb trees. Basically, if you're in the wilderness and a bear picks a fight with you, you've had it.

Stay cool, I told myself. It was probably just a bird, or a fox... or maybe a pig or... a... a werewolf! Yep, I knew it – that definitely sounded like a were-wolf – or a tiger at the very least.

'Oh look,' I whispered to myself in a surprisingly detached way, 'my worst nightmare appears to be coming true.'

Whatever was out there was clever, prowling just out of sight – probably sharpening its claws or waiting for reinforcements. All of a sudden, I knew with total clarity that I couldn't spend the night here on my own – I'd go mad. I had to get off this mountain right away. I knew getting back down in the dark would be dangerous, but I had made the decision to retreat. I packed my bag in seconds and wrapped the blanket tightly around me. The fire was beginning to die down, so I took a burning branch for a torch and reluctantly doused the embers with the remains of my water. The violent hiss and smoke made me jump and my eyes stung as they strained to adjust to the murky gloom. For several minutes, I crouched motionless in a low, defensive stance, breathing hard, listening, waiting. I held my sword in one hand, the flaming torch (actually, it was more of a smouldering twig) in the other. Finally, despite my better judgement telling me to curl up into a foetal ball and stay put, I began moving down the mountain. I turned in a cautious circle round the camp, then set off back down the river valley, scanning the darkness constantly for any signs of attacking beasts as, occasionally, I heard distant crashing noises in the undergrowth behind me.

I nearly broke my neck several times sliding across smooth rocks and tripping over tangled branches. I reminded myself that most mountaineers died on the descent, but after what seemed like an eternity of panic-stricken stumbling I emerged from the undergrowth at the top of the dam and stood by the edge panting, looking out across a vast expanse of cold night sky. It was beautiful and humbling. Silvery-grey silhouetted clouds drifted past and tiny pinpricked stars dotted the horizon. Far away in the valley, I could just make out the shining lights of Yoshiwara; it made the feelings of remoteness seem even more intense, as if I was gazing down at the earth from a distant, alien world.

I picked my way carefully to the edge and turned one last time to stare back into the mist. In a rare moment of lucidity, I reasoned that whatever was out there was most probably harmless, but then again, I didn't want to stick around and test this new theory out. I threaded the sword through the straps of the rucksack, then, very cautiously, I sat down and began edging towards the top of the ladder on my backside. I put my feet on the first rung. The hilt of the sword immediately caught on the concrete lip of the dam, and rather than calmly unhooking it, I began to panic, thrashing around desperately to release myself. Suddenly, the sword jolted free and for a split second I was slipping out of control. My hands lurched forward, grabbing the rungs tightly and I pressed myself hard in, gasping with fear. There was an utterly black void below me, but I knew how high up I was. There was no doubt about it – if I fell off now, I would die.

'CALM THE FUCK DOWN, SAMURAI!' I shouted at myself, without the slightest hint of irony. I really hoped Bryan made it back from Tokyo or else no one else would know I was up here. It would probably be weeks before anyone in the factory noticed they were running low on boxes and alerted someone. I forced myself to start moving again, giddy with fear and glimmering in a cold sweat. It's one thing to live your life as if you're dead when things are going well, I reflected, as I eased myself hesitantly down, rung by rung, but I really didn't fancy dying – not just yet.

It seemed to take an eternity in the dark, but finally I reached the ground and collapsed, drunk with relief. I kissed the ground and vowed never to go near another ladder as long as I lived. After all, what did the *Hagakure* know? The samurai probably didn't even have metal ladders.

The path was easy to find again and it quickly led me back past the deserted wooden lodge and on to the safety of the warm Tarmac road. And now, from the security of safer altitudes, I was starting to wonder: was I just a total coward? What would most people have done? Common sense immediately told me: most people wouldn't have been stupid enough to go up there on their own in the first place.

I laughed. I was definitely a coward, earnestly studying kendo to try and prove to myself... what, exactly? That I was hard? That I was capable of doing what Bryan did? That I could become a master? That I wasn't scared of dying? It was ridiculous; it was normal to be scared of dying, for God's sake. Sure, it all sounded good in theory: become a martial-arts acolyte in Japan, studying the way of the sword – all very romantic. But deep down, I knew I was kidding myself; I was scared of everything. In fact, it was quite fitting that I spent all my time making cardboard boxes: I was a real paper tiger.

I located the bike in the hedge, tied the sword back on and wearily began the long downhill descent. Still, I thought to myself cheerfully. At least I'm alive – which was more than could be said for most samurai.

It took a great deal of faith riding into the darkness; the absence of light felt like a heavy pressure against my eyeballs. I had to weave back and forth to help slow myself down, and I also discovered that it was virtually impossible to avoid the frequent and deep potholes. Suddenly, there was a large, sickening jolt and I felt myself flying through the air in slow motion. The last thing I remember thinking (other than, Noooooooooo), was that the mountain was never going to let me get down alive.

When I came to, I was lying stretched out on my front with the bike on top of me. Searing, red-hot pain immediately shot down my arm, and my mouth tasted of blood. How much time had passed? Had I been knocked out? Moving the bike to one side, I struggled to my feet and hopped up and down, like an anxious child, trying to soothe myself. I had to get back to Yoshiwara, get to Suzuki-san's house; he'd know what to do. I gathered my stuff up, wrapped the blanket tightly round my wrist as a makeshift splint, then picked up the bike and tried to assess its roadworthiness. It seemed to be in one piece, but the brakes were steaming hot and the pads felt as if they had melted. I was going to have to improvise or else I'd never get home.

I balanced tentatively over the crossbar and set off again with both feet skidding on the floor to slow me down. Steering with one arm and an elbow was also a challenge, and each pothole proved to be more painful than the last. For the next couple of hours, I freewheeled, wobbled and skidded down the mountain road cursing my stupidity, and occasionally screaming when I hit a particularly big bump. After what felt like an eternity of virtually blind and one-handed mountain biking, a single point of light loomed in the distance. It was my old friend – the vending machine. I pulled up in front of it and gratefully bought a bottle of water. I immediately poured some over my head and downed the rest in one – all the while thanking God for the genius who decided to place a roadside vending machine right here. I collapsed in the small pool of yellow light and examined my injuries. I had taken the skin off my knees and hands, and my wrist appeared to be quite spectacularly broken. I moaned with nausea and with frustration at my foolishness. Naturally, I didn't have any health insurance and I was fairly certain I was going to require some kind of expensive operation.

I have no idea what time I eventually made it to the 7-Eleven, but having finally recovered from the shock of me stumbling in, covered in blood, bowing and saying, '*Konbanwa, Odana Yama – ouchy*' ('Good evening, Mount Odana – ouch'), the shopkeepers rang Suzuki-san. (Luckily for me, Yoshiwara was a small enough place that they knew exactly who I was.) Suzuki-san immediately came and picked me up and took me back to his place. I looked like a dazed survivor from a plane wreck. He winced when I showed him my wrist, and administered cool compresses and paracetamol, then laughed with joy and astonishment as I mimed my adventures. I was exhausted and delirious, but adamantly began trying to show him my copy of the *Hagakure*. He examined it carefully, nodded knowingly, and put me straight to bed.

*

An apprentice near a temple will recite the sutras untaught.

Anonymous

11

Doctors, Cockroaches and Temples

After a fevered night of throbbing pain, Suzuki-san bundled me into the van at first light and took me to see his friend, who he described rather ominously – with the help of a dictionary – as 'the Kendo Bone Doctor'. The doctor lived about half an hour away in a large Merchant Ivory-style bungalow surrounded by shady palm trees and terracotta pot plants.

We were escorted into a cool, clean practice room with a leather orthopaedic bed and framed acupuncture charts hanging on the walls. The doctor spoke to me slowly in a soft, reassuring way. I sat there politely listening and not understanding a word, all the while thinking that although this was nice, and maybe a bit of acupuncture would be relaxing, I was in a great deal of pain and we really should get to a proper hospital. Finally, he began to examine my swollen and tender wrist. He spent a long time cradling and prodding it, concentrating, as if he was listening for something.

I was starting to get a bit frustrated – it all felt a little 'alternative'. Yes, it's broken, I thought. Come on, stop feeling my bloody aura – I need a hospital.

The doctor appeared to come to a decision. He got me to kneel down and motioned for Suzuki-san to stand behind me and hold my elbow.

What on earth is he doing now? I thought with indignation. Suzuki-san grasped me firmly with an apprehensive frown. I still hadn't worked it out.

Then, the doctor took my wrist in both hands and…

… oh shit. It suddenly dawned on me what was about to happen.

With an almighty crunch, he snapped the bone back into place in one sickening, lightning-fast movement. For a split second, I was completely out of my body, looking down in violated disbelief. Far off in the distance, I heard my blood-curdling, high-pitched lady-scream. Then I shot back to reality, as he administered a few more agonising manipulations for good measure.

Suzuki-san's expression was a mixture of horror and hilarity. The doctor calmly re-examined me and seemed satisfied with his work. He splinted my wrist and placed it in a sling. Then his wife popped her head round the door and produced some tea. I downed a cup gratefully, still shaking and sweating profusely. I was high on adrenaline and, I suppose, relief. At least it was all over. I wouldn't need to go to a hospital – no expensive medical bill headaches. It felt like a very Japanese solution – very kendo – but don't get me wrong: had I realised what was about to happen, I would certainly have needed to be pinned down.

After thanking the doctor and presenting him with a gratefully received bottle of whisky, we drove back to Yoshiwara, laughing with relief while Suzuki-san did impressions of my screams. There was no malice in his teasing. In fact, it felt like quite the opposite, and seemed to have the effect of transforming the whole excruciating experience into a huge triumph over adversity.

As we approached his house, Suzuki-san suddenly skidded up on the side of the road and began pointing excitedly through my open window. It took me a little while to process what I was looking at, but the morning clouds had parted and there, in all its iconic majesty, was Mount Fuji. It was an absolutely colossal sight, towering above us like... well, like a massive fucking volcano.

'Toby-san, challenge,' said Suzuki-san walking his fingers up the dashboard with an air of mischief. 'Up Fuji Yama,[1] bigu ouchy.'

I paused and looked at him. There was something in the way he said 'challenge' that suggested that an expedition was a foregone conclusion. Suzuki-san seemed to have the mysterious ability to communicate a huge amount through a few well-chosen words. I nodded in silent acceptance and narrowed my eyes with resolve. Mount Fuji. It was a pilgrimage: you hadn't really been to Japan until you'd climbed it, and it was mandatory for any martial-arts aficionado. But now, as I cradled my damaged arm and dented ego, I couldn't help feeling a note of caution. Bryan had said it was a seriously harsh climb; there were plenty of stories about people dropping dead from the altitude and the sheer exertion. In fact, an old Japanese proverb stated: 'Everyone should climb Fuji Yama once – but only a fool climbs it twice.' Apparently, to date, Suzuki-san had climbed it about 20 times.

I spent the rest of the day at Suzuki-san's house resting, relieved not to be in acute pain or falling off a mountain. I vegetated on the sofa, watched telly and met some of his numerous teenage children. They appeared briefly around lunchtime, drifting through the kitchen, bleary-eyed, staring into the fridge in hungry bewilderment, as teenagers do. His wife, Shizuesan, also put in an appearance. She was friendly and welcoming and immediately began cooking and offering me pillows and medicines before disappearing again. It was strange

---

1. Mount Fuji (Fuji Yama), 12,388 feet.

watching the Suzuki household come and go. Everyone seemed to live very separate, disconnected lives.

Bryan arrived late in the evening in a state of genuine concern. Suzuki-san had phoned him and he came straight from the station.

'Christ, I leave you alone for five fucking minutes,' he laughed, poking at my sling. 'What the hell happened?'

We shared the edited highlights of our weekends. It seemed that Tokyo had gone well for him and Kazue was planning on coming to stay in Yoshiwara for a holiday. A holiday? Great! My mood lifted. I wouldn't be able to make cardboard boxes for a while, but at least the house wouldn't be empty all day. Okay, so I wouldn't have any money either, and that was definitely going to be a problem, but what choice did I have? Looking on the bright side, it would be a good opportunity to get to know the area and maybe study some Japanese.

The following week, I headed down to the factory to show my arm off to the boss, who apparently suspected that I might be making it all up in order to get out of working. I performed a heart-wrenching show of remorse and tried my best to insinuate that I felt as though I had let the whole company down. I even picked up some cardboard wistfully, then placed it back down again with a misty look in my eyes. My theatrics were made all the more challenging by the intense joy welling up inside me at the prospect of several weeks of chilling in the sunshine – albeit completely penniless.

At lunchtime, there was a small ceremony for the old lady, who was finally retiring. We all stood in a sombre circle as the boss made a long and presumably moving speech. People began welling up, and the boss faltered and stuttered. We hung our heads with respect and I marvelled at this unrestrained show of corporate, yet seemingly quite genuine, emotion. Eventually, the Puganought, lips quivering, tears streaming down his face, presented the old lady with some flowers and the boss handed her a sealed envelope, practically headbutting the floor in humility. The old lady laughed and tried to shrug off all the unwanted attention. She had lived too long to get emotional about it and had a definite twinkle in her eye that spoke volumes to a fellow box packer. Everyone said their goodbyes and expressed their regret that she was going. Then, quietly, she wheeled her bicycle away down the dusty road for the last time, flowers protruding from the basket, and gazed back at the factory, waving at the assembled workers. Bryan sprinted after her for a final unorthodox farewell hug.

'Gambatte,' she called to us faintly from the distance. I climbed up on a stack of palates and did my best bow. There was that word again: Gambatte – 'Endure', 'Hang in there', 'Do your best'.

I would miss the old lady's wise, calming presence. As she became a dot on the horizon, I was sure I could hear the faint sound of her whooping with relief, kicking her heels together on the soft summer breeze.

That evening, contrary to all my instincts, I returned to the kendo class. I really wasn't sure if I'd survive another session, but in the spirit of perseverance I went along. I entered the *dojo* feeling delicate and apprehensive. It was still hot and stuffy, but nowhere near as intense as the first time. Everyone had already heard the hilarious story of the frail Westerner who had ridden up Mount Odana and broken his wrist, but they all seemed genuinely concerned.

Takagi Sensei inspected my arm and nodded almost imperceptibly, as if he wholeheartedly approved. Then he bowed, strode off and began furiously belting the hell out of some poor unknown masked student, as if the very sight of my injuries had brought on some kind of uncontrollable fit of bloodlust.

My own training that night, out of necessity, involved stepping up and down the hall, trying to master the kendo footwork. Suzuki-san was extremely exacting about the correct posture and explained that this was a good opportunity to practise the basics. He spent a long time adjusting me and demonstrated a remarkable ability to instantly project himself forward with astonishing speed and force. It seemed that the strength of kendo lay in co-ordinating the body as one highly concentrated unit. The weight rested in the toes, hips slightly tilted towards your opponent and then, bang: the attack was driven by the legs, as the sword was simultaneously raised and then returned to the en-garde position in a relatively small movement. It made the difference between hitting someone with the strength of just your arms, compared to running into them with all your weight. I stumbled along behind Suzuki-san, awkwardly failing to imitate his power and finesse. He studied me with intense concentration, his expression suggesting he was slightly bemused by my incredible natural ineptitude, mulling over the immense challenge that teaching me the art of the sword was going to present. Still, I repeated the movements with uncharacteristic determination.

It was certainly a relief not to have to spend the whole lesson in *seiza* or be repeatedly hit on the wrists and head, but after several hours of repetitive sliding on the hard, polished floor, much to my embarrassment, my bare feet finally started to develop blisters and bleed.

Later, having drinks at the parrot bar, I showed the kendo teachers my blisters. They all thought this was utterly fantastic and loudly congratulated me. Nabi-chan assured me that now I was 'really learning'. I wondered if I turned up the following week having lost a leg I would receive a standing ovation.

On Thursday, Kazue arrived. I was moping about the Ninja House, successfully avoiding doing anything, when she suddenly appeared at the doorway with a rucksack as big as she was and an acoustic guitar slung across her shoulders. She looked as though she was heading off to India for a gap year. Dumping her stuff, she collapsed in the middle of the room and lit a cigarette.

'Wow,' she said, looking around frowning. 'It's like… a haunted house.'

We chatted politely and I made tea. Kazue was a born-and-bred Tokyo girl, and it was obvious that Bryan had omitted to tell her about the unique 'rustic' nature of the place. In fact, arriving in Yoshiwara was probably as strange for her as it had been for me. She peered into the bathroom with trepidation and walked around the fruit trees silently, investigating delicate orange-and-black spiders hanging from sticky white cobwebs. Her expression said it all.

We talked all afternoon; it was a relief to finally speak to a Japanese person who understood English. She told me about her experience of living in London and I complained about making cardboard boxes. She sympathised, as she'd just quit her job in a clothes shop and was at a loose end. It was a brave thing to do. Japanese people rarely left a job voluntarily and I could see that she was uneasy about the future.

When Bryan came home, it was clear that he was really pleased to see her and we all went out to a local restaurant where, after some complicated negotiations with the chef, I ordered vegetarian *tempura*, rice and boiled vegetables. This was no small achievement, and the waitresses giggled and stared at me as if I'd just ordered roasted dick. Bryan chose the meatiest pig trotter soup I'd ever seen and proceeded to wave bits of it in my face, as if it might convert me.

Kazue turned out to be easy-going and quickly fitted in with the slow pace and routines of the countryside. It was nice having some company. For me, she was an unending source of fascination and I bombarded her with questions about language and Japanese traditions, which she always did her best to answer. In return, I tried to teach her advanced and obscure elements of English, such as regional accents and hip-hop phrases from the 1980s. There is something intensely surreal about hearing a Japanese person saying, 'Oi am a cider drinker' in a thick Devonshire accent, or declaring, 'She is mega-fly girl, whereas I am whack homeboy.'

I probably should have felt like a gooseberry, but somehow, with the three of us there, it seemed to work. Bryan and Kazue didn't make me feel too uncomfortable and, apart from the occasional rustling of late-night passion behind the thin sliding screens, it was cool. (On those occasions, I would quickly grab a *shinai* and take a discreet walk down to the train station to practise my sword strikes under the flickering platform lighting.) We never mentioned these things openly, but sometimes, the next morning, I would whisper in a mockingly shocked way to Bryan, 'Man, what the hell were you guys *doing* last night?'

Time passed slowly as I waited for my wrist to heal. A thick blanket of prickly heat permanently hung over Yoshiwara and the stifling nights were punctuated by the abrasive whines of angry mosquitoes and distant rumbling trains. I did a lot of sliding up and down the *dojo* floor – more than even the most conscientious kendo student ever should – until I felt confident that I could forcefully step towards even the most determined attacker.

Bryan continued to work every day at the paper factory while Kazue and I vaguely attempted half-arsed home improvements, lounged in the garden and went for walks. The house was gradually coming together. The original kitchen had been located next to the bathroom but was lost beyond all hope beneath a mountain of boxes and grimy old tools belonging to Suzuki-san's dad. Instead, we had managed to build our own small, functional kitchen, having rescued a (relatively) old fridge, rice cooker and a small gas stove from other people's rubbish. Unfortunately, as soon as we began to cook proper meals in the house, the dreaded invasion of the cockroaches began. At first, I glimpsed the occasional red flash scuttling across the corridor, but now they were breeding and growing bigger and bolder by the day. We would be sitting on the floor eating dinner when a fat, 2-inch, armour-plated behemoth would suddenly make a dash for it across the *tatami*, causing all of us to leap around in panic, trying to kill it with kendo swords, pots, pans or anything else close to hand. They were utterly indestructible. Even when Kazue tracked down a can of bug spray that was so toxic it probably contravened every health-and-safety law under the sun, they would scurry away unperturbed. All we could do was obsessively clean up any food crumbs and resign ourselves to the fact that we had an infestation (as, apparently, did most of Japan).

Over the next couple of weeks, the kendo teachers went out of their way to be sociable and spend time at the Ninja House. It seemed as though they felt personally responsible that I'd hurt myself, and I was humbled by their concern.

One day, Kazue and I were taken on a day trip high up into the mountains by Nabi-chan and Suzuki-san. It was exciting to finally get out of Yoshiwara again. Nabi-chan took us in his big, shiny, Japanese-style Cadillac. It suited him perfectly. It practically oozed funky guitar riffs, and he drove it like a total kendo bastard. Every other car was a challenge, an opponent, and he was taking no prisoners.

After a couple of nausea-inducing hours weaving through the mountains, we pulled up outside the entrance of a large temple complex. Suzuki-san put his hands together and did some comical chanting, then ushered us all inside. Nabi-chan tried to explain something about the place, but ancient religious history was a tricky subject to translate and despite Kazue's best efforts, all I could really glean was that it was a Zen temple and very old – which I had kind of suspected already.

We climbed upwards, through a network of beautiful mossy paths ringed with thick pine and bamboo. Solid wooden buildings were artfully camouflaged among trees and frozen cascades of jagged grey rocks. In the calm temple atmosphere, we all gradually became quiet and began to wander off on our own, lost in personal contemplation and admiration of the natural beauty and solitude. Black-robed monks padded silently along the passageways, their pale shaved heads glowing from the shadows. As they went about their business, they moved with solemn purpose, neither rushing nor wasting time, as if they knew there was nowhere else to be other than right here, right now.

A ceremony was under way behind closed doors in one of the larger halls. Subdued chanting and chiming bells drifted through the site, carrying the melodies of a thousand years of unbroken practice. There was a sense of peace here that felt infinite, as if it could easily swallow up the delusion and ugly noise of the entire world.

It was something I had previously only ever experienced second-hand through books on mindfulness, films and other people's anecdotes. Even now, I was keenly aware that I was a spiritual tourist just passing through. I imagined kneeling down in front of the monks, enraptured by their words of wisdom – but just as I was about to get lost in one of my stereotyped kung-fu acolyte/Zen fantasies, I caught myself in time and stopped. Small-minded adolescent daydreams were out of place here. Instead, I sat on a stone wall and watched an old monk weeding a vegetable plot, crouching behind a slatted wooden fence. It was such a normal, down-to-earth sight.

So simple – the wisdom of such an approach could be easily overlooked. I watched the monk for some time, then strolled over to one of the magnificently decorated shrine rooms. I took my shoes off and knelt down on the gigantic blocks of interlocking *tatami*. Everything was polished and immaculate. My eyes drifted across the altar, statues of Buddha, fresh flowers, candles and the soft blue smoke of pungent, smouldering incense. Then, my gaze rose upwards towards a spectacular black, painted dragon, stretching across the entire span of the roof. The detail was exquisite and the design complex, yet perfectly balanced. I knew next to nothing about Japanese art – or any kind of art, in fact – but the mental clarity and vision of the artist who painted this were immediately apparent. I thought about the many long-forgotten generations of people, who, like myself, must have sat quietly, right here in this meditation hall, rooted to the spot, staring up in awe.

Some time later, Kazue tracked me down and announced that it was time to leave, as we were going to a mountain festival. We drove for a few more miles, then pulled off into a field of long, swaying green grass packed with randomly parked cars and excited-looking people. In front of us, a raised stage was filled with performers in kimonos playing gigantic drums.[2] They danced and sang, while overexcited children ran about flying brightly decorated kites.

We sat in the middle of the swirling throng on white plastic garden furniture, drinking beer and soaking up the atmosphere and remarkable scenery. There was a definite country-fair feel to the celebrations and it wasn't long before everyone (with the exception of Kazue) was predictably drunk. Suzuki-san and Nabi-chan were, as usual, acting larger than life, loudly toasting everyone and trying to get embarrassed girls to pose with me in photographs. They ended up dancing around arm in arm, falling over and crashing into groups of bemused-looking locals. If it was normal for a group of middle-aged kendo teachers to act this way, I never saw anyone else doing it.

By the early evening, we had sobered up a bit and sat on an ancient stone bridge eating corn on the cob, watching the crowds ebb and swell. To one side of us, a large gang of tough-looking teenagers blasted out gangsta rap from the back of a low-rider convertible. It seemed weirdly out of place. A tiny old lady wandered over and asked them to turn it down. I braced myself for the first shooting of the night, but they responded immediately, collectively bowing and apologising, without the slightest hint of attitude.

Later, beacons were lit up and down the valley and fireworks began to explode across the night sky, raining down on us in dazzling brilliance to ubiquitous roars of 'Oooh' and 'Aaah'. Nabi-chan told me that the Japanese call them 'fire flowers'. It was a fitting name and the bangs and sparkling bursts went on for hours. They were a tradition at summer festivals, with deep booming sound and colourful luminous radiance. I marvelled at the amount of money it must have cost to put on such an impressive show.

As we drove home through the night, everyone was tired, happy and

---

2. *Taiko* – or, more specifically, *kumi-daiko*, an ensemble of *taiko* drums.

talked softly. I fell asleep to the mesmerising wash of passing headlights and the repetitive swaying of zigzagging mountain roads.

*

And those who were seen dancing were thought to be insane by those who could not hear the music.

Friedrich Nietzsche

12

The Dance of the Migrant Worker

A few weeks later, my wrist was sufficiently recovered for me to return to work.

Early one morning, before the heat of the day had properly taken hold, I found myself sitting cross-legged in a dewy field outside the paper factory, watching a pair of beautiful, intertwined white cranes grooming each other. Mount Fuji dominated the horizon and the air was clear and still. It was a timeless oriental scene, as depicted on countless lacquered box lids and fine bone-china plates. The birds took flight and my spirits rose along with them. I rubbed my wrist, pulled a tight bandaged support over it and, rising, strode purposefully towards the factory. I felt strong; I was ready to make paper again, ready to train. Unsummoned, the theme tune to the *Rocky* films stirred in the depths of my mind and I clenched my fists with determination. The factory would be my *dojo*; boredom, sweat and monotony my deadly opponents. God damn it, I'm going to make the most cardboard boxes ever, I thought, as I fired a few shadow punches into the air before marching inside, eyes narrowed with resolve.

Bryan was midway through setting up the first paper-reel change of the day. I saluted him, headed straight for the cardboard and got stuck in. For the next few hours, I kept my internal dialogue to a whimper and focused completely on the task: pick up cardboard, fold it, stack it. Perfect. Pick up the pace now – work those boxes.

The morning flew by. After lunch, I even began helping Jobsworth move some pallets and, by the early evening, I had been promoted back on to the production line, still struggling, but this time putting my heart and soul into it. Only MC Squared looked disappointed to see me back. He ordered me around, signalling gruffly with his chin. I ignored his hostility and did whatever I was told. I wasn't entirely sure why he hated me so much – I was genuinely trying to fit in, and certainly wasn't intent on usurping his authority. Maybe he disliked Bryan and, by default, me? Perhaps it was racism? Xenophobia? Or, as I suspected, it was simply that he was a total and utter bastard. Stay cool, you need this job, I told myself after each rude MC order, but it didn't stop me conjuring up disturbingly brutal revenge fantasies.

For the rest of that week, I ate, breathed and lived work. At the end of each day, my T-shirt would have white salt rings on it from the constant sweating, and I would fall asleep as soon as I got home. Fanatical commitment was the only way I could survive. Although I was still a long way from winning any respect from my co-workers, at least I was no longer a hindrance and was finally beginning to feel as if I was close to earning a place on the team.

Back at the *dojo*, I'd actually advanced to wielding a sword again. Although we were only training a few times a week, classes were still far more gruelling than I had anticipated in the UK. I spent my time repeating basic movements and strikes till my arms trembled with muscle fatigue and I dripped with sweat.

Suzuki-san and Nabi-chan helped improve my posture, getting me to slide up and down with a *shinai* pressed hard into the small of my back. I looked ridiculous, but nobody stared or laughed and I felt I was gradually starting to understand the basic theory, if not the actual technique of generating enough force and speed to make an attack. The relentless aggressive striking felt very unnatural to me, but there was a good reason for the tactic: kendo didn't worry about defensive movements – there was no time. The theory was that your first mistake or hesitation would be your last. Studying the teachers sparring, I gradually began to gain an insight into their practice. It was a bloody-minded but positive attitude – a determination in the face of adversity. It didn't matter if you were young or old, male or female; it wasn't even about aggression, although you could be forgiven for thinking so. It was about being in the moment, or being hit. A split second of self-doubt or any kind of backing down left you wide open. It was brutal, but under the surface I could see a mental and physical awareness that reflected kendo's Zen roots. It was a practice that required an acceptance of reality and the immediate situation at hand, win or lose, life or death, and developing the awareness to deal with it skilfully.

I asked Aono-san about this theory and, after laughing and reminding me how young and naive I was, he agreed in typical Yoda-like fashion.

'Kendo and Zen… same,' he said, mopping his brow with a cloth. 'Mmm, yes, like monk sitting in *zazen*: when mind too much thinking, sometimes teacher hit them with stick.' Then, whack – without warning, he suddenly slapped me really, really hard on the head. 'TOBY-SAN – WAKE UP!' he roared, and burst out laughing again.

I nodded with pain and tried to ignore the creeping feelings of violated resentment. I think that Aono Sensei already knew something about me that deep down I still only suspected – that I was never going to become a kendo master. I knew he had the measure of me, but my ego wasn't quite ready to admit it yet. Still, he had a memorable way of getting his point across.

Meanwhile, my new-found dedication to gaining enlightenment through hard manual labour was being tested to the limit. The relentless tedium of work was so intense, it was mildly hallucinogenic. I longed for something to happen – anything!

One afternoon at the factory, Bryan produced a small but powerful ghetto blaster he'd found in the office. He pulled out a couple of CDs, plugged the player in and pumped up the volume. Everyone stopped in their tracks, staring in amazement. The work was so repetitive that any variation in routine was startling, and this simple act was utterly transformative. It was a blast of fresh air, a revolution; it was 1967 all over again – the Summer of Love.

Music brought a magical new dimension to the factory. It shouted out, 'You are not a machine; think for yourself and question authority.' Well, at least it did to me. For the rest of the day, the box packing seemed to happen by itself as Bryan took us on a journey through his CD collection. Toni in particular perked up and even showed us a few of his disco moves. He promised to bring some of his music in – much to our apprehension. Unsurprisingly, MC Squared and the Puganought were suspicious, as if their brains were struggling to process this affront to routine. They hadn't been consulted and didn't like it at all, but it didn't stop anyone from working, so what could they do? They were apparently dimly aware of Japanese pop music, but seemed disorientated by funk and hip-hop and visibly scared by drum 'n' bass. They hung about in their usual places at the back of the factory, looking forlorn and undermined. The boss came out, grinning idiotically and tapping his foot like an embarrassing dad. He then appeared to realise he had absolutely nothing whatsoever to say and went away again. It was as if the whole factory was having a great big psychedelic freak-out. Well... relatively speaking.

The following day, the boss rolled up in his big, expensive boss car, playing a hideously bland pop version of drum 'n' bass at full volume. He slid the window down and poked his head out, waving a pile of brand-new CDs at us, desperate for some kind of acknowledgement. We smiled back and nodded at him. After he'd gone, Bryan sighed and shook his head at me. 'Living proof you just can't buy cool.'

Later in the week, Toni produced a home-made tape. It was much worse than we could have imagined. Comprised of about five or six poorly recorded, Arabic-style turbo-disco tunes on a loop, it made cheesy western pop seem like high art. Most of the lyrics were in English, but obviously written and sung by people who didn't actually speak the language. Perhaps I missed the subtle nuances, but the song most painfully etched into my brain, and rendered in the style of a high-pitched anthem, went something like:

> *Sharey sharey lady, because I am a lonely.*
> *Sharey sharey lady, riding through the night.*
> *Sharey sharey lady, looking for adventure*
> *Because my heart is going, looking in the night.*
> *(Repeat… a lot.)*

Much to our horror, we soon realised this was Toni's only tape and he was hell-bent on playing it continuously. Jobsworth and Sami were initially delighted by the chintzy commercial sounds. They grooved around the packing tables, clicking their fingers, arms held high in the air, pursing their lips and gurning at each other, but by mid-afternoon, even they were beginning to look jaded. Every time the music was due to finish, Bryan, Toni and myself would glance twitchily at the stereo and begin edging towards it – Toni with his tape and us with anything else… anything. The Summer of Love was over and the battle of the stereo had begun: Toni versus all other types of music.

Shimizu-san and Akio stayed out of it – they didn't seem to care – and the Puganought and MC Squared clearly viewed music as just another thing to stand around ridiculing. Bryan and I, however, regarded it as a lifeline to sanity. Tensions between ourselves and the Iraqis steadily rose. I began to fantasise about jumping up and down on Toni's tape as he knelt on the floor, begging for mercy, while the rest of the factory looked on and cheered. It was amazing, just those same few songs, literally, EVERY – BLOODY – DAY!

Toni would happily sing along, mullet rippling in the breeze from the table fans, gold jewellery glinting in the sunshine, with a huge, vacant grin on his face. In his mind, it was always Friday night at the Baghdad Ritzy, a hundred Iraqi girls crowding round as he titillated them with his playful moves. Toni looked like a Bollywood version of John Travolta – but, secretly, I couldn't help but admire his awesome sense of style.

For some time, Bryan and I had been developing a form of communicating over the din of the spinning paper machines that relied almost entirely on facial expressions. It had reached new levels of subtlety. I would throw him an agonised look across the factory floor that clearly said, 'Well, here we are. I guess it's not really surprising.' To which he might raise a single eyebrow, thereby answering, 'Yes, we are indeed truly screwed. But look on the bright side – if we can survive this, we can probably deal with anything.'

One day, after MC Squared had just rudely ordered me to do something by tapping me on the chest and saying, 'Oi, *ima, ima*' ('Do it now') in his ugly, monotonous voice, instead of ripping his poisoned heart out of his chest and feeding it to him, I stood behind a pile of pallets, seething with anger and frustration. I was hot, tired, hungry and bored, with ten solid hours of packing to look forward to, but I was also weirdly... elated. It felt as if things couldn't get any worse. I had to laugh. And then, very, very strangely, I began to dance about on the spot.

Bryan wandered round the corner, stopped, took one slightly concerned look at me, then lit a cigarette and sat down to watch. After a few minutes, he joined in, weaving in and out of the pallets in a kind of spontaneous, deranged conga. Our crazy moves perfectly expressed the raw frustration of working every day in a foreign sweatshop. And so, the Dance of the Migrant Worker was born.

Over time, the moves evolved into a definite set sequence: lifting your arms and legs alternately in the air, skipping on the spot and wiggling your fingers like a really enthusiastic Morris dancer. The philosophy was simple: you had to give it everything you had. There could be no holding back. And most important of all was the facial expression – a fixed grin that said, 'Woooooohooooooo, look at me. I'm cramming an entire day's worth of happiness into my five-minute break.'

We would dance the Migrant Worker whenever we were close to breaking point, as a way of letting off steam in an otherwise bleak situation. When no one was looking, one of us would covertly start to dance and the other would quietly follow suit. It was childish and absurd, but it reminded us to laugh at ourselves. A couple of times, I noticed MC Squared and the Puganought catch a glimpse of what we were doing and stare at us in disgusted bewilderment. It made it all the more fun to know that our dance totally baffled and offended our joyless supervisors. Eventually, we stopped caring who saw us. To the other workers, we were just kids anyway – freaky foreigners, no matter how we acted. We figured we might as well give them a reason to laugh.

But as the weeks turned into months, the exhausting work began to take its toll. Although we were earning money and getting physically fit, our mental health was unquestionably starting to suffer. Trivial annoyances between Bryan and me and the MC and the Puganought transformed into bitter resentment, and we would frequently end up finishing late in the evening, due to their zealous need to complete extra paper runs, dog-tired and way too frazzled to go to kendo. The challenge of surviving the Factory of Dreams was beginning to eclipse the urgency I felt to master martial arts.

Every day, Bryan worked the left-hand row of machines under the pursed-lipped authority of the Puganought, while I was on the right side, overseen by MC Squared. They were rapidly turning into petty, lazy tyrants. We started to view them as vindictive POW guards, who would take any opportunity to throw their weight about. Everyone hated them, but they took particular delight in bossing us around, possibly because we were Westerners, but certainly because we didn't try to cover up our disdain for them. In my feverish daydreams, I imagined the MC as a fat pig standing on his hind legs, dressed in a Japanese officer's uniform, barking orders. I would wrestle his machine gun off him and re-enact a surreal fusion of *The Great Escape* and *The Bridge on the River Kwai* on a daily basis. I would, of course, first take the time to surgically stomp the shit out of him before riding off down the paper conveyer belts on my imaginary motorbike to freedom. We discussed the situation with the kendo teachers, but they all agreed that we couldn't confront them. Nabi-chan, being a successful retired businessman, took particular exception to our complaints and said it was our duty to put up with our supervisors' failings, regardless. They were our superiors, and we should just ignore tensions and work hard. Kazue explained that these kinds of work situations were all too familiar in Japan – the dark side of *senpai–kohai*.

Meanwhile, the boss remained utterly unaware of pretty much everything that happened in his own factory and continued to bumble around his office, showing off his latest purchases of fishing equipment. One day, his dad (the real boss) put in a brief appearance on a routine visit from his larger factory in Numazu. A slick, grey-haired businessman, he exuded all the over-confidence of an executive banker. His arrival had the comical effect of making everyone go arse-kissing and bowing crazy, as if they were in the presence of a living god. Much to our delight, though, he'd travelled in America and spoke a bit of English. He stopped to practise with me and Bryan, as if he was on a royal walkabout, while the rest of the crew stood around ashen-faced, not understanding a word. Welcome to my world, you bastards, I thought, revelling in their discomfort.

'So, how you like working here?' the boss enquired.

I'd been in Japan long enough now to know how to play the game. 'It's tough… but good work,' I replied. 'Nearly everyone works so hard.' I couldn't stop my gaze from flitting towards MC Squared, who was staring down at his shoes.

'Mmm.' The boss nodded, sizing up the situation like Columbo. I felt he could easily read between the lines. He turned around and said something gruff and forceful in Japanese to the supervisors.

'You tell me if they give you problem. Maybe you come to China, we open new factory soon. We need good workers... Many prostitutes there – very cheap.'

'I... er... Thank you,' I said.

He patted me on the back and everyone returned to their work stations, looking a bit worried.

Bryan was laughing like a maniac. 'Holy shit, did you see their faces?' he said.

For a long time afterwards, MC Squared and the Puganought didn't hassle us. But it was only a matter of time – such a brazen insult in the workplace wasn't going to be forgiven easily.

*

Not till we are lost, do we begin to find ourselves.

Henry David Thoreau

13

Runaway Holiday

So far, unlike Bryan, I had seen very little of the rest of the country and was starting to yearn for a change of scene. Most of the time, I existed in a child-like world of mimes and grunts, although my Japanese had improved a little. Now, instead of just hearing a blur, I could at least decipher actual words and sentences. It was also becoming clear that a lot could be achieved by just describing English things with a Japanese accent – *milku* ('milk'), *toiret* ('toilet'), *kikuboxshingu* ('kickboxing'). I was also able to talk commandingly about hot weather and how hard, tiring or painful things were. But I really had no idea how to go about learning the language and spent a lot of time pestering Bryan and Kazue – then immediately forgetting what they had just taught me.

My arrival in Japan seemed to be causing Bryan to rediscover his 'British-ness'. I would frequently incite a sense of moral outrage in him by pointing out minor irritations that he had previously learnt to tolerate and ignore. It was his relationship with the boss that clearly caused him the most annoyance. The boss was getting richer by the day, and the company was expanding faster than we could keep up, but Bryan was still working himself into the ground, and getting comparatively little for it. What with that and the patronising, rude treatment at the hands of the MC and the Puganought, it was becoming intolerable, and time for some militant action.

We had both now earnt enough money to start thinking we seriously deserved some time off. The summer break loomed, but sadly, in Japan this barely amounted to a long weekend and was nowhere near enough time to do anything really constructive. We decided that enough was enough – we were having a holiday regardless.

'Mother fuck this place,' shouted Bryan one day, as he pulled up in the forklift truck. He beckoned me to balance on the forks at the front then proceeded to raise them up and recklessly drive around, ranting about something the Puganought had just done or said to him.

'Let's just go,' he called up to me. 'We should do some travelling. We could hitchhike, maybe make it down south. What do you say?'

He began to lower the forks, but pressed the wrong button, causing them to lurch forward, leaving me hanging by my fingertips for dear life about 25 feet in the air.

'Okay, okay, I'm up for it,' I cried. 'But for Christ's sake, don't kill me first.'

The Puganought, who'd been observing from the shadows, now stepped forward and issued Bryan and me with a stern warning in Japanese. The MC watched from a distance with a great big, fat satisfied smile on his face. For once, it was fair enough and Bryan bowed and apologised without the slightest flicker of rebelliousness (but the subtle look he flashed me a moment later said otherwise).

The summer break arrived and we put our plans of escape and adventure swiftly into action. Bryan hadn't even entertained Kazue's idea of asking the boss for time off. When work at the factory resumed the following day, we would be anywhere other than Yoshiwara, and our slave-driving boss would just have to deal with it and perhaps even attempt some work himself for a change. As ever, Bryan was confident things would work out, and I went along with it. I wasn't sure it was a great idea, but in the heat of the factory, standing beside a mountain of cardboard, the allure of being anywhere else had just been too tempting.

So one balmy evening, we found ourselves standing on a deserted motorway slip road holding a piece of cardboard with the characters for Nagoya – the nearest big city – scrawled on it. Kazue had returned to Tokyo, apparently to have a hot shower, and we were feeling carefree and rock 'n' roll.

It hadn't really occurred to us what we would do when our small amount of money ran out, and we certainly weren't thinking of the consequences. Escape was pretty much the sum total of our plan. We managed to get a couple of short lifts, and ended up at another isolated lay-by late at night. An ominous damp fog rolled in and the roads were eerily quiet. Just as we'd given in to the prospect of sleeping in a ditch, a pair of slow-moving headlights stopped in front of us. The car's windows were blacked out and it had large '50s-style tail fins, shining metallic radial wheels and whitewall tyres. We opened the door and introduced ourselves to the driver, who continued staring straight ahead, cigarette dangling from his lip, totally impassive and intimidatingly cool. He was a serious-looking man, muscular, in his forties, dressed in a high-collared black shirt and dripping with attitude.

'I'm not sure if this is a good idea,' I said quietly.

'Yeah… me neither,' whispered Bryan.

We climbed into the back seat, having both agreed it was a really bad idea.

'So, er… where have you come from?' asked Bryan casually.

'Tokyo.'

'Aha... um.... cool. Where are you heading?'

'I'm here on... *business*,' replied the driver without taking his eyes off the road.

Bryan and I glanced at each other fearfully. It was clear that whatever this business was, it didn't require any further questioning.

We drove for an hour or so, in tense silence. Finally, he pulled up at a service station and announced that he was dropping us off. We jumped out and he drove away slowly like a phantom in the night. We headed towards the reassuring normality of a convenience store, feeling as though we'd just had a brush with a very dark, dangerous person.

'So what did you make of that?' asked Bryan softly.

'Scary,' I said. 'Serial killer?'

'Yakuza hit-man... definitely.'

The Yakuza were the Japanese mafia. They didn't normally bother Westerners – not unless you were really stupid or very unlucky – but, nevertheless, they were definitely the wrong people to mess with.

'Why do you think he gave us a lift?' I asked.

'I don't know. Perhaps he needed an alibi or something. I've never met any real Yakuza before. Nice car though.'

'Yeah, although I reckon the trunk was probably rammed full of semi-automatic weapons and dead bodies.'

A little while later, as we were buying some food, we suddenly noticed our Yakuza assassin standing near the entrance of the shop staring at us.

'Holy shit,' exclaimed Bryan, reaching for a magazine to hide behind.

I squeezed in next to him and pretended to examine an article in detail. We peered furtively out of the shop window into the darkness.

'Where's *Top Snipe* when you need it?' I joked.

'Seriously, what is he up to?'

As we began to scan the store for possible emergency exits and potential improvised weapons, the Yakuza hit-man abruptly turned around, got back in his car and drove off.

'Oh my God, that can't have been a coincidence. What the hell did he want? Do you think he's going to try to kill us?'

It seemed unlikely we'd managed to annoy anyone to the extent that they'd organised our executions. Unlikely, but not impossible. Whatever he was doing was seriously creepy though, and the very last thing on earth you ever wanted to meet hitchhiking late at night.

After a long time loitering in the shop pretending to read magazines, we headed back outside. We tiptoed around the service station, peering into the darkness and wishing we'd got the bus. Eventually, we found ourselves irresistibly drawn to a roadside vending machine that sold beer.

'Welcome to civilisation,' said Bryan, happily patting it like a trusted old friend and emptying his pockets of loose change. It wasn't long before we had entirely forgotten about our mafia friend and were deep in animated discussion about how to deliver the perfect round-house kick.

Following several more trips to the vending machine, our next lift was in the early hours of the morning from a group of off-duty American Marines looking for a late-night party. Following the Second World War, Japan still had a permanent American military presence, but it must have been covert in Yoshiwara.

It was shocking to suddenly be confronted by a group of giant, muscular Westerners. A gargantuan, thick-necked jock jumped out of a van and asked us if we knew where they could get a drink.

'Gee, er, a bar I guess?' answered Bryan dryly in a ropey American accent.

'Sorry,' I said. 'We're British. I mean, he's just joking, er…'

The American laughed and shook his head. 'Well, I knew that already, chaps,' he said in an excellent plum British accent, right back at us without missing a beat.

They took us to the nearest town and, in the course of the brief journey, our American alter egos were born – 'Rock Poseidon' and 'Brad Schapelli'.

'Hey Rock,' said Bryan later as we propped up a bar, squeezed in among a line of colossal, shaven-headed GIs. 'Y'know what…?'

(Authentically long American pause.)

'… What?'

'I just, like, totally love that British *Monteey Pythohn*.'

'Well, heck, Brad,' I answered. 'Sure, I guess.'

'I say, can we get you chaps a beer?' asked a Marine, sounding like a pipe-smoking RAF pilot.

'Hell, yeah,' we called back.

The Marines had 12 hours' leave to fit in as much drinking and rock 'n' roll as was humanly possible in rural Japan. We couldn't compete, but we did our best and fulfilled our dreams of sleeping in a ditch.

The following afternoon, we were on the road again. As we waited patiently for someone to stop, it occurred to me that hitchhiking was a bit like being on stage, although in this case the audience were whizzing by. The occupants were safe inside their cars, either staring, carefully sizing you up and assessing your suitability, or scowling at the horizon, desperate not to notice you.

Having done my fair share of hitching, I had developed a sophisticated system for thumbing down a lift. First, the right body language. Standing face on, honest, yet turned slightly, beckoning, as if to confirm you were heading in the right direction. Then there was the complex issue of facial expressions and eye contact. A gentle smile, but never outright grinning, which immediately denoted madness. Any serious glowering and you may as well be standing in your blood-stained pants holding a machete. It was best to act polite-casual, only making direct eye contact when they got close, as if to say, 'Oh, why yes. I would like a lift. To be honest, I'm so non-threatening and comfortable here, I'd nearly forgotten where I was going.'

Finally, the mental discipline. Too much urgency, and a sense of desperation and frustration and resentment loomed. A subtle desire to move on was best, coupled with a Zen-like acceptance of standing on the spot for ever if necessary.

However, for some reason my expertise seemed to be a little rusty, and we'd been forced into a detailed study of the seldom-appreciated nuances of motorway slip roads. We chatted, smoked, watched insects scuttling over the hot, dusty kerb and threw pebbles at road signs. It took a long while before anyone gave us a second look, and as the sun beat down, we lolled barefoot on a grassy bank, dozing and taking it in turns to hold our sign up and bow at passing traffic.

Eventually, a friendly trucker took pity on us and we rode in his luxurious cabin several hundred miles west. He was relieved that Bryan spoke Japanese, and asked the usual questions: where were we from, did we like Japan, why were we standing by the road waving our thumbs at him (we were the first hitchhikers he'd ever seen)? Finally, he dropped us in the desolate, industrialised outskirts of Nagoya. It must have been around eight o'clock at night and, in the absence of much passing traffic, we resorted to playing *Deer Hunter* Roulette[1] by the side of the road. It wasn't long before we were drenched in beer, staggering along the hard shoulder randomly waving at passing cars. To our surprise, a tiny, beaten-up old Nissan flashed its lights and pulled up. A young couple kindly offered to give us a lift into town. We squeezed ourselves and our

---

1. *Deer Hunter* Roulette involved shaking a can of beer for several minutes then placing it back into the pack and theatrically screaming at the next person until they picked one and opened it against their head – in homage to the harrowing scene from the film *The Deer Hunter*, where Robert De Niro and Christopher Walken are held captive by the Viet Cong and forced to play Russian Roulette against each other.

bags into the back seat, damp, stinking of alcohol and trying to make reassuring 'Don't-worry-we-won't-kill-you' hitchhiking chit-chat.

Arriving in the city centre, we had just stopped at a set of traffic lights when we spied a couple of bullies in the street pushing a salaryman around. Inebriated office workers were ubiquitous in Japan and could often be seen weaving their way home from an evening of entertaining clients. They were easy pickings. The bullies were shouting and slapping at this particular man as he clung to his briefcase, bowing his head in fear.

'Shit, look at that,' cried Bryan.

'I wonder what's going on. I really think we'd better call the police.' I leant forward to try to speak to the young couple. 'Er... Police?... *Policu*?' I was at a loss trying to come up with the appropriate mime. 'Hey Bryan, how do you say...?'

Without warning, Bryan suddenly leapt out of the car and ran across the street straight into them. In a split second, he'd attacked the thugs kendo style (minus the sword), by pushing them and letting out blood-curdling *kiai* shouts.[2] Amazingly, the bullies immediately turned tail and ran away, as did the salaryman in the opposite direction. The couple in the car looked as though they were about to cry. I cleared my throat, thanked them politely for the lift and explained that they needn't worry as we were '*bushi*',[3] and that here would do just fine. With that, I gathered our bags and jumped out of the car.

Bryan was staring at his shaking hands in a state of disbelief, marvelling at his newly discovered vigilante powers. I'd never seen him do anything like that before. His response had been pure 'spirit of the samurai'. Hell, he hadn't even used a sword! I couldn't help but feel impressed. If I could just somehow rewind the situation, maybe I could also muster up the courage to... I cringed – surely that was the least *bushido* thought any aspiring ninja had ever had? If I was honest, my suspicion that I just wasn't cut out to be a kendo master was growing, and if proof were ever needed – that was it.

'Come on, Superman. Let's get out of here before they come back,' I said.

Bryan scanned the street, carefully checking to see if any more civilians were in trouble. 'I'm Batman,' he replied in a gravelly voice, then wandered after me.

Nagoya turned out to be depressingly expensive and even the cheapest hotel

---

2. *Kiai* – a battle cry; an exhalation or union of breath and power released at the moment of striking.
3. *Bushi* – 'warriors': the Japanese equivalent to declaring yourselves knights in armour.

room seemed like an insane waste of money. Instead, we found a small park with a deserted playground and slept underneath a plastic climbing frame.

We drifted through the city, hanging out in terrible bars and wasting a great deal of money on seemingly nothing in particular. Gradually, the realisation that we would probably have to return to the factory after all began to dawn on us. First though, seeing as we were already several days late for work, we needed to speak to the boss and beg for our jobs back. We loitered in front of a phone booth trying to swallow our pride and summon up the nerve to ring him.

'Oh Jesus, what are we doing?' murmured Bryan.

It took several abortive attempts to make the call. When we finally got through, Bryan began giggling uncontrollably. He passed me the phone and sat down on the pavement, head in hands.

I stared into the receiver and tried to muster all the language skill I possessed. The conversation went something like this:

Boss: '*Moshi moshi?*' ('Hello?')

Me: '*Aha, oh… er, Shachousan, Toby desu ka do.*' ('Aha, oh… er, hi Boss, it's Toby.)

Boss: '*Toby-san, daijoubu? Doko desu ka?*' ('Toby-san, are you okay? Where are you?')

Me: '*Umm… Er… atsui desu.*' ('It's hot.')

Boss: '*… uh.*' ('… oh.')

Me: '*Shachousan… genki desu ka? Yoshiwara atsui desu ka?*' ('How are you, Boss? Is it hot in Yoshiwara?')

Boss: '*… ah… hai, chotto atsui desu…*' ('… Er… it's a bit hot, yes.')

Me: '*Ahh, honto… so desu ne.*' ('Oh really? Hmm – how interesting.')

Bryan was curled up with laughter. I shoved the phone in his face and ran away to watch from a safe distance. He pulled himself together, and he and the boss chatted for a while. His expression started to relax. It looked as if things were going to be okay.

'So what did he say?' I asked, hopping about nervously once he'd hung up the phone.

'It's cool; we've got our jobs back. I can't believe we just did that.'

'Was he angry?'

'No, not angry. A bit confused. I told him we wanted to work for him again, but it would take us a few days to get home. I said we were young and naive, but very sorry. I think it made him feel all fatherly and boss-like. The Japanese love that kind of stuff. Don't worry – we'll soon be back with our beloved boxes.'

I whistled with relief through my teeth. 'You know when the MC and the Puganought hear about this, they're going to make our lives fucking hell on toast.'

'So what's new?' said Bryan, grimacing as he picked up his bag. 'Remember we're young, naive and *western*. Come on, let's go celebrate.'

With that, we bounded off to the train station, dancing the Migrant Worker with every ounce of unbridled holiday joy we had left.

*

Pain is the best instructor, but no one wants to go to his class.

General Choi

14

A Kicking in Kyoto

We decided to spend our remaining holiday time immersed in culture, visiting Kyoto – the ancient capital of Japan. There was just enough money left for a final blowout, so we bought some tickets for the Shinkansen – the bullet train. It lived up to its reputation for being amazingly fast; it was like flying at ground level. Sitting among sharp-suited businessmen, we rocketed along in air-conditioned luxury, and by lunchtime we were roaming the streets of Kyoto.

We took in a few of the sights, admired some beautiful temples and tagged ourselves on to groups of tourists following guides with loudhailers. I wondered about the fanatical need to view old buildings and absorb the shallow bullet points of history that people seemed to develop when on holiday. 'Ah, an old building. Oh, steeped in history, is it? Wow, when's lunch? Honey, get a picture of me standing in front of that authentically dressed local; look he's bowing to us. God, the Japanese are SO polite.'

By the late afternoon, we were wondering what on earth we were doing there. We took an unimaginative and ill-fated detour towards the nearest bar and our moods began to spiral into depression. Time was running out and we'd soon have to head home. That afternoon, we drank like condemned men, and by the early evening we were in a hideous state, complaining about work, Japan and kendo, and generally feeling sorry for ourselves.

Around ten o'clock, the place started filling up with people, and a small group of Westerners wandered over to our table.

'Hey you guys, mind if we join you?' They were Americans – teachers, judging by the straight-laced look of them.

Bryan flashed me a look of glee.

'Sure thing, bro. I'm Rock and this is Brad,' I said in my finest West Coast accent.

'Join the party dudes,' Bryan drawled.

'Hey Rock, Brad, nice to meet you. This is Chad, Josh, Todd 'n' Rod, and I'm Randy. Can we get you guys a beer?'

'That'd be, like, awesome,' I replied. 'Budweiser – light.'

'So where are you guys from?' asked Chad.

'Oh, y'know… LA, New York, kind of all over?' I said, my accent wobbling and stalling halfway through the sentence.

There was an awkward lull in the conversation.

'You're British, right?' Chad squinted at me, flashing a lukewarm smile.

'Yep.'

'Okay. That's funny.'

I hoped they were too confused by our 'quaint Britishness' to take real offence.

'So… where do you guys teach?' Chad asked.

'We don't.'

There was an audible gasp of amazement. The vast majority of Westerners living in Japan end up teaching English – enduring a daily nightmare of singing, 'If you're happy and you know it, clap your hands' to bored children, and realising that they didn't understand the first thing about their own language and couldn't discern an attributable adjective from an interrogative pronoun if their lives depended on it. We were a rarity.

'We work in a paper factory for a bunch of… of… wankers,' blurted out Bryan emotionally.

'A bunch of what?'

'Oh, you mean assholes, right?'

The cultural divide was growing wider with every sentence. The Americans were clearly starting to regret sitting at our table.

'Hey, you guys are jokers. You're like, real funny,' declared Randy, trying desperately to lighten the mood.

'We ran away and… and now we're fucking pissed,' slurred Bryan.

'Pissed… You mean drunk, right?' said Chad uncertainly.

'Urgh, forget it,' drooled Bryan, and he challenged Todd to a game of pool.

It was a disaster. Bryan appeared to have developed some kind of Tourette's syndrome. Every time Todd potted a ball, Bryan would mumble swear words and insults under his breath.

Todd was extremely tolerant, but somewhere down the line his patience ran out. 'Hey, hey, what? What the fuck? What did you just fucking say? You wanna fuck me! Man, fuck you. I'll kick your fucking ass,' he exploded, slamming the pool cue down and gesticulating like a rapper.

Bryan swayed on his feet, smirking. 'Fuck you,' he slurred again, quietly to himself staring at his shoes.

'O-kay,' I shouted, choking on my drink and jumping up between them, laughing apologetically. I led Bryan firmly back to his seat.

The Americans calmed down and asked me to keep a handle on my good buddy. Bryan apologised and I explained that it had been a long day and to just ignore everything we said.

Bryan leant over the table, rocking backwards and forwards on his chair, holding my gaze. 'Why do Americans always have to talk so much shit before they have a fight?' he whispered, looking innocently at me through one bleary eye.

'I don't know,' I snapped, 'but you're not doing much for international relations. From now on, don't say another word unless you run it past me.'

Bryan stared into his drink, looking amazed and hurt.

'Er... hmm. Gosh, what's gotten into me?' he said with genuine surprise, then went quiet for a long time. Sometimes it was confusing trying to live the life of an honour-bound samurai warrior, particularly when on holiday.

It was quite insightful talking to the Americans about life in Japan, but it occurred to me they were living in a bit of an artificial bubble. They spent their time either in schools or clean, air-conditioned flats, or drinking their wages away with other teachers at Western-themed bars. I'd been in Japan for about three months now, but with the exception of the increasingly erratic kendo practice, I'd spent most of my time in the paper factory. Although I was convinced I was having a more authentic experience in Yoshiwara, I couldn't help but feel a bit jealous.

The early hours of the morning arrived and our conversations degenerated into a blurry mess. Bryan had wandered off to the toilets and failed to return. I found him attempting to goad some worried-looking Japanese guys into playing pool with him and suggested it was time to go. We finished our drinks, shouted goodbye to everyone, then stumbled outside and headed straight for an all-night noodle bar. The streets were empty, and having bought some food, we collapsed under a willow tree to eat it. Next to us, a sparkling stream gently bubbled away and a picturesque humpback bridge completed the rustic Kyoto ambience.

Bryan went back to the shop for second helpings. When he reappeared around the corner a few minutes later, it was clear that something was very wrong. He took a few wobbling steps before his legs buckled and he collapsed on to his knees, staring vacantly at me. It looked as if someone had emptied a bucket of blood over his head.

'HOLY SHIT!' I cried, leaping up and grabbing him.

'I... blurg... don't know... what... the...' he gasped, spitting blood all over me.

I was suddenly stone-cold sober. My first thought was that he'd been stabbed, and I began desperately searching for puncture wounds. His eyes and lips were swelling up from punches, and he was incoherent and in shock. Finally, I found the source of most of the bleeding – a small cut on his head. My heart was racing as I scanned the streets, firing myself up to defend us from further assault.

The noodle-bar shopkeeper ran out waving at me. 'Yakuza, you go – you go quick. QUICK,' he shouted, looking scared.

A bolt of electricity shot up my spine. I had no idea what Bryan had done or said to get his head kicked in, but if he'd picked a fight with the Yakuza, then this was going to be serious. There was definitely a time and place to stand and fight, but after some brief but honest reflection over what was about to come charging round the corner, I'd concocted a fairly detailed mental image of several Westerner-hating ninjas – with guns. I grabbed our bags in a state of blind panic, pulled Bryan's arm across my shoulder and dragged him off into the night. We stumbled and ran, looking back to see if any gangs of tattooed, sword-wielding gangsters were chasing us. After about ten minutes, I slowed the pace, feeling fairly certain no one was following. I tried hailing a passing cab, but as soon as he saw the state of us the driver sped off.

Bryan was able to speak a bit now and seemed to be okay. I began firing questions at him: 'What the hell happened back there? What the fuck did you do?'

'I… I don't know, really. It happened so quickly. I was just standing there. I didn't do *anything*. I didn't even see anyone coming. I suddenly felt someone punch me in the back of the head, and then the next thing I knew I was on the floor and some guys were stomping the shit out of me. And then they just ran off.' He dabbed at his face painfully with his T-shirt. 'I swear, I didn't do anything!'

'Hmm, okay, come on, Batman, let's get the hell out of here.'

We set off towards the darkest street I could find. There was no way any hotel was going to take us in this state. Eventually, we found a small car park and slept shivering between two cars.

The following morning, we were woken unceremoniously by an old lady prodding us with an umbrella.

'You can't sleep here,' she complained.

Our faces were buried in our coats, but as soon as we sat up and she saw the state of us she ran away – probably to call the police. Our hangovers were deservedly horrific and we looked and felt like sick, anxiety-ridden tramps. The swelling on Bryan's face had started to go down, but two shining black eyes were developing and he was covered with dried blood. We were both in desperate need of a wash.

'Uhhr… My God, what the fuck happened last night? What did we do?' Bryan groaned, rubbing his jaw.

'Oh, well, it was fairly routine y'know. After offending the entire expatriate community of Kyoto, you managed to get beaten to a pulp by the Yakuza… and now there's probably a ransom on our heads. Well, on yours at least.'

'Ah… right… yeah… that makes sense.'

We found some public toilets, cleaned ourselves up, then wandered aimlessly through a labyrinth of backstreets, lost and miserable. We pulled our hoods up tightly, trying to avoid people's gazes.

It wasn't long before we decided to call it a day and go home. Bryan was mortified about what had happened. This was his first-ever real kicking and we still had no idea what he'd done to deserve it – although it was fairly easy to imagine him drunkenly stumbling into a gang of Yakuza killers, declaring himself a master of kendo and shouting, 'Which one of your geishas wants to dance?'

'Shit, this is really, really bad,' he moaned. 'The kendo teachers are going to kill me. Street fighting in Japan is considered shameful if you study martial arts – it's a big no-no. People who cause trouble get thrown out of *dojo*s.'

'Well, it wasn't exactly a fight,' I pointed out truthfully. 'More of an assault.'

'They won't see it that way; I'm just going to have to hide until my black eyes go down.'

After a gloomy journey back that lasted the entire day and most of the evening, through thin, drizzling rain, we had both done enough introspection about our runaway holiday to feel genuinely young and naive.

Back in Yoshiwara, we spent the entire next day lurking in the shadowy recesses of the Ninja House, overwhelmed by a deep, hungover sense of self-loathing and embarrassment. That evening, as was increasingly their habit, the kendo teachers came round. As the sliding paper screen rattled open, Bryan let out a doomed moan and pulled a blanket over his head. They knelt down around the table and beckoned him to come and have a drink. He called back weakly that he wasn't feeling well, coughing loudly for effect, as if he was phoning in to work to pull a sickie.

'Eh?' they called him again with bemusement. I held my breath; it was like watching a train crash in slow motion.

'*Bryansan, drinku,*' they urged him looking perplexed and a little hurt.

Nabi-chan got up and began playfully poking him through the blanket. 'What's the matter with you? You're being rude.'

After pleading illness a few more times, Bryan reluctantly sat up, head bowed, braced for a roasting.

'Ohhh…?' A ripple went round the room, then gradually a chuckle and finally, outright, raucous delight. They asked what had happened and nobody seemed outraged or dishonoured in the slightest. Bryan was limp and flushed with relief. They calmly explained that they'd all had fights when they were younger – it was clearly no big deal. They began showing us various teenage scars and reminiscing about past battles. Apparently, street fights were quite rare in Japan – although, when they did happen, people tended to get killed.

This was an unexpected and interesting reaction. As we sat chatting and laughing, all of a sudden it occurred to me that none of them had ever mentioned *actual* fighting or street self-defence before. The more I thought about this, the stranger it seemed, considering kendo was, after all, supposed to be a fighting art. It was clear that the kendo teachers didn't give much thought to violent confrontation – at least not with strangers – and surprisingly, they seemed all the happier for it. Certainly, none of them had tried to give us the impression that they were 'hard' or ever hinted at possessing mystical combat secrets. We questioned Suzuki-san about this, and his answer made me sit up and take note. Bryan translated. He said that, 'Kendo is for cultivating mind and body and spirit. It should be used to help others, not to hurt people. It is a way of peace, and a way of honour, and this is the true essence of *budo* – the way of the warrior.'

'*This* is why we train,' Nabi-chan said. 'Not for fighting, but for "fighting spirit". Understand?'

I nodded. A thoughtful, manly stillness pervaded the room.

'*Kampai*,' whispered Takahashi Sensei, chinking his glass gently in a mournful salute.

Their words struck a deep chord in me. Of course, it was good to know how to look after yourself, but this rarely required becoming an invincible terminator. Many years ago, I had been at an aikido[1] class when my training partner became angry and said that I wasn't grabbing him forcefully enough to make it 'street effective'. I remember stepping back and gazing up at him – he was six-foot tall, with a shaven head and bristling with muscles and tattoos. I wondered who on earth he thought was ever going to attack him. I'd be the first to admit that I was never much of a fighter, but I'd experienced real aggression and violence when I'd worked in mental health – enough to realise

---

1. Aikido (合氣道) – 'the way of harmony' – is a Japanese martial art which specialises in developing *ki* (氣) (*chi*) or 'energy'. It involves learning to redirect and apply and receive force, usually through a refined system of locks, throws, holds and weapon work.

it wasn't something I enjoyed. Okay, so I wasn't exactly sparring with the SAS, but knowing some martial arts had definitely helped me avoid getting hit and gave me the confidence to deal with some tricky situations. I quickly realised though that, however effectively I resolved a physically threatening situation, I always came away feeling bad. Having someone attack you is an intensely upsetting (and obviously quite painful) experience, no matter what the outcome. Of course, every adolescent male dreams of making themselves unbeatable, but despite what a lot of people would like to think, invincibility is an enduring martial-arts myth. Sure, you can train to improve your chances, but when you find yourself passing on a night out with good friends in order to punch blocks of wood while some angry teacher shouts that your sloppy technique would never stop a man armed with a spear, it may be time to address some of the bigger issues in your life. It was clear to me that fighting was something I was happy to avoid, but the ability to defend myself was still important to me. A friend once put it very succinctly: 'Fighting involves trying to hurt someone, but self-defence is largely about trying to stop them hurting you – or better still, not having a fight in the first place.'

Suzuki-san and the rest of the teachers clearly weren't motivated by my concerns. They felt that life was hard enough without having to fantasise about confrontations that hadn't happened yet. They weren't training for uncertain challenges; they were doing it for the here and now. The universal challenges of ego, fear, laziness, illness and old age were inescapable, and therefore much more terrifying and worthy opponents.

Returning to work was a humbling experience. The boss looked at us with sad, puppy-dog eyes through the office window. We were his naughty, prodigal sons – but at least we were home. Back on the factory floor, the MC and the Puganought's smug silences and feigned indifference told us in no uncertain terms that our punishments would be administered slowly and with great delight. Jobsworth Jalal was acting as though we'd been demoted to agency staff toilet lickers. He ordered us around with military fervour and even tried to twist the knife by acting pally with MC and the Pug – as if in the space of a few days our unauthorised absence had somehow resulted in them bonding into loyal mates. In fact, they just totally ignored him. Even Toni behaved like a jilted lover and tortured us by playing his tape over and over and over, until Sami, for the sake of everyone's sanity, confiscated it.

Time passed. We kept our heads down and tried to rein in our barely concealed loathing for everyone. And we even refrained from dancing the Migrant Worker quite so often.

*

The nail that sticks up gets hammered down.

Japanese proverb

15

The Night Train

It was midsummer, and the draining humidity was gradually being replaced by a fierce, bone-dry heat. We wore flip-flops, thin cotton *keikogi*[1] and T-shirts. And even that was too much.

When we weren't slaving our guts out at the factory or soaking up the air conditioning at the 7-Eleven, we lolled about the house in our pants in front of an ineffective electric fan. Every day, we gazed out through the open shutters watching bees, *semi* and butterflies darting around the dense green foliage of the garden. It was therapeutic and provided a tranquil respite from the insanity of work. You could spend hours just sitting quietly as a fascinating microscopic world of insects passed by. The plum trees were alive with marauding black ants and red spiders hung motionless in the shady eaves of the house, waiting patiently for the heat of the day to pass.

Sometimes, early in the morning – when the air was cool and fresh – Suzuki-san's elderly parents wandered in to tend the vegetables. They strolled around, weeding and watering plants like helpful pixie gardeners, then disappeared again. Occasionally, I'd wake to see Suzuki-san's dad gazing in at us, chuckling to himself at the irony of his ancestral family home being full of big-nosed, round-eyed foreigners. It must have been strange for them. After all, they'd lived through the war – a time when Westerners would have been regarded as deadly enemies, devils even.

Like most old people, they talked about the past nostalgically, and I was sure my grandmother would have got along just fine with them. Apparently, the kitchen had once been bombed during an air raid and Suzuki-san's mum ended up with a piece of shrapnel buried in her neck. They chuckled fondly to each other as they recounted the story, as if it had all been hilarious. That was old Japanese people for you: the word 'tough' doesn't even come close.

---

1. *Keikogi* – 'practice clothes': a uniform for martial arts, usually made from white cotton, referred to as *gi* in the West.

Despite valuing our free weekends above all else, one steaming-hot Saturday we managed to waste the whole glorious day inside, sheltering from the blinding light and playing on Bryan's PlayStation. We were deeply immersed in a game involving ninjas called *Tenchu* ('Stealth Assassins'). It had only just been released and was clearly designed with us in mind. You controlled a sword-wielding assassin moving through a dark underworld of ancient castles and ghostly, candle-lit temples in feudal Japan. The scenery was artfully rendered with maple forests and snowy oriental gardens but, unlike most games, it required stealth and cunning, rather than random button bashing. Sadly, having just missed out on the computer revolution, I found that every time my character was attacked, like me, it panicked, failed to open simple doors, repeatedly ran into walls and ate all its supplies. I gave up and lay on my back listening to a soundtrack of strangled guards and decapitated warlords. By dusk, Bryan was well and truly stuck, having spent about three hours failing to get past a particularly tricky level. He was muttering to himself feverishly and shouting in a deranged, mocking voice.

I wandered about the garden, absentmindedly launching into sloppy martial-arts techniques, wondering if I was ever going to improve and moving in sporadic bursts of concentrated violence in an attempt to upset the twilight rush of hungry mosquitoes. I seemed to be developing an immunity to their bites – either that or the combination of noodles and *sake* in my blood was putting them off.

The front door slid open and Kazue poked her head in, back from Tokyo and looking bright and refreshed.

'Hey, how was your shower?' I called.

'Nice.'

She leapt on to Bryan's back, causing his ninja character to fall off a rooftop and die – much to his annoyance.

'How was holiday?'

I wandered over and poked my head through the open shutters 'Yeah, erm... good. We went to Kyoto.'

Bryan threw me an exasperated look.

'Ahh, Kyoto very beautiful.'

'Yeah, well. I don't think either of us will forget it in a hurry...'

Kazue had brought back some anime DVDs she insisted we watch. I wasn't particularly enamoured by the prospect of spending the entire evening watching cartoons, but Bryan was about to beat his PlayStation to death with a hammer and outside the light had faded to a dense tropical blackness. So we cracked open some crisps, put the lights out and settled down to watch *Grave of the Fire-flies*. Any concerns about it being childish were quickly laid to rest, as it turned out to be pretty much the cartoon equivalent of *Schindler's List* – a gut-wrenchingly tragic story of orphaned children scrabbling to survive during the Second World War. Halfway in, and Kazue was a weeping mess. Bryan and I sat stoically staring at the TV screen, bottom lips quivering, determined to hold it together and not cry in front of each other.

'Christ… this is so… *sad*,' said Bryan, his voice cracking. 'Pause it for a sec, I… I'm just… nipping to the bathroom.'

Five minutes later, he returned looking red-faced and puffy-eyed.

'Yeah, I'm just gonna… nip to the bathroom too,' I said, rubbing my eyes as though I had hay fever.

Afterwards, we sat around feeling drained. Kazue sniffed and dabbed at her face with a tissue.

'Well… cheers for that life-affirming movie, Kazue,' said Bryan sarcastically, breaking the silence and picking up the next DVD. 'Round two, anyone?'

'Oh Jesus – seriously, I don't think I can handle it,' I moaned, lying back on the floor.

'It's okay, Toby-san,' sniffed Kazue reassuringly. 'This one will make you feel better.'

If *Grave of the Fireflies* had been a shocking depiction of wartime suffering, then *My Neighbour Totoro* was the perfect antidote. In fact, it went a little too far in the other direction and I found myself welling up again at the heart-warming, innocent tale of two young girls moving into a dilapidated country house with some magical forest-dwelling, Shintoesque[2] animal spirits that lead them into otherworldly adventures. The film captured their childlike joy as they got to know their new home and became accustomed to the delights of rural life. It might have been the fact that I'd been staring at a computer screen in a darkened room for most of the day, but I couldn't help comparing their experiences to my own here in Yoshiwara (albeit with slightly less smoking, drinking and sword fighting in their case). We fell asleep in front of the flickering TV screen, exhausted by the unexpected ordeal of watching a couple of cartoons.

At some point in the early hours of the morning I was woken by Kazue urgently jabbing at me and telling me to crawl under the table. I was sleepy and confused and there appeared to be a gigantic train rumbling past the house. I

---

2. *Shinto* (神道), literally, 'the way of the spirits' – the indigenous spiritual traditions, folk law and mythology of Japan.

lifted my head and peered into the darkness. Everything was shaking and rocking and the shutter doors were rattling like crazy. In the distance, I could hear booming, crashing sounds. I lay back, marvelling at the rudeness of late-night train drivers.

Kazue was insistent, and I could see her now trying to wake Bryan, who just kept batting her away and rolling over. I stared up at the ceiling for a minute and watched the lampshade dance wildly about. Kazue crawled back over and carried on trying to get me to put my head under the table. I wriggled my way underneath and fell back to sleep, after noting with irritation that Japanese people could be really bizarre. If I was snoring so badly, then why couldn't she have just said so?

It was mildly surprising waking up under the table with Kazue.

'Earthquake last night,' she said. 'Only little though.' She stretched over and kicked Bryan. 'Some people very lucky it was small one.'

I was a bit disappointed at having hallucinated my way through my first-ever earthquake, but Japan lay across four tectonic plates, so it seemed likely there would be further opportunities to hide under the table.

Suzuki-san turned up mid-morning, hobbling and groaning with pain. He'd put his back out at work, and shuffled in clutching at the walls theatrically. He explained that he was on his way to see the Bone Doctor, adding a resigned 'ouchy' and a few comical sound effects.

Bryan and Kazue weren't going anywhere in a hurry, so I offered to tag along with Suzuki-san. He explained that he hadn't noticed the earthquake during the night, but had woken up with all his cats in bed with him – an ominous event, as he was convinced they were psychically controlled by his wife and sent to spy on him. He called them '*neko-spy*' ('cat-spies'). I wondered what Suzuki-san's relationship with his wife was like. Every time we were drinking and a cat wandered past, he would hide his beer and whisper, 'Shhhh, *neko-spy*, wife spy.'

In the cool, clean practice room of the surgery, Suzuki-san lay stretched out on the creaking leather couch as the Bone Doctor slowly started feeling his way down his spine, prodding, sensing and listening. Suzuki-san stared back at me with a nervous expression. We both knew what was coming.

CRUNCH.

For the next few minutes, the doctor's hands played him like an accordion. I could barely contain my amusement – it was such a novelty to see him having a hard time for a change.

'*Ouchy desu ka?*' ('Does it hurt?') I joked.

He howled with a contorted grin on his face. I urged him to '*gambatte*' and '*fighto*' until tears of laughter were streaming down both our faces. By the end, even the doctor was smiling. It was some of the most vigorous back cracking I'd ever witnessed, but Suzuki-san was soon standing up, realigned and in one piece again.

As we headed into town to get some lunch, I did some impressions of Suzuki-san's cries, while he laughed and reiterated the fact that Japan was '*kibishi*' ('difficult').

We stopped at an American-style roadside diner and ordered *gyoza* (Japanese dumplings). I wasn't sure exactly what these were, but as we squeezed into the fast-food cubicle, Suzuki-san waved my concerns aside and assured me they were '*oishi*' ('delicious'). I swallowed apprehensively. Eating out in Japan was always a minefield of awkward social faux-pas for me: 'Ah, our most honoured guest, please sit down. We have been saving all winter to give you our finest cuts of meat. Our ancient grandmother has selflessly hand-suckled this calf for you, and our children have gone without, just so we could show you our delicacies... You're a *vegewhat*? Oh... well, then – perhaps just a bowl of raw blood and fish.'

A waitress brought a collection of small, steamed, crimped packages, drenched in an aromatic dark sauce. They smelled delicious. I hesitated. I didn't want to appear ungrateful, but...

'Er, *Suzuki-san... vegetarian... desu ka?*' ('Are these vegetarian?') I asked, twirling my chopsticks around nervously. (I'd long-ago learnt to handle them like a pro.)

He laughed rather too loudly for comfort and assured me they were, but his eyes were twinkling again. I felt sure he was having me on, but I wanted to believe him so badly. My mouth was watering; I was starving and yearned for something other than noodles. I took a bite and found they tasted every bit as good as they looked. We greedily devoured several platefuls, then leant back in our chairs satisfied, sipping tea and chatting in broken Japanese and mime. It was that warm, laid-back, Sunday-afternoon vibe. On the diner's radio, the universally familiar melodies of Bob Marley (patron saint of travellers and beach cafes) played. They conjured up images that were so fantastically out of context I had to smile. Here I was, an Englishman, sitting in an American diner with a Japanese kendo master, listening to reggae. I guess globalisation has some benefits.

Outside, among dusty, white concrete buildings and webs of tangled pylons, traffic swooshed past and, rising above it all, Mount Fuji propped up a boundless blue sky.

At the *dojo*, the sliding doors had been left open and the last rays of the evening sun flooded the hall. We sat on the floor, stretching our legs as people arrived and got changed. Bryan opened our kit-bag and the most ginormous cockroach we'd ever seen sprang out and proceeded to scuttle about him in panicked circles. He leapt back in shock, then danced up and down trying to step on it and kill it with his *shinai*. To anyone watching, he must have appeared to have spontaneously broken into an insane jig. It was pure comedy gold. I watched the teachers' bemused expressions and shook with laughter as the cockroach made a break for freedom and Bryan nonchalantly went back to stretching without missing a beat. His cheeks glowed crimson with embarrassment as he stared straight ahead.

'I think we should probably wash our kit,' he said, meekly looking around.

'Hmm,' I agreed, wiping mildew off one of the *hakama*. We knelt in *seiza* for a few minutes, watching the class unfold.

'Oh, Suzuki-san and I went into town and ate *gyoza* today,' I said, offhandedly.

'*Gyoza?*' He turned to me with surprise. 'Are you sure?'

'Yeah, delicious.'

'But they've got meat in them.'

'No, not these ones, these… were… veggie…' Before I finished speaking, I realised my mistake. Who the hell was I kidding? God, I really *was* young and naive.

Bryan shook his head pityingly, put his helmet on and strode off, looking for a fight. I knelt quietly on my own for a few minutes, ruminating. I felt nauseous – as if I should probably make myself throw up or something. Then again, for the first time in a long time, I wasn't actually starving hungry.

I watched the kendo teachers going through their paces. With their masks and body armour, it was only possible to tell them apart through subtle differences in their physical characteristics and fighting styles. Nabi-chan was enthusiastic and unco-ordinated, Suzuki-san had just the right balance of strength and experience, while the unmistakable master, Takahashi Sensei, was powerful, domineering and utterly terrifying.

Who were these people? Collectively, they were the kendo teachers, but as individuals I barely knew them at all. Japan seemed to have this relentless way of showing you the power of the group over the individual, rounding off your outspoken Western opinions and habits. I wondered how long it would be before I too was a raw-fish-guzzling, socially responsible, workaholic team player. I stood up stiffly and began swinging my *shinai* in slow, deliberate over-head strikes, then walked submissively over to join in with the rest of the class.

*

Fall seven times, stand up eight.

Japanese proverb

16

Buy Low, Sell High

Autumn crept up on us, as the stifling temperature finally gave way to cool, crisp days dappled in sunshine. Things felt more normal now, and I could generally get through work without quite so much internal turmoil and outrage. Paper-reel changes and box packing were almost entirely automatic, and I seemed to have become as capable of hard work as any of the others.

One day, a new worker arrived – a Chinese man called Huang. He was in his fifties and spoke a little English. He blundered fretfully through the box packing, bumping into people, tying himself in knots and generally upsetting the delicate balance of the factory's carefully honed system. I understood exactly what he was going through, but although I was sympathetic, I was still shocked by my visceral urge to want him to just fuck off and get out of the way. I had to remind myself that just a few short months ago, that was me. In time, he too was demoted to the solitary shame of making cardboard boxes. I smoked a cigarette at the entrance and stood watching him. He gazed about, bewildered at the indescribable dullness, his face a picture of despair.

'Oh dear God, no,' I thought with detached revulsion, as I found myself irresistibly compelled to show him how to make a cardboard box properly: the student had become the master! The ethereal, Jedi-like ghost of the old lady materialised before me. 'Yes, Toby-san,' she seemed to whisper. 'You know it be true.'

Huang was a government official from Beijing who had come over to learn the ropes for Shachou-san's dad's new Chinese factory. I tried to make him feel at home by explaining that I was a kung-fu[1] aspirant, but his eyes immediately glazed over.

'Oh...' he said in a derisive, bored manner. 'So you like... Bruce Lee, Jackie Chan?'

---

1. *Kung fu* – literally, 'skill acquired through practice or hard work' – a generic term describing many different styles of Chinese fighting arts. It's mainly used in English; the Chinese tend to use '*Wu Shu*' meaning 'martial arts'.

'Of course,' I replied. 'But not just films. I'm into real martial arts too. And Chinese philosophy – y'know, Daoism,[2] the *Dao De Jing*,[3] that kind of thing.'

'Wha… You… You know Lao Zi!'[4] he spluttered, as if I'd just boasted an intimate knowledge of the Chinese nuclear programme. He wandered away, eyeing me suspiciously, then went to inform his superiors.

The following weekend, we took the train to Numazu to try to buy some warm clothes. Bryan managed to find a woolly hat, while I acquired a ridiculous hooded top with the words 'Bear Surf' embroidered on it that was too small for me. We'd been wandering around the local shopping centre all afternoon and were just about to go home when we stumbled across a small sports shop selling skateboards. Bryan practically fainted with joy, having been a semi-professional skateboarder in his teens. He immediately bought a deck and dazzled a small group of shoppers with an impromptu display of tricks. He urged me to do the same, promising that he could teach me, but I was already wise to skateboards and knew that I only had to look at one to injure myself. It was a scientific fact that once you were old enough to drink and lust after girls you stopped bouncing when you hit the floor. We'd even coined a name for it: 'False radness' – the erroneous belief that in spite of your advanced age and physical decrepitude, you're still able to engage in extreme sports, do the splits or break-dance. Bryan had broken so many bones during his career that his doctor had eventually ordered him to give it up. The last time he'd skated, we'd been living in London. One evening on the way home from the supermarket, we came across a massive half-pipe in the local park. We sat and watched for a while before Bryan could contain himself no longer, borrowed a board from some kid and left a gang of teenage skaters speechless.

'Man… check out that old dude,' I'd heard a kid sitting near me whisper.

'Yeah, he's wicked, mate,' I said, trying to be 'down', then immediately regretted it. His crew glowered back with an expression that clearly said, 'Fuck off, Grandad.'

Inevitably, Bryan's final stunt involved snapping his wrist. No one else noticed, but I could immediately tell. He wiped out hard, then leapt back up, his expression contorted into a face-saving fixed grin. He jogged back towards me,

---

2. Daoism (Taoism), referring to the Chinese concept, religion, philosophy and culture of *Dao* ('道'). Pronounced *Dō* in Japanese. Like Zen, it is difficult to describe in fixed language and has various meanings and usages. Most frequently translated into English as 'The Way', 'The Path' or 'The Natural Principle'.

3. *Dao De Jing* (*Tao Te Ch'ing*), *The Classic of The Way and its Virtue*.

4. Lao Zi (Lao Tzu), literally, 'Old Master', the legendary author of the *Dao De Jing*.

cradling his arm and mouthing swear words. As we walked to A & E, still carrying our shopping, he groaned through clenched teeth, 'False radness... Next time, remind me I'm too old for this shit.'

Back at the factory, it turned out the smooth concrete floor made a perfect skate park. Bryan shot up and down the aisles, entertaining people by popping ollies (jumping in the air with the board) and spinning in alarming circles. For the Iraqis, it was yet further confirmation that we were mere children and they were rock-hard he-men. Toni couldn't resist having a little go, but immediately fell flat on his face. He hobbled away, waving a dismissive hand as if to suggest he was merely verifying that skateboarding was an immature waste of time. The very next day though, to everyone's surprise, the Puganought turned up on a scooter. He trundled up and down with startlingly unself-conscious abandon, looking like a wobbly toddler showing off. It could have only been more tragic if the boss had appeared on a pink bike with stabilisers (which, admittedly, was always a possibility).

'Like you said,' I whispered smugly to Bryan, 'you just can't buy cool.'

Several days later, the boss approached us to ask for a favour. He wanted our help entertaining a couple of American businessmen. They were touring paper factories in the area, looking for a new packaging supplier for a big mobile phone company. It was potentially a massive order, and Shachou-san was anxious to create a great impression and cut a deal – except his English wasn't up to small talk, let alone the finer points of negotiation.

That evening, we were invited to join them for dinner at an expensive local restaurant. As usual, we were late and jogged the few miles there discussing banqueting etiquette and our newly formed, hard-arse business and entertainment strategies. We'd do some casual chit-chat, put them at ease and then blam – we'd seal the deal. It was exciting. No longer were we simple migrant workers; now we were rising to the dizzying heights of, well, geisha girls.

'Buy low, sell high,' I shouted out, exuberantly.

'Branch out and go for growth,' Bryan called back. 'And remember, don't stand your chopsticks up in the rice – it's bad luck.'[5]

'Got it. And we pour the drinks for the Americans first, right? Then Shachou-san and finally the rest of us.'

---

5. At Asian funerals, chopsticks are often placed upright into bowls of rice upon the altar in the same way incense is offered.

'Check. Oh – and don't use the term *chan* when you address the boss's wife.'

'What? Why not?' I stopped jogging for a minute to catch my breath. Bryan always said 'Kazue-chan'. I'd just assumed it was the female equivalent of s*an* ('Mr').

'No, it means, er…' He began to laugh. 'Well it's a bit like "cutie" or "baby".'

'What?' My blood ran cold. Up till now, I had been using the term *chan* with every single woman I had met – the boss's wife, the old lady at the factory, the 7-Eleven staff, the female kendo teachers, even Suzuki-san's wife. Amazingly, in all that time, no one had said a word or even raised an eyebrow. I tried to imagine a Japanese person turning up at home and calling everyone 'baby'. My face flushed with embarrassment.

'You bastard, why didn't you tell me?'

When we finally arrived at the restaurant, a large assembly of waitresses greeted us. We were guided into a stylish private room featuring bamboo screens, flowers and a sunken dining area. The boss sat fidgeting with his wife and eight-year-old son, dressed to the nines and looking as awkward as hell. Next to them were two chunky, suited, middle-aged Americans who were obviously tired and a bit bored. No one was talking, and it felt like we had chanced upon a bunch of virgins on an awkward first date. The boss leapt up with relief and chided us for being late in that fake jokey way that made it quite obvious he was bloody fuming. His wife glowered at me with the cold, dead eyes of a shark. I silently resolved to never speak to her after tonight. We politely introduced ourselves (having agreed that it might be diplomatic to forgo the Rock Poseidon and Brad Schapelli routine), and Bryan passed cigarettes around, then ordered steaks and a huge amount of beer, while Shachou-san bombarded me with questions to translate for his guests. I wasn't quite sure precisely where he had got the idea that I was suddenly able to understand Japanese, but no one appeared to notice that I had little clue what the boss was saying, so I just asked the Americans polite questions and tried to put everyone at ease. The boss didn't know what we were saying anyway. Occasionally, I stroked my chin, nodded and threw him some 'negotiations-are-going-well' looks.

The Americans seemed like nice, normal guys who would rather have been at home having Sunday lunch with their families than engaging in the mystifying world of Asian business deals. A few drinks in though and the tension started to evaporate. It turned out that their trip had so far consisted of a series of hideously formal meetings, and they were extremely relieved to meet some

English speakers and kick back a little. The boss and his wife sat mutely sipping *sake*, while we chatted away and got down to the serious business of getting slaughtered. A few hours later, the boss and his new associates were getting on swimmingly and had totally given up trying to translate anything or talk shop. The boss's wife had taken their son home and Shachou-san lay slumped with his arm around the Americans as we toasted each other and bonded over fishing anecdotes and how great everything was. By the time we left the restaurant, we were all best buddies and had been invited to small-town America for camping trips and barbecues. The boss tearfully hugged us goodbye in the car park and wobbled off home looking happy. No one had mentioned paper or any deals, but that was the Japanese way. First, you created a harmonious relationship with your customers and then, only when you were family, did you talk money.

A couple of days later, Shachou-san discreetly took us to one side and announced that the Americans had placed a large order. He thanked us for our help, bowed, then glided away, looking smug.

'*What?*' whispered Bryan, in a now familiar tone of disbelief and outrage. 'Is that it? The least we deserve is a bonus or a day off. The tight-arse.'

'Maybe,' I said, feeling disappointed, yet somehow unsurprised. 'I guess he just assumes we'll do whatever's good for the factory out of sheer loyalty. Still, at least we now know we're capable of brokering high-powered business deals.'

'Oh, come on. Who the hell are we kidding? You need qualifications to get anywhere in this world and, as far as I recall, we're qualified to do exactly fuck all. In fact, we're overqualified – we're astrophysicists at the university of stupid. Basically, we're stuck here slaving our guts out while the boss gets rich. Shit, that order must be worth a fortune.'

Word got out that we'd helped with the business dinner, which only added to the general atmosphere of bitterness. The boss had taken *us* – the children – out to dinner. Jobsworth slammed boxes about in a strop and refused to talk to anyone for the rest of the day. This time, we felt even more cheated than usual. We'd only been trying to help, but somehow, yet again, we had managed to offend and alienate everyone. I began to realise that working in Japan was more of a minefield than I'd previously imagined. In the eyes of our co-workers, we couldn't do anything right. If we rocked the boat, we were ostracised; if we helped steer the boat towards prosperity, then we were getting above our station.

As we lay on the wooden pallets outside and stared up at a damp, grey sky, the paper machines continued to whir away in the background and the air stank of cold sweat and disillusionment.

'We've really got to get out of here,' I said weakly.

Bryan didn't answer. He didn't need to.

*

When you change the way you look at things, the things you look at change.

Wayne W. Dyer

17

A Bowl of Ramen

Winter was coming. The temperature continued to drop and soon the draughty old Ninja House was as cold as a tomb. We started to close the shutters at night and swaddle ourselves in layers of clothes and blankets. Once the sun had set, we'd spend our free evenings huddled around the table complaining and drinking tea. Having a bath had turned into a major exercise in agonising *misogi* ('ritual purification'). The word for cold, *samui*, was now as familiar and well used as *atsui* had once been.

Life in Yoshiwara was becoming a little too Spartan for comfort and perhaps inevitably, relations between Bryan and me were also starting to feel strained. We were both frustrated and disheartened. Work was physically exhausting, kendo was gruelling and ego crushing, and the house, amazingly, continued to attract mosquitoes and cockroaches, despite the chilly weather. We began communicating less and less, and our interactions were soon almost monosyllabic. Day-to-day living was weighed down by our sour moods and petty squabbles.

At first, it was just little things, but soon everything we did or said to each other seemed to grate. I was *seriously* fed up. Fed up with not speaking the language properly, fed up with being too hot or too cold, fed up with work, fed up with everyone's constant insistence that we were young and naive and needed to persevere, fed up with hanging around the train station late at night because Bryan and Kazue were boning each other senseless in the living room. Equally, Bryan had had more than enough of my moaning, enough of having to translate for me most of the time, enough of me relying on him. Even Kazue seemed to have retreated into a half-life of daytime telly and sleep. It felt as though we were all depressed and starting to take it out on one another.

The climax of hostilities came to be symbolised by a simple bowl of *ramen*. As a vegetarian, noodles had become my staple dish. One day, I left a half-finished bowl on the dark wooden floor of the kitchen area. Bryan curtly told me to clear it up. It was reasonable enough, but I took extreme umbrage at being *ordered* to do it. Something inside me snapped and I refused. Why the fucking hell should I? Why couldn't someone do something for me for a change? I'd had enough of Bryan and being told what to do. To hell with everything! The bowl remained there for an entire week, festering in silent rebellion. And during all this time, Bryan and I didn't exchange a single word – which I suppose was a testament to our respective stubbornness.

It was a miserable and lonely week. On the Friday evening, a sharp, stormy wind whipped through the deserted streets of Yoshiwara. Coming home to the house that night felt like returning to a damp, inhospitable cave. I forced myself into the garden for my hundred practice strikes with the heavy *suburito*. Half an hour later, I stepped back inside, steaming with sweat and feeling mean. Bryan sneered at me derisively. I sat down opposite him, poured myself a shot of *shochu* and lit a cigarette. After sitting in silence for a long time, snake-eyed like gunfighters, we began draining shot after shot of cheap *shochu*, taking it in turns, staring in silent loathing while the bowl of *ramen* continued to rot and attract flies. The tension was unbearable. My emotions flitted between childlike rage and an urge to fall about laughing. I seriously wondered if I was heading for a nervous breakdown.

Kazue was leaning against a wall, her face frozen in a mask of disapproval. Suddenly, she stirred.

'You guys seriously need to sort shit out,' she snapped abruptly. 'NOW.' Then she stood up and marched off in disgust.

Kazue was always calm. We knew that if she was that pissed off, then things were becoming critical. Several minutes of excruciating silence passed. We grimaced and squirmed.

'Don't know what *her* problem is,' mumbled Bryan, wrinkling his nose and avoiding my gaze.

'Yeah... Jesus,' I said, raising my eyes to the ceiling.

We both cleared our throats, before going back to staring into the distance. Then – and I don't remember specifically how – at some point, we began to talk. More out of boredom, I think, than any particular desire for reconciliation. As usual, we discussed anything other than our feelings or the situation at hand. And eventually, true to form, the conversation gravitated towards martial arts – except this time there was a definite air of drunken confrontation.

After half an hour of lame verbal sparring concerning the ever-pressing issue of what style was best, I'd had enough of beating around the bush. I went in for the kill.

'If you ask me,' I said in a dramatic, calculated challenge, 'kendo doesn't work. In fact, it's stupid.' (Admittedly, not one of my finest propositions, but it hit the target.)

Bryan's eyes rolled into the back of his head with outrage and his muscles shivered. He sat bolt upright, grinding his teeth and practically drooling at the approaching conflict.

'No…' he declared loudly with an equally weighty retort. '*You're* stupid. You never really wanted to learn kendo, anyway. I've sweated my balls off to get where I am.'

'Okay, I'll show you what I've learnt right now in the garden.'

Outside, a ghostly wind rattled the wooden shutters and the house creaked and flexed like an old sailing ship. Our bloodshot eyes simultaneously flicked to the pile of *shinai*s standing in the corner.

'I'm going to make you eat that bowl of *ramen*.'

'Yeah, well *I'm* going to—'

The door slid open and Kazue wandered in and sat down between us.

'Hiya,' she said flatly.

'Oh, hi,' we replied in unison.

'Have you sorted shit out yet?'

'Yeah. Yes, definitely. Uh-huh, it's fine.'

'Good, I'm going to Suzuki-san's house for hot shower. See you later.'

With that she left and we resumed our showdown, almost without missing a beat. I poured us both another shot of paint stripper, held it up to the light and squinted at Bryan through the greasy glass.

'Fuck you,' I spat in mock salute.

'No… fuck *you*,' he toasted back.

That was it. We both leapt for the swords and began whacking each other senseless before we'd even made it outside. Almost immediately, we managed to smash the overhead lampshade, showering broken glass everywhere and plunging us into semi-darkness. Despite being drunk, Bryan was still way too quick with a *shinai*, so I launched myself into him and we ripped through the sliding paper screens, crushing them into splinters. Bryan retaliated, missed and swept the contents of the table across the room. We jumped up, staggered into each other again and sent the fridge and the contents of the kitchen flying. For a brief while, we loosely retained the pretence of an honourable martial-arts face-off, stoically punching, blocking, kicking and locking. But then the red mist descended, and we totally lost the plot and started wrestling each other. The emotional floodwaters had burst and six months of sheer frustration came pouring out. The next ten minutes were a blur of escalating violence, angry grunting, shattering furniture and gratuitous destruction.

Abruptly, I snapped back into reality, to be confronted by Kazue standing over us, shouting as we rolled around on the floor attempting to throttle each other. She'd rather unfortunately cut her shower short.

'You… you… wankerists!' she shouted. 'What have you done?'

Very slowly, we relaxed our grips and sat up dazed, rubbing our necks, and coughing and blinking.

'What – are – you – *doing*?' she screamed, looking around in horror.

We stood up slowly, heads bowed and blushing. She glared at us both, then turned around and immediately marched out again. Cautiously, I surveyed the wreckage as a creeping feeling of embarrassment and anxiety spread through me. I swallowed hard. How would we ever be able to face Suzuki-san or his parents, let alone pay for the damage?

'Whoops.'

'Er… hmm.'

'Well… um, I guess that settles that,' I said quietly, pretending to inspect one of the swords.

'Yeah… yeah. I guess so,' said Bryan, rubbing his back and picking shards of glass out of his socks.

Amazingly, neither of us appeared to have sustained any serious injuries. The room was trashed though – broken screens, ashtrays, bottles, books, food and body armour were strewn across the stained floor. The fridge was lying on its side leaking water and buzzing loudly. And underneath it, I found the crushed remains of the festering *ramen* bowl.

'Never get between a man and his noodles,' I joked lamely.

Bryan nodded and began sweeping up the debris. A little later, I scooped what was left of the *ramen* into a bin liner.

'Ha! I win,' said Bryan, quietly.

I paused and flicked a bit of stinking *ramen* at him, then reached for the nearest sword.

'Now you're getting it,' he said with a grin.

Kazue returned late in the evening from Suzuki-san's house, after reluctantly trusting us enough to be left alone whilst she went for a hot shower.

'Think I'm going back to Tokyo again,' she said resolutely.

'Okay,' said Bryan, meekly.

In the face of overwhelming awkwardness, I put the kettle on and went to get some *milku*. By the time I got back, the atmosphere had improved, their differences clearly resolved without the destruction of any more furniture.

In fact, on closer inspection the damage wasn't really too bad. We managed to repair or clean most things, and the next day found some replacement screens in one of the outbuildings. The *tatami* floor was another matter though. It was badly stained with trodden-in ash and dirt and needed urgent attention. After a lot of futile scrubbing, we decided to buy fresh mats. They were expensive, but a great improvement, imparting a pleasant aroma of dried grass, which permeated the house.

Things really started looking up when Nabi-chan popped round and donated a small gas fire. We did our best to insulate the main room and plugged up most of the howling gaps. The temperature had improved and it felt as though we'd been saved from a rather gruelling survival situation.

One Monday, for no apparent reason, Bryan and I massively overslept. Perhaps it was the relief of a warm night's sleep, or maybe just the stress of the previous week, but we woke up around ten o'clock, confused, as we hurriedly rushed to get ready for work – which involved little more than standing up and leaving the house.

'Do you think we're going to get into trouble for being late?' I said as we stumbled sleepily towards the factory.

'I don't know,' said Bryan. 'I don't think it's ever happened before in the whole history of Japan.'

We made a very public display of jogging around the factory doing the polite morning rounds of '*Ohayo gozaimasu*', then put our guilty heads down and dived straight into working. After about ten minutes, the boss came out and hovered behind me, not saying anything, but clearly trying to act stern and reproachful. It irritated me immensely.

Okay, so I'm late, I thought. For God's sake, deal with it. Sorry for not making you richer. What do you want me to do? Commit *seppuku*?[1]

I was so desperately tired and cold that I didn't really care what he thought anymore. Part of me wanted to find the words to tell him to take his job and shove it up his arse. But my limited Japanese vocabulary resulted in me stammering, opening and shutting my mouth like a goldfish. I began to well up with the sheer frustration of my lot. Finally, and much to my surprise, I started to weep.

Surprisingly, the boss's eyes also began to glisten. We stood there speechless, both looking at each other, crying our eyes out: me from despair and

---

1. *Seppuku* – 'cutting the belly', also known as *hara-kiri*; ritual suicide by disembowelment, used by samurai – and government – as part of the *bushido* code of honour.

exasperation; the boss, mistakenly touched by my seemingly genuine regret at being late and letting the team down.

'*Daijoubu, Toby-san… daijoubu*,' ('It's okay') he eventually said, patting me consolingly on the back and walking away looking satisfied.

My sense of self-loathing knew no bounds. I really was a total failure. I couldn't even tell my boss to piss off.

The rest of the morning was wretched. My hands were numb with cold, and the taunting sounds of 'Sharey sharey lady' droned on and on in the background. I had reached rock bottom.

'So this is what I've come to?' I whined pityingly to myself.

Shimizu-san wandered over and stood next to my station on the packing lines. He appeared sympathetic to my internal turmoil. He didn't speak for a long time and seemed to be mulling something over in his head. Finally, he put his hand on my shoulder and said very seriously, and with a great deal of effort, 'Toby-san, change… your… mindu.'

I stopped what I was doing and looked at him questioningly.

He said it again, more confidently this time, and with even more conviction: '*Change your mind.*' Then he turned away without waiting for an answer and went back to work.

Something inside me felt as if it had popped. I stood up straighter and a smile broke through my sad, embittered expression.

'Of course…' I marvelled. 'How brilliantly simple.' I'd always imagined such profound revelations only came after arduous training with an enlightened master on a mist-shrouded mountain. Then again, these are precisely the kind of assumptions that obscure the real gems that are inevitably right under your nose. I stared out through the open doorway, lost in contemplation and wonder. Actually, it *was* a bit misty out there. And there *were* mountains in the distance. And work was undeniably arduous. I chuckled. Shimizu-san's simple words had cut through my troubled mood like the sun coming out after a rainstorm.

The rest of the day was the same as ever, but I felt as if something had changed. I had gained a fresh perspective. Or, rather, I had let go of an old one.

*

One who chases two hares catches neither.

Japanese proverb

18

DJ Ladies Love and Blighty Four

After the noodle incident, Kazue returned to Tokyo. We kept on at a fairly subdued pace for several weeks and did little else but work, sleep and practise kendo. My enthusiasm for being hit on the head was definitely waning, and martial arts mastery now seemed a remote prospect at best. The Factory of Dreams continued to grind, but although Bryan and I shared the common attributes of apathy and low self-esteem, they were underpinned with the unlikely, yet nagging belief that we were destined for great things. In a spirit of desperation and blind optimism, we began to hatch a new and exciting plan which came to preoccupy us in a way that's only possible when doing hard, menial, physical labour for 12 hours a day and spending your evenings being hit with bamboo swords.

It was simple: together we would make the funkiest music known to man and get ourselves a record deal. Having left school at the height of the dance music explosion of the early '90s, we had music and DJing in our blood. Bryan already had a laptop, but this would require some expensive equipment. I was going to save up for some decks, and he would buy a sampler and some speakers. We were amazed that we hadn't thought of it sooner. Actually, it had occurred to me before, but money, work, scratched floppy disks, and insanely complicated music-editing software always seemed to get in the way. In England, we'd both been obsessive record collectors and spent a lot of time 'making tunes', or rather, sampling snippets of obscure records, adding a predictable drum beat and perhaps a hip-hop lyric of someone shouting the words 'hip-hop' every eighth bar, then drinking ourselves unconscious, secure in the knowledge that we had managed to finally lay down 'The One'. As anyone who has ever made music will know, coming up with great ideas for tunes is easy, but finishing them is another matter.

'Listen,' said Bryan one lunchtime at the factory, as he sat astride a gigantic roll of paper, slurping away on *natto*.[1] 'We've seriously gotta do this music thing.'

'Yo. For real,' I said excitedly. 'We gots ta get paid!'

'What?'

'Er, we've got to get paid, make some money.'

'Right, exactly. I'm fed up with working for these patronising morons. If we can record some tunes, it could be our ticket out of here and we could get a decent job. But I'm not messing about anymore. This is serious – we've got to be committed.' With that, he slid down from the paper roll and pulled out a magazine cutting. It was a picture of a grey rectangular box with rows of impressive-looking knobs and a thin, green LED display.

'The AKAI S5000 Sampler,' he said, his voice trembling slightly. 'Brand new,' he added, carefully studying my reaction.

'Okay... What can it do?'

'Well, it samples. And... and... Shit, what can't it do? Just look at it. With this beauty, nothing can stand in our way.'

I had to agree. Over the next few weeks, we spent as little cash as was humanly possible and bided our time. As McJobs go, the pay wasn't too bad and anyway, so far, Suzuki-san had refused point-blank to accept any rent money. By mid-December, we had amassed an impressive wad of crisp yen notes that were crying out to be spent; finally, we were ready to put our plans into action.

It was a few days before Christmas, and we headed straight into central Tokyo on a fast train, chatting away in excitement, with a weekend of factory-free fun and serious shopping ahead of us. After the stagnant backwaters of Yoshiwara, the exhilaration of arriving in the city again was so powerful it was actually mildly anxiety provoking. Our silver train snaked its way through endless suburbs of tightly packed identikit housing. I melted back into my seat and peered past the reflections of the window. In the distance, I could see immense glass-and-steel buildings breaking up a deep bronze skyline. As we flew towards the heart of the pulsing metropolis, I trembled with anticipation. It felt as though I was returning to civilisation after a long expedition into the wilderness.

On arrival, we pushed forward through a heaving crush of people on to the subway system. I gawped at the crowds, wide-eyed like a hillbilly – it almost as intense as arriving for the first time. Giant chrome escalators ferried us up towards the rushing noises and cold air of the outside world. The winter streets rumbled and shook with action. Shoppers hurried past, wrapped tightly in warm coats and scarves. Traffic, flashing lights, steaming vents, exotic aromatic takeaway food and indecipherable billboards assaulted my senses.

Finally, after a disorientating march, we arrived at Kazue's house. She lived

---

1. *Natto* – traditional Japanese soya beans, protein-rich and fermented with grass bacterium; extremely smelly with a thick brown gooey texture, rather like snot; definitely an acquired taste.

with her family in a high-rise block of flats behind a busy downtown shopping street. We were welcomed inside and I was introduced to Kazue's mum – a tiny, reserved woman who seemed surprisingly calm about having her home descended on by two lumbering Western men. Kazue seemed pleased to see us, and we were led into the living room and immediately plied with food and drink. It was such a novel experience to be in a clean, central-heated room. The place was minute by Western standards (Bryan described Tokyo flats as 'rabbit hutches'), but it was luxurious compared to the Ninja House. After a long-dreamt-of hot shower, I felt utterly spoilt by the delights of long-forgotten modern amenities. We lay underneath a *kotatsu* – a heated, knee-height living-room table – and basked in front of the mesmerising glow of a giant flat-screen TV. It took all of ten seconds to fill Kazue in on the news from Yoshiwara, then we announced our intention to make it big in the music world. To her credit, she refrained from collapsing on the floor in hysterics. In fact, she didn't bat an eyelid and calmly offered to drive us to Akihabara[2] the next day.

After a brief tour of the flat, Kazue took me into her room and dramatically threw open the cupboards lining the back wall. They were piled high with row upon row of toy robots still encased in their pristine boxes. She then proceeded to deliver a lecture on *Gundam* (a Japanese cartoon robot franchise – according to Kazue, the Japanese equivalent of *Star Wars*) about which she was clearly passionate. It was quite startling, and a little scary. In England, toy robot collections usually belonged exclusively in the realm of prepubescent boys.

We bedded down for the night on soft futon mattresses in Kazue's room. As I drifted off, I tuned into the distant but ever-present background noise of the city, reflecting on the continually surprising nature of the Japanese.

We slept late and woke to the heartening sounds of Kazue's mum cooking breakfast. She presented us with a healthy mixture of *miso* soup[3] and 200 cigarettes that she'd won the previous night playing *pachinko* (a form of Japanese pinball), of which she was a consummate master.

Kazue went off to collect the car from the garage and her mum sat us down in front of the TV and put on a kendo competition that she'd recorded for our benefit. It turned out to be a grand final between two high-ranking masters, and we were instantly hooked. To the untrained eye, kendo competitions can come across as slightly chaotic, with a lot of hitting and screaming and seem-

---

2. Akihabara – literally, 'Field of Autumn Leaves', but better known as 'Akihabara Electric Town', the place to buy computers, cameras, music equipment, etc.

3. *Miso* soup – a traditional dish, usually made with a thick paste of fermented barley or soya beans.

ingly random scoring. I'd seen them before, but this was different. In a massive arena, crammed to capacity, two ancient *kendoka* faced each other, barely moving. They appeared to be perfectly matched, frozen in an en-garde position, locked in an internal battle. For the longest time, they remained stock still, sword tips barely touching, sensing each other. Very gradually, they began to circle, searching for an opening. The huge crowd was going wild with all the atmosphere of a World Cup final. In a fight like this, the physical form was almost secondary; they were probing for a lapse in composure, a momentary break in mental concentration. The commentators were gabbling with excitement and we were glued to the screen in fascination.

For several unbelievably nail-biting minutes, the match continued as a dead heat. Then, one of them let their guard down – only for a split second, an almost imperceptible dip in the angle of his sword and a tiny wobble as he settled back into his stance. He was just testing the water, but it was all his opponent needed. Quick as a flash, his entire body shot forward and struck hard. It was a perfectly co-ordinated lunge to the throat (*tsuki*) and he took victory to win the championship. We danced around the room shouting for joy and hugging Kazue's mum as the strike was replayed over and over. It was the most exciting kendo fight we'd ever seen, an incredible demonstration of timing and composure under pressure. The two swordsmen calmly bowed to each other and returned to the edge of the arena, where they knelt down and began checking their equipment and packing it away. There was no punching the air in celebration or glowering with defeat. It was impossible to tell from their expressions who'd won and who'd lost, and it occurred to me that being totally awesome at sword fighting was wasted on the wise and humble.

Ten minutes later, we were cruising downtown Tokyo with Kazue driving her dad's giant Mercedes, still reeling from the unexpected excitement of the kendo match and banging out deafening tunes loud enough to make the car shake. Whenever we pulled up at traffic lights and junctions, people stopped and stared, no doubt wondering who it could be making such a racket in the rumbling, blacked-out ride. We were shamelessly showing off and loving it. I put on 'Man of Steel' – a drum-and-bass classic and, more recently, a paper-factory stereo anthem.

'Shit, this fucking rocks,' shouted Bryan, biting his bottom lip. 'We should so make something like this, y'know, with that sort of… "bwarp bwaaarp" sub-bass sound.'

'You mean "wooarp, woooooarp",' I said.

'That sounds like Bow-Wow in Japanese,' added Kazue.

We drove on through cavernous underpasses and vertiginous flyovers, heading towards Akihabara Electric Town. Kazue dropped us at the edge of a busy shopping plaza. As we got out of the car, the music was still thumping, and several people stopped to check us out. After all, we were foreigners, and clearly not businessmen, teachers or backpackers – maybe we were famous? Or maybe we were just annoying them. It was hard to tell.

Akihabara was full of affable gangs of loitering teenagers, who hung around posing, desperate to be noticed, perhaps get their faces on the cover of a magazine or maybe hook up with a celebrity. Like most things, the Japanese didn't do style, music and fashion by halves, and many of them resembled flawless clones of their subculture heroes. Here, it was fairly easy to identify people's musical allegiances. If you liked hip-hop, you wore reversed baseball caps, tracksuits and gold chains. If you were a Goth, a little patchouli oil and some eyeliner simply wouldn't do – full face paint, a leather cape and a fencing sword were required. And if you liked manga, well, you became a living, breathing cartoon character.

Bryan led me towards a giant music superstore. Its windows were lit up by video screens showing girls performing 'Para-para' – a kind of synchronised-vogueing dance craze in which stony-faced models simulated stacking bricks to a kind of hard Euro house or trance music. A bit like insane line dancing. It was deadly serious, very bizarre and never ceased to amuse me. Inside, the floor groaned under the weight of expensive consumer treasure. I immediately began subconsciously trying to calculate the number of cardboard boxes required for such an operation. After we'd spent a few minutes wandering the store, weak-kneed and wide-eyed, a shop assistant resembling a neon mannequin with white peroxide hair strutted over to us.

'Heeeeey, you guys DJs?' she asked in a squeaky voice, looking us up and down, before presenting us with a business card. It read 'MC CHILL – DJ PROMOTER'.

'Oh yeah,' I said. 'Yes, um, I'm DJ… (cough) er, Ladies Love and this is…'

'Blighty Four,' said Bryan quickly, with an air of feigned indifference. 'We're from London; just passing through, y'know.'

'Oh… kay,' she said uncertainly. 'I've not heard of you guys.'

'No, you wouldn't have,' quipped Bryan. 'We're very underground.'

We both nodded, trying as hard as we could to look cool. It was all very uncool. She wandered off, clearly sensing our desperation. We kept her card though; we weren't quite ready to face the general public just yet, but it was surely only a matter of time.

'So… where does Blighty Four come from then?'

'It's what the boss's son calls me; he can't say my name properly. Actually, I quite like it… Well, it's better than DJ Bryan.'

'Hmm, fair point.'

'I see you're still "DJ Ladies Love" then,' said Bryan, smirking. The pained way he spat out the words made it sound like DJ Massive Twat.

A friend had christened me one night at a memorably bad party in East London. I'd waited patiently by the decks all night with my records in a queue of angry, puffa-jacketed, bad-boy raver DJs, all intent on playing the hardest techno known to man. Finally, in the early hours of the morning, I was allowed on, but immediately cleared the dance floor with a terrible recreation of the DMC Mixing Championships. Only a solitary drunk girl remained, swaying in front of me, gurning and waving her arms about as if she was trying to fight off imaginary wasps. My friend Sarah had sidled up, surveyed the scene and mockingly declared that I was now officially 'DJ Ladies Love' – as in the rapper LL Cool Jay (Ladies Love Cool James). Somehow, the name stuck, but it was always more of an aspirational title.

The shop was an Aladdin's cave of high-tech equipment. Racks of expensive technology lined the walls, and turntables and mixing desks were laid out seductively on display. I'd had my sights set on buying a couple of Technics 1210s (the DJ industry standard), but then something else caught my eye – something I'd never seen in England… A pair of brand-new silver Vestax PDX-2000 turntables. Built for scratching, designed by world-champion turntablists, they glinted softly in the light with the alluring promise of technical prowess and artistic integrity. Underneath, a sign in English read:

> PDX-2000 is awesome design. Strictly for super professional DJ only. High torque, quick response. Fine and wide pitch control, DC motor, most best performance…

'Strictly for super professional DJ only'… Would I have to pass a test or show some kind of ID? I wondered. I ran a hand covetously over one of its pristine slipmats. They were my Stradivarius. I quietly reasoned that my lack of previous DJing success could only be explained by not having had a pair of these babies.

While MC Chill was boxing them up for me, Bryan had located the AKAI S5000 sampler and was deep in prayer. A shop assistant was running through a dense operating manual with him and beads of sweat were forming on his brow as he tried to decipher some of the Japanese writing.

'Can you understand any of it?' I asked.

'Erm, well I think this character might mean "wood"; and that's definitely the one for "mountain".'

'Perhaps it says, "Not for use in forests or up a mountain?"' I suggested.

'Oh shit, we'll work it out.'

We tracked down some small but powerful monitor speakers and a mixer, handed over an obscene amount of cash, then wobbled outside, proudly carrying our tickets to fame and fortune.

The afternoon sky hung low, with thick, yellowish clouds overshadowing the endless traffic and shuffling shoppers. It didn't take long to locate some record shops and escape the biting cold. Soon, we were eagerly thumbing through piles of rare and collectable vinyl that would have been almost impossible to get back home. After several hours of fevered crate digging,[4] we'd amassed an impressive pile of tunes. Sadly, though, after working out the cost, it quickly became obvious that we could probably afford just one, maybe two at a push. I bought a couple of battle breaks[5] and a few of my favourite albums and resolved to give up eating when we returned to Yoshiwara.

It was starting to get dark when Kazue came and picked us up again. We stowed our bounty in the boot and after some painful indecision ended up at a bizarre Irish-themed pub in Roppongi – an area famous for nightclubs and bars. It was disorientating stepping out of futuristic Tokyo into a basement lined with dark Victorian wooden panelling and sepia pictures of gnarled Irish farmers – like stumbling on to the set of a wildly inaccurate period drama. Groups of testosterone-fuelled English teachers and businessmen mingled at the bar, talking loudly, guzzling frothy European beer and chatting up giggling Japanese girls. Everyone looked sophisticated, well groomed and well paid. Over the din of the crowd, I caught snippets of macho, big-city conversations between large rugger-bugger banker types on foreign deployment from the wine bars of central London, with nicknames like 'The Dan-ster' or 'The Steveonator', showing off their plumage to each other: 'Hey big guy, still making a mint with those offshore accounts?', 'Top man. Rob-o, you old tosser!', 'I'm on the Sony portfolio now – got a bloody Porsche for my bonus!'

It was as if we'd landed on another planet. In fact, just hearing English being spoken was a novelty, and I felt utterly alienated by the fake Western surroundings. I gazed down at my own shabby, factory-worn clothes and rough worker's hands; I looked like a country bumpkin. I took comfort in the belief

---

4. 'Crate digging' – searching for rare or unusual vinyl to sample, as in 'digging through a crate of records'.

5. 'Battle breaks' – records comprised of samples, sound effects, dialogue and drum loops for mixing and scratching.

that eventually all our suffering would be worth it; once we had made a fortune with a multi-award-winning album, things would be different. Maybe then I could have another attempt at kendo mastery, when I'd sorted my shit out first. Kendo was undoubtedly hard, but kendo and working at the Factory of Dreams – that was nigh on impossible.

'When we're rich and famous, I'm going to start importing cider and call it "Scrumpy Jap". Then I'll get a Lamborghini and crash it into the paper factory and just leave it there and not even claim on the insurance,' enthused Bryan as our conversation drifted towards the familiar fantasy world of what we were going to do when we escaped he Factory of Dreams.

'No, I think you would buy paper factory,' said Kazue. 'Then you get Toby-san to come and work with you, and you could both order each other about and say "Oi" rudely and make boxes every day.'

'Hmm, I think I might employ Jobsworth and MC Squared to be my DJ managers,' I said. 'I'd pay them to carry my vinyl… Seriously though, I might travel… I don't know, maybe even go back to uni.'

'Go back? You never went in the first place. And, anyway, they won't let you in without maths.'

'Oh, well. Perhaps I'll just buy a mansion in the countryside and become an eccentric hermit then. Every day, I'd chill in my garden hammock listening to tunes and making home brew.'

'Christ, yes… Bliss,' said Bryan, shutting his eyes and picturing the scene.

I closed my eyes too and tried to block out the claustrophobic, smoky, theme-pub chatter, imagining the warmth of an English summer's day on my face, a lazy bumblebee drifting past, cricket on the radio, the distant sound of children's laughter…

Then… whack – Kazue hit us both on the head.

'You guys are like sad little old men,' she said, shaking her head in pity.

After a while, Bryan and Kazue got chatting to the people on the table next to us. Everyone was speaking Japanese at full speed, so I sipped my drink quietly and watched Mariah Carey murdering some kind of hideous Christmas pop song on MTV. As she cavorted around in a bikini on a fake snowdrift, it occurred to me that it was quite a challenge to feel Christmassy in Japan. Like most British expats at this time of year, I began to picture an idealised vision of the festivities – friends and family back home all getting on well, gathered around a hearty open fire in Christmas jumpers, sipping mulled wine, with Slade's 'Merry Xmas Everybody' playing on a crackling gramophone.

I was woken from my daydreaming by Kazue introducing me to a plump, depressed-looking Japanese girl. She was wearing a Santa Claus hat and was clearly my gooseberry double from an adjacent table.

'She is single too,' said Kazue with a meaningful nod. 'Do your duty, Toby-san. Go on, speak Japanese to her,' she added, before leaving us to die of humiliation while everyone sniggered from a distance.

The girl looked as unenthusiastic about the situation as I felt. Any chemistry between us was definitely going to have to involve test tubes. As far as I could tell, she introduced herself as 'Tomato' (but it was noisy in there). I discovered that she worked as a typist in an office, enjoyed watching TV and eating fish, didn't like music and was definitely not interested in the way of the warrior in any sense whatsoever. Never in the history of mankind had two more incompatible people been forced to endure polite matchmaking conversation.

'So... TV... good,' I said, barely able to conceal my disenchantment.

'*Hai, honto suki desu*,' ('Yes, I really like it') she replied, her mouth stuffed full of crisps. Then, staring at me inquisitively, she asked, '*Friedu potato suki desu ka?*' ('Do you like chips?') with a sudden, genuine curiosity.

'... *suki desu*,' ('Yes') I said, while turning round and mouthing 'Fuck off' at Bryan, who was convulsing with laughter at the other table. It wasn't long before we'd given up on small talk and were staring into our drinks, each wishing the other would drop dead.

We left in the early hours of the morning to the piped melody of 'Auld Lang Syne', which is played at closing time in much of east Asia, always in an easy-listening, lift-music style for some weird reason.

Outside, Roppongi seemed to have transformed itself into a gaudy fairground of coloured lights, seedy hostess clubs and 'love' hotels that charged by the hour and were almost certainly never frequented by lovers. The air was sharp and cold, and we walked quickly through the thinning crowds, dodging the tourist vultures that were an ever-present fixture on the streets. Apprentice Yakuza wannabes hassled anyone who looked lost or likely to follow them into some godforsaken strip club where they could safely part them from their wallets. It was entertainment on an industrial level. We'd all had enough though, and I was relieved to finally get back into the car and escape the soulless, hollow-eyed, homogenous nightlife.

*

Karoshi – a noun meaning 'death caused by overwork' [*ka* ('excess') + *ro* ('labour') + *shi* ('death')]

19

Merry *Christmasu*... Now Get Back to Work!

The next day was Christmas Eve and, as much as we would have liked to go out and celebrate, it was time to head back to Yoshiwara and get to work.

Coincidentally, that morning, Kazue received a call from an old high-school friend who wanted to come and visit. He was called Krisu, an unusually Western name for a Japanese person, although, to some extent, he sounded typically Japanese – a young apprentice salaryman who secretly felt trapped by his job and spent his life stuck behind a desk, loosening his tie in rebellion and dreaming of being a massive, rampaging, manga-style robot. Kazue joked that he was '*bon-bon*' – a 'poor little rich kid'. He had a car, though, and was up for driving, which solved the immediate problem of getting ourselves and our equipment home. I felt sad about leaving Tokyo, but we were keen to try out our new kit and, despite all the odds, we were finally starting to feel a little bit festive.

Christmas in Japan is overwhelmingly a commercial event and not a public holiday as it is in the UK. Bryan did cynical impressions of confused, brow-beaten employees marching to the 7-Eleven to buy tiny, shrink-wrapped yule-tide cakes which, for some inexplicable reason, had become a Japanese tradition – 'Merry Christmasu... Now *get back to work*.'

We laughed, but the truth was we were facing an increasingly urgent dilemma: were we going to have another unauthorised holiday? Neither of us wanted the stress of causing yet more ill feelings at the factory. Tensions had eased a little, as we'd been generally keeping our heads down, but the thought of spending Christmas break making cardboard boxes was more than we could handle. This was *Christmas*, after all; it was our moral duty, surely, to make merry by binge-drinking, watching crap TV and stuffing our faces with food. In the absence of any decent excuses, we decided to take some time off on 'religious grounds' and pray for divine intervention.

Krisu rolled up late in the afternoon in a tiny, knackered Ford Fiesta that looked wildly out of place on the slick streets of Tokyo. He parked, leant out of the window, shouted '*Oss*',[1] waved a couple of bottles of wine at us, then jumped out and launched into a group hug. He threw me a high five and bowed, and I offered him a cigarette, which he examined with interest until Kazue berated him, reminding him of the fact that he didn't smoke (they'd been classmates since kindergarten and had the kind of relaxed, informal friendship that was rare in Japan). Krisu tossed the cigarette away, laughing, and began beating his chest like Tarzan. He was clearly a total nutter.

We said goodbye to Kazue's mum, thanking her for the hospitality, then somehow managed to squeeze ourselves and all our boxes and bags into the tiny car. I would miss the brief oasis of comfort that was Kazue's home.

By the time we'd got going, the afternoon was drawing in and a few isolated snowflakes were starting to fall. The roads were quiet and we sped through the city, making good time. Kazue insisted on driving, as Krisu was too scary behind the wheel and lacked her psychic ability to detect speed cameras.

Once we were well under way, it became apparent that we'd forgotten to bring a corkscrew for the wine. It seemed like a long shot, but in the absence of any 24-hour hardware stores, we swerved into a service station and I leapt out and mimed opening a bottle to the pump attendants.

'Er, *konbanwa… corkuscrewu… kudasai?*' ('Good evening… corkscrew… please.')

The attendants stood to attention for a second, looking unsure, glowing in their pristine white dungarees and smart matching caps. All of a sudden, one of them raised a finger in comprehension.

'*Hi, chotto matte kudasai,*' ('Just a moment, please') he shouted and ran into an office, returning with a beautiful, shining silver corkscrew with roughly the same amount of ceremony as if I were being awarded Excalibur. I tried to give them some money, but they were having none of it.

'*Dozo,*' ('Please, take it') they cried, bowing low. And as we drove away, they continued to bow in unison, waving us off until we could no longer see them.

'Wow,' I said. 'Now that's what I call customer service.'

'Hmm, it's kind of normal in Japan, I think,' said Kazue, looking proud.

'It's a Christmas miracle,' said Bryan, going misty-eyed.

'*Oss!*' shouted Krisu and began opening the wine.

---

1. *Oss* – a cry of encouragement common in martial arts and sports that denotes fighting spirit. Made up of two characters meaning 'to push' and 'to suffer', it's a bit like shouting, 'Come on!'

An hour or so later, we were cruising along, tipsy and in high spirits, and, lacking a car stereo, united in a rousing Christmas singalong. Kazue and Krisu didn't know any English carols and we'd never heard any Japanese ones (if they even exist), so we just sang the *Star Wars* theme tune. (*Star Wars* was both mine and Bryan's first-ever experience of going to the cinema, and it blew our impressionable four-year-old minds – little wonder that we ended up interested in Asian philosophy and sword fighting. Kris and Kazue also grew up with it. There's a deep sense of bonding to be gained that transcends language and cultural barriers from agreeing on the coolness of things.)

'Staaar Waaaaaars, Stahahahaaaaaaa Wars, Stahahahaaaaaaa Wars, Staaaaaar Waaaaaarrrrs.'

We belted it out with passion at the tops of our voices, then, to finish with, Krisu broke into a unique and moving rendition of Darth Vader's anthem (sung in a clear falsetto voice): 'Darthu Sader... Darthu Sader... Darthu Saduuuuur.'

Just beyond the steel barriers of the motorway, dark, forested scenery lurked, and remote, jagged hills cut into a blue twilight. I wiped condensation from the window with my sleeve. The road arced its way across massive bridges and steep, shadowed valleys. Sporadic lights of distant towns and villages shimmered in the distance. Japan was a tough, mountainous country and flat, fertile land was at a premium. Almost every available inch seemed as though it was being used for some purpose. The drive home gave me a real sense of scale, and I thought about what a difficult journey this must have been before train lines and roads were blasted through the rocky terrain. A quick visit to Tokyo could easily give the impression that Japan was entirely insulated from the natural world and completely at ease with modern technology, but people retained a surprisingly traditional mindset and a deep sense of longing for the past. Out here in the darkness, there were still some wild, unforgiving ancient places. For the majority, this wilderness had been all but obscured by concrete and neon, but the mountains and forests existed, beyond the reach of development, and by their hard, forbidding nature continued to endure.

Thick flakes of swirling snow were beginning to pile up on the windscreen wipers and Kazue strained to see out through the dim headlight beams. She drove cautiously and we were soon skidding along, following slushy lorry tracks on the whitening road. By the time we crawled into Yoshiwara, the storm had taken hold and a winter flurry covered the sleeping landscape. We fell out of the car into another world, laughing, shouting, throwing snowballs and sliding down the thin, icy alleyway towards the Ninja House. It was freezing; we hurriedly unloaded our stuff and headed inside to get the gas fire going. The house was perfectly still and quiet, insulated from the deluge.

Krisu paused at the doorway for a moment, soaking up the old-fashioned décor with a sentimental smile. He patted the wooden beams affectionately and breathed in the smell of freshly cut *tatami*, while talking softly to Kazue.

'Krisu says it's like returning to childhood,' Kazue told us.

We warmed the place up and sat surrounded by boxes and bags, pulling out bits of equipment like excited children unwrapping their presents. It turned out that Krisu had brought along a small movie-screen projector, which he rigged up to our new speakers and pointed at one of the faded white walls. In a moment, a multi-coloured, hyper-real picture with crisp surround sound transformed the room into a state-of-the-art cinema. We lit some candles, wrapped ourselves in bedding, turned the fire up and watched some lame, eye-candy sci-fi film about Mars. I fell asleep, floating through space, orbiting the giant red planet, drifting through the darkness in slow motion.

Christmas Day dawned frozen and still. I peeped through the shutters at the dull, overcast morning. A few scattered bird tracks spiralled out over the white rooftops of the garden sheds, and icicles hung low from the rusty tap. Lots of snow equalled no work, which meant that everything was truly fresh and magical – divine intervention had come through. Father Christmasu had left the best present possible: a well-timed holiday. I nodded in thanks towards the shrine. The angry red doll eyed me back mysteriously.

Krisu only stayed till the afternoon. The main roads were clear and, as is the Japanese way, he needed to get back to work on what would have been Boxing Day if the Japanese celebrated it. Although it seemed crazy that he had come all this way for one night, he didn't seem to mind. We waved him off outside the house, singing a parting chorus of 'Star Wars', and promised to hook up the next time we were in Tokyo.

By the early evening, it was time to get the festive celebrations under way. A roast dinner was way beyond the remit of the kitchen, but we managed a mean curry and some garlic potatoes. I peeled the veg and made tea. Kazue crafted small, decorative origami birds to hang around the house. And outside, the snow began to fall again.

It felt good to be cocooned safe inside. Steam billowed from the cooking pots and we cranked the gas fire up till the room was sweltering. Just after dark, it occurred to me that I should probably confront the elements and ring my family, what with it being Christmas Day. I wrapped myself in a parka jacket and crunched across the frosted streets towards the 7–Eleven.

It was business as usual in the outside world. As ever, the staff were standing awkwardly to attention waiting for a rush of customers that never came. I bought an international phone card and headed out to a telephone booth. I keyed in the thousand–digit security number and eventually heard voices, echoing and distant.

'HELLO! WHAT? Yeah, it's me, Toby. TOBY. Yeah, fine, yep, still in Japan... I... I said, I'm still in Japan... Yes, I'm eating enough.'

It was unreal, and reinforced the fact that I was a long way from home, but it was reassuring to hear that life there was continuing as normal.

When I returned to the house, I decided to place my hilarious surprise snowball attack on hold. Bryan had plugged the sampler in and was staring at the operating manual in horror as the sheer complexities of it began to dawn on him. I hovered in the doorway, brushing snow from my shoulders. With each turn of a page, he looked increasingly confused and outraged, as if he were thumbing through some really obscene pornography.

'So, what's the deal with it?'

He let out a primeval groan, dropped the manual on the floor and wrapped his arms tightly around his head to prevent it from exploding.

'Not so good, then?'

'Oh God. It's like trying to decipher ancient hieroglyphics. I think I've just wasted a grand and a half on a stupid lump of metal that doesn't work. I should have just got a cardboard box from the factory and drawn some knobs and dials on it.'

Kazue sat silently with her back to us, watching telly. It was obvious I'd missed some kind of furious argument.

We ate Christmas dinner in a subdued mood. Bryan brooded underneath a dark cloud, fidgeting and slapping at a particularly hardy mosquito that kept trying to land on his neck. He gazed back at the sampler like a jilted lover. Eventually, he seemed to visibly crumple, placed his chopsticks on the table and lifted his chin.

'Go on then,' he sighed. 'Just fucking eat me.' He turned to me with a defeated look on his face, like he was about to cry. 'Why is it *everything* I ever try to do turns to shit?'

'Oh, come on... not everything,' I said. 'You can speak Japanese, you do kendo... Er, hats look good on you.'

'Do they?' he asked, suddenly perking up a little.

'Actually,' suggested Kazue, 'I think it's because—'

'Don't answer, Kazue,' said Bryan, quickly. 'It was meant to be a rhetorical question.'

'Uh?'

'It's just a figure of speech, y'know. Like when you ask a question, but you're not really looking for an answer.'

'I see,' said Kazue. 'English is so weird.'

'It's not that weird,' said Bryan.

'Is weird,' said Kazue.

'Jesus,' I said. 'Look, you're both weird, okay?'

We sat quietly for a few minutes, each lost in our own private thoughts, listening to the hiss of the gas fire.

'Well… PHHHHRRRRRRP,' I said, breaking the silence with the most cynical impression of a party blower I could muster. 'Merry Christmas, everyone. Now where the *fuck* are all my presents?'

'Here's your present,' said Bryan, punching me hard in the arm.

'Oh no, I got you the same!' I said, slapping him round the head.

Slowly, a smile crept upwards from Bryan's mouth, finally breaking through to his eyes.

'You must be so glad you came here.'

'Come to Japan, have a few laughs, spend all my time getting hit on the head by kendo teachers and work in a paper factory every bloody day? Are you kidding? This is like being the *real* Karate Kid. I wouldn't miss this for the world.'

Later, Suzuki-san and Nabi-chan arrived with a couple of large bottles of *sake*. They were keen to celebrate Christmas, in the same slightly quaint way the British sometimes have a go at Thanksgiving, Bastille Day and Diwali. We showed them the turntables, which I'd proudly set up in a raised alcove on one side of the room. Nabi-chan couldn't understand it: why on earth had I brought *two* record players? I switched it all on and gave them a few minutes of frenzied scratching and mixing. They were bewildered. Why did I keep touching the records? I was going to break the needles. Why didn't I just let the music play? I guessed hip-hop had yet to reach the Japanese martial-arts community in any meaningful way, so I turned it off and sat back down defeated. Kazue put on an easy-listening Latin-jazz CD and they all breathed an audible sigh of relief. I pulled out some crisps and peanuts, remembering that Japanese drinking sessions were modelled on a kind of late-night '60s cocktail-party ambience. Normality was resumed.

We talked for a long time in broken Japanese until I lost the thread of the conversation. I swayed back and forth with my eyes half closed, head swimming with *sake*.

Suzuki-san leant over and poked me awake. '*Ashita wa Fujiyama*... Kendo challenge.' ('Tomorrow, Fujiyama.')

'Huh? But... but I thought you couldn't climb Fuji Yama in the winter?'

'No, not the mountain,' said Bryan, 'the rollercoaster. It's called Fujiyama – the rollercoaster of fucking doom! There's no work tomorrow because of the snow, and Suzuki-san says he'll take us. Seriously, it's mad.'

'*Fujiyama rollercoasteru, saiko desu,*' ('Fujiyama is incredible') agreed Nabi-chan.

'Biggest ever,' added Kazue.

I'd never been on a rollercoaster before and could only picture an ancient wooden one I'd once seen, but not actually ridden, in Great Yarmouth in England.

'*Kendo testu,*' Suzuki-san reiterated, eyeing me sternly. Apparently, this was a serious test of my nerve as a martial-arts acolyte. If I could handle Fujiyama, I could handle anything the kendo masters would throw at me. In the Yoshiwara kendo school this was a bizarre, but essential initiation.

'Sure, I'm up for it. Why not?' I said, relieved that I wasn't going to have to climb up a volcano. 'Sounds cool.'

We did some *kampai*'ing and toasted each other. And although I wasn't entirely certain, it seemed as though everyone was regarding me with pitying amusement.

*

If things seem under control, you are just not going fast enough.

Mario Andretti

20

Riding the Rollercoaster of Doom

I felt sick as we cruised down the slushy concrete highway towards Fuji-Q Highland – the gigantic amusement park that was home to 'Fujiyama King of Coasters'.[1]

I was becoming increasingly convinced I wouldn't enjoy it, or even survive the experience, but Suzuki-san continued to pressure me with that hard-to-resist, *sensei*-type encouragement: 'Japan *hardo* – kendo challenge, *fighto*', etc. I pondered the possible connections between rollercoaster riding and the way of the warrior: feeling the fear and doing it anyway? Going beyond fear? Practical self-defence at fairgrounds? I couldn't help wishing these lessons could be learnt in a slightly more traditional setting. Perhaps safely on the ground in some concealed jungle monastery with Suzuki-san imploring me always to believe in myself and 'fight for honour', to which I would respond by nodding with sudden clarity, flexing a pumped bicep and kicking a tree in half.

Bryan and Kazue gave me a more familiar roasting.

'Come on, man, do you want to stay a pussy for the rest of your life?' said Bryan.

'Pussy-san,' agreed Kazue, nodding seriously.

I didn't, but what had seemed like an unmissable experience a few hours earlier, now, in the harsh light of day, felt like a very bad idea. In fact, it was starting to dawn on me that there were few things as likely to bring on a drowning sense of anxiety than attempting to ride the world's biggest rollercoaster with a massive hangover, following a night of hard drinking. However, peer pressure in Japan is a serious matter, so I bowed to popular consensus and began trying to mentally prepare.

The weather had broken and the snow lay piled in scattered icy clumps. The amusement park was definitely open for business, and Bryan and Suzuki-san

---

1. In 1996, it was the highest and fastest rollercoaster ever built, with a 259-foot drop and travelling at 130km/h.

were depressingly excited. As ever, Kazue was impassive, indifferent even. I was the only one who would rather be convalescing in a darkened room listening to ambient music and sipping water.

By the time we arrived at the theme park, I was green and sweaty. I held my head out of the window like a carsick dog, lapping at the fresh air. I fell into the car park and retched a few times. In the distance, a tall fence surrounded the immense black steel girders making up the base of the rollercoaster. I could hear the ride picking up speed, beginning its terrifying, rumbling descent to earth, the screams of petrified passengers occasionally catching on the breeze. I stared upwards until my neck hurt, taking in the spaghetti-like construction of the track. It looked impossibly thin and flimsy, bright-red flags billowing from its highest points. Apparently, it was shut down in high winds – I swallowed hard and hoped for a blizzard.

'You are gonna fucking *love* this,' shouted Bryan, skipping gleefully towards the entrance, arm in arm with Suzuki-san. I wondered how it was possible for him to have known me for so long, yet be so wrong about what I would love. Kazue lit a cigarette, breathed the smoke out in a sigh and looked me up and down.

'I think… you will… shit pants,' she said, as if she'd spent a long time mulling it over. It didn't sound like idle speculation. Then she wandered off to join the others.

Fuji-Q Highland turned out to contain an infinite world of horrors for the nauseous and the hung over: non-stop techno, flashing lights, candyfloss and spinning fairground rides. Bryan, Kazue and Suzuki-san didn't waste any time, and jostled their way through the crowds with me in their wake to begin queuing up for the rollercoaster. It was bright and cold, and I shivered in the winter sun. We stood in line, chatting away, gradually moving closer and closer to the ride. Behind us, a couple of bored schoolgirls giggled and played on their mobile phones, as relaxed as though they were waiting at a bus stop. My stomach cramped and my mouth tasted of metal. As we got nearer, I noticed even Suzuki-san and Bryan were starting to look a bit unsure. Their chatter became quieter, less boisterous. Only Kazue seemed unaffected. Phew, I thought, *everyone's* shitting their pants.

By the time we were close to boarding, we were shuffling restlessly on the spot, cresting a wave of collective anxiety as any last remnants of bravado evaporated.

'What the *hell* are we doing?' said Bryan, staring up at the imposing track, as if the penny had finally dropped.

'Ouchy,' cried Suzuki-san, burying his head in my shoulder.

'Seriously... what *are* we doing?' I said. 'I mean, why are we putting ourselves through this? What are we trying to prove? Hang on... haven't you guys
all done this before?'

'Well, yeah, sure, but it seems like a long time ago now. And anyway, we
were drunk. Still, I... I don't remember it being quite this high,' said Bryan.

I'd noticed the emergency exit stairs marked 'Chicken Run'. Would it
really be so shameful? We could leave right now; perhaps pretend that Suzuki-
san had suffered a stroke and we needed to carry him back down. Go for a cup
of tea... a nice walk... maybe a snooze? Watch some paint dry – *anything*.

Finally, we were at the front of the queue. It was time. Kazue caught my
eye and began laughing. She still looked impossibly relaxed. When it came
down to it, she was the only one of us who had any real balls.

'You are massive... girl blouse,' she called over to me.

I danced about on the spot, shaking the tension from my arms and trying
not to throw up.

'It's girl's blouse; *girl's* with an s,' I said, correcting her as we clambered into
the carriage.

'Ah, sorry, you are massive *girl's* blouse.'

I tried not to burst into tears as the restraints were lowered and locked into
place. Everyone let out a low murmur. This was it; there was no going back.

We pulled out of the tunnelled hangar with a lurch and started the long
climb to the top. The occupants of the other carriages sounded like they were
beginning to feel it now, with a few timid shrieks and cries.

The carriage juddered and clicked, as a thick, oily chain dragged us ever
upwards. An icy landscape came into view and the cold air made my headache
throb. Far below, crowds of tiny, pixelated people were scattered across the
amusement park. I clung to the safety bar with white knuckles and focused
on Suzuki-san who, with hands clasped together, hail-Mary style, had begun
the Buddhist chant '*Namu myoho renge kyo*' (meaning, literally, 'To honour or
devote oneself to the wonderful law of the Lotus Flower Sutra'), much to the
amusement of the people behind us. The ascent seemed to take forever, but
finally we levelled off at the very top for 20 or 30 feet, inching slowly towards
the drop-off. We were so unbelievably high up, my brain was having trouble
processing the situation. Panicking strangers were shouting now, geeing each
other up and bonding with cries of '*Oss*', '*Gambatte*', etc.

Then time slowed down; everything became silent.

'Oh look,' I said, 'you can see Mount... F... F... Mount Fuji-
aaaaaaaaaaaaaaaaaarrrrgh!'

We tilted forwards and dropped face down into the most spectacular free fall imaginable. I was almost tipped out of my seat, weightless, pressed up hard against the restraints, literally flying. Everyone was screaming, but amazingly, I didn't seem to care anymore. In a split second, my fear transformed into a pure endorphin rush, and I knew I wanted to dedicate the rest of my life to riding the world's biggest rollercoasters. As we levelled out at a blistering 135km/h, grimacing from the G-force, my only thought was that I immediately wanted to go again. The next big drop had me screaming for joy. Then we rocketed through some unbelievable twists and turns and I held my hands high, shouting my head off like a fearless lunatic. All too soon, it was over; we slowed down and rolled into the hangar, gasping and puffing with relief.

In front of us, another ride was being loaded up with a fresh crew of pale-faced, trembling passengers.

'*Abunai*,' ('Danger') Suzuki-san called out to them.

We laughed and waved at them to run away; very few people had the courage to laugh back. We clambered out, limp with exhaustion and headed down to ground level. TV screens displayed pictures taken at the precise moment when you suddenly realised that you weren't going to die and this was actually great fun. I looked as if I was having some kind of epiphany, so I bought a print, if only to remind myself of a fleeting moment of hangover-conquering alchemy. We went and rode some of the other attractions, but with the possible exception of a rusty Ferris wheel that creaked alarmingly and swung about at the top, seemingly held together by one single thin metal bolt, everything else seemed tame in comparison.

By the end of the day, there seemed like nothing else for it but to ride Fujiyama King of Coasters one more time (I now addressed it by its more respectful full title). Before we were even halfway along the queue, I began wondering how the hell I could be so stupid to put myself through this for a second time, and as we were securely fastened into the carriages, my anxiety returned with comic vengeance. I'd got away with it once; surely this was kicking fate in the nuts.

The slow ride to the top was every bit as scary as the first time. My mouth went dry, my knees trembled and a heavy weight of annoyingly self-constructed dread pinned me to my seat.

'Oh look, there's Mount Fuji againaaaaaaaaarrrrg!' I said again. Quickly followed by, 'Waaaaahoooo, come on you motherfucker, is that all you've got?'

On the way home, I lay draped across the back seat of the Suzuki-wagon, staring at the roof, shattered by the emotional rollercoaster of riding the world's biggest rollercoaster. I wasn't sure if I'd passed my kendo bravery test with flying colours, exactly, but I had at least survived.

We spent an uneventful New Year's Eve at home. The kendo teachers had gone to be with their families, so we did what any lost, lonely foreigners would do: rented Stanley Kubrick's Vietnam-war epic *Full Metal Jacket* on DVD, drank some venomous red wine (which was genuinely called 'Frenzy') from the 7-Eleven, and passed the evening doing impressions of marine-drill sergeants, screaming across the table and showing our 'war faces'. Around midnight, we wrapped up warm and wandered over to the local temple.

A mellow crowd of pensioners were huddled around a crackling bonfire, sipping hot *sake*. They waved us over and poured us shots. We were welcomed into the celebrations and took our places round the fire.

There was a nice, small-town vibe; no one seemed that concerned about the passing of the year or particularly excited about the arrival of a new one. Kazue began chatting with an elderly couple. She then introduced me to our next-door neighbours at the Ninja House. I didn't recognise them at all, but Bryan and I did a synchronised formal bow. They knew all about us, of course, and I couldn't help mentally replaying various loud, drunken sessions and shrinking a little. Kazue said they thought my sword practice was going very well. I felt acutely embarrassed as I pictured myself trying to swat mosquitoes with my *shinai* in the garden, loudly mixing on the decks or taking a sneaky piss in the bushes late at night.

'I think we'd better keep it down a bit at home,' I said to Bryan, who was blushing slightly and obviously thinking the same.

'Yep,' he said awkwardly, trying to avoid eye contact with them.

People queued at the shrine in an orderly fashion to ring a cast-iron bell with a long, plaited rope hanging from it. They clapped their hands together solemnly, bowed and said a prayer in front of a larger version of our shelf shrine with the angry red doll. I asked Kazue about New Year traditions.

'Yeah, well, uh... the bell symbolises change... or something,' she said, watching the ritual unfold with a puzzled expression. 'I know what it means, but I can't really explain it in English.'

'Hmm, ever thought of becoming a tour guide?'

We laughed. I understood what she was getting at though, and conceded that most Westerners couldn't tell you what our festivals mean either, particularly in another language. She did, however, mention that the red doll at the Ninja House was called Daruma and had something to do with martial arts, maybe originally from China. Bearing in mind that this was, essentially, still pre-internet times, the mystery seemed destined to continue for a while. I liked the idea that our local deity was a fierce warrior. I stared up at this giant doll's head. It still looked pissed off, and in the gentle candlelight seemed to emanate a wrathful, ethereal power. It was tantalisingly exotic. As I stood by the fire, watching the procession of worshippers streaming past, I realised that in all the time I'd been in Japan, Daruma had managed to totally elude any explanation. Why a disembodied head? Why so angry-looking, and what was with the big, staring eyes? Even the earliest Elizabethan missionaries to Japan were probably more informed than me. When I'd asked Suzuki-san about it, he'd performed some totally baffling mimes that Bryan and I could only watch in complete bewilderment. I decided I would have to bite the bullet and ask Aono Sensei. Surely being a Zen monk and speaking a little English meant he would be able to explain it, albeit in an intimidating and deeply patronising manner.

It seemed fitting to offer a quick New Year's prayer. I passed Bryan my drink, and joined the queue for the bell. When my time came, I gave it a confident ring and slapped my hands together.

'O, mighty Daruma, please help me to become a worthy martial-arts student, and er, world peace please… *domo arigato gozaimasu*,' ('thanks') I said in a loud, clear voice, then stepped to one side to allow the conveyer belt of worshippers to continue. No one took any notice of me. Silently, I made a secret appeal: 'Daruma, listen, it's me again. I appreciate that world peace is a big ask, but if at all possible, martial-arts mastery would be great – and a new job would really help. Seriously, I can't keep this cardboard box shit up for much longer… Oh, and a girlfriend. And maybe some new vinyl. And… and…' It suddenly occurred to me that this was more like a wish list for Father Christmas than a prayer to a revered deity. I wandered back to the bonfire slightly humiliated by my childish neediness. Whoever Daruma was, my pitiful wining was unlikely to impress him. Besides, he probably didn't speak English anyway.

The holiday had come to an end, and now a dark, gloomy January set in. The winter sun struggled to rise and its half-light barely lasted through to the early afternoons. What was left of the snow lay in dirty puddles of melted water, and the fetid stink of pulped paper seemed to hang in the air. Yoshiwara felt more remote than a ghost town on a bank holiday.

Now, more than ever, the pressure to extract ourselves from this bleak situation weighed heavily on our minds. It was only the kendo that seemed to really make any sense, but even so, regular practice was becoming more and more difficult to achieve due to late finishes at the factory. One night, we arrived at the *dojo* after the class had already started, fuming. It had been a tough day and our dickhead supervisors had been a real pain in the arse, ordering us around and doing very little themselves. I was really starting to suspect they were engineering the late finishes just to annoy us.

Bryan was sure of it. 'They're just jealous of us,' he said, as he put his mask on with gritted teeth. 'There was no reason for those last few runs on the paper machines; I swear they're doing it deliberately.'

'What's their fucking problem then? What have we done to them?' I sort of knew the answer to this, as we made very little effort now to disguise our disgust at the way they spoke to us.

'Who cares? Come on, let's go.' He motioned for me to spar with him. We were both in the mood for a fight.

I donned my helmet, bowed and took up my position opposite him. First, we got into a slow rhythm of moving up and down the *dojo*, performing head strikes, each time getting stronger, harder. I kept my head up and hit him back as hard as I could. Bryan didn't flinch. He was much faster than me, but I wasn't going to back down, not tonight. I soaked up his strikes and focused on getting a few good, solid revenge hits back. We screamed at each other, pulling our war faces and trying to dominate the centre ground. It was deeply cathartic. I felt the frustration flow through me, each sword strike a channel for my hatred of MC Squared. In my mind, I destroyed him: Oi, Toby-san. Move those boxes now. Nooooooo – move them yourself, *twat face*!

Smack, crack, whack.

Bryan looked as though he was similarly releasing a long day's worth of pent-up resentment and rude treatment against the Puganought.

Bang. He hit me incredibly hard on the wrists, making my sword shake, but my adrenaline was flowing and I barely felt it. I went at him double time, completely unconcerned as to how many times I got hit, which was lucky, as he basically beat the living shit out of me.

By the time we were finished, my ears were ringing. Suzuki-san and Nabi-chan were standing to one side, watching and, surprisingly, laughing. Suzuki-san spoke with us, and Nabi-chan gave me a thumbs up.

Bryan translated, looking pleased. 'Suzuki-san says our form is terrible, really sloppy, particularly yours. But our fighting spirit is improving.'

'That's good,' I said, taking my glove off and rubbing my wrist, which I could now feel was starting to swell.

Nabi-chan stepped forward and motioned for me to come over and spar with him.

'*Toby-san, fighto.*'

I stood up, trying to focus myself again, as the fighting spirit suddenly seemed to drain away.

'*Gambatte*,' called Bryan, with a chortle.

'*Bryan-san, fighto*,' said Suzuki-san, in an uncharacteristically deep, intimidating voice.

Bryan's smile faltered. It looked as though we were both in for some hard lessons.

Back at the Ninja House we were still preoccupied by our music-making struggles. It took a great deal of deep breathing, phone calls to Tokyo and patient help from Kazue to sort the sampler, but eventually all our equipment was doing what it was supposed to do. Finally, it was time to let the creative avalanche loose – time to make tunes.

Here we go… Any minute now…

But our minds went blank; we'd spent so long getting to this point, we didn't know what to do. We sampled drums loops, old movies, synthesiser licks and obscure vinyl rescued from junk shops, and hey presto – the same old predictable, unfinished shit. Most evenings degenerated into each of us pursuing solo activities, plugged into headphones, lost to our private dreams. I scratched and played my battle-records in infinite cut-up juggles on the decks to the roar of an imaginary appreciative audience. Kazue watched telly and Bryan sampled. He'd often spend weeks crafting a single break; the same loops over and over again, doctoring it with imperceptible subtlety.

'Listen,' shouted Bryan excitedly one evening, as if he'd just made radio contact with an extra-terrestrial. 'Do you hear *that*? Do you hear that high-hat – the way it kind of fades out… into the reverb?'

'Mmm, not sure… What about if you were to add a seriously loud sub-base sound just there: boom, kick-a-boom-boom. Whaaaarp.'

'Hmm… Perhaps I could do some scratching over the top. Y'know: beep ahhhhhhhh fresh.'

'Yeah… yeah. Maybe.'

'Beer?'

'Please.'

Meanwhile, in the Factory of Dreams, our minds clung to the fading memories of Tokyo thrills and rollercoaster rushes. It took time to get back into the swing of things and come to terms once again with the gaping void that was work.

One day, I found myself looking out from behind my cardboard boxes (now a tower of origami masterpieces) that acted as an office wall in our open-plan environment. I paused for a minute, watching the ingrained, predictable choreography of our routine: the Iraqis straining to lift the heavy boxes in their sweat-stained army shirts, Bryan and Shimizu-san changing the spools of paper offcuts, Akio, the MC and the Pug organising the next gigantic reel to be fed into the machines, the boss with his feet up in the office, grinning and playing on his mobile phone… Huang, the Chinese guy, had left. I guessed it had been too much for him, or maybe something better had come along? In the factory, information was handed down on a need-to-know basis. I needed to know how to make cardboard boxes – period.

I wandered outside into a cold, dark drizzle to take a solitary break. From the shadows, I stared back through the sliding metal doors, carefully studying everyone's expressions. Bitterness and determination were etched into their faces. This was hard, painstaking, unglamorous work. They had no choice; escape wasn't an option. But me, on the other hand? Man, what the hell was I *doing* here? I wondered. It wasn't that I considered menial work beneath me. Far from it. But I clearly wasn't very good at it. This really wasn't going anywhere. Realistically, we were never going to earn enough money, get promoted, make a hit tune or master kendo. We were free to leave Japan at any time. So what on earth was keeping us here? What was keeping *me* here? Why didn't I just do myself a favour, get on the next plane home and forget this stupid kendo/paper-making/slave-driven life? I had no answers…

But I did have a sudden and genuine concern that we might be running low on cardboard boxes – I'd changed since I'd been here. I wasn't quite sure how, but something was different. I promptly threw my cigarette butt into an oily puddle, shivered and marched back into the fray.

It was turning into a long day, but everyone else appeared to be pushing themselves as hard as ever. The team was reaching unprecedented levels of efficiency. There seemed like little else for it but to join in.

Usually, once I was warmed up and had broken sweat, my body seemed to take over, but I noticed that I was feeling unusually spaced out – even for me. The whir of the machines sounded louder and my head felt blown up like a football. I tried not to give it much thought and, in the absence of anything else to do, I just went at it harder.

Box load after box load of paper was mounting up by the packing tables. We wrapped and stacked the pallets ready for shipping, grunting from the effort, tongues hanging out, eyes vacant like cattle. I shone with sweat and my body moved like a caged animal, repeating the same actions again and again till I was gratifyingly numb. I urged myself onwards, hands flying into the boxes like daggers. Four cardboard strips folded into perfect triangles... *Oss* – it was already done. Removing the paper reels from the machine – *hi-ya* – two at a time! Three lengths of tape to seal a box, my fingers blurring before me – *ichi-ni-san* – then move on. Masterful, beautiful, like a fast-flowing river, deadly, efficient, like a... a...

'What the fuck are you doing?' interrupted Bryan.

'Huh?'

'You're talking to yourself!'

'Oh... really?' I said, unclenching my teeth and trying to look sane. 'Well, ha, I'm just such good company.'

He stared at me suspiciously.

'Are you feeling okay?'

'Sure, great. I think?' I paused for a minute to catch my breath. 'Actually, now you mention, it I do feel a bit hot.' I put my hand on my forehead. I was burning up. The glands around my throat felt lumpy and sore. For some time, I'd been aware of a hole in my back tooth. I got the occasional twinge – nothing bad though, just enough to remind me it was a problem. I'd done my best to chew my noodles on the other side and hope it would go away, but I was suddenly conscious that it felt as if I was harbouring some kind of raging infection. I poked around in my back molars and winced. My jaw was swollen, and no sooner had I become aware of it than the pain started to increase. This was a schoolboy error – when travelling or living abroad you don't lose your passport, you never carry stuffed toy animals through customs for that shady guy you met in the departure lounge and you *always* make sure you get your teeth fixed before you go!

I stood for a while, rubbing my face. Sami came over to see what was wrong. I pointed at my tooth and he nodded with sympathy and poked at some pressure points on the back of my neck. For a while, it helped, but little by little, I could feel things overtaking me. It was close to the end of the day, so I soldiered on – less due to any heroism, but more from a lack of knowing what else to do. I dreaded to think what might happen to a patient who went to see the Bone Doctor with toothache.

Finally, Shimizu-san wandered up and uttered the single merciful word I spent every day longing to hear: '*Owari*' ('Finish' – even now it gives me a thrill to hear it). I was about to duck out of the traditional '*Osaki ni*' routine of begging everyone to forgive me for having the audacity to leave work (I thought I was in too much pain to care), but somehow, when it came down to it, I was surprised to discover I couldn't bring myself to pass on the formalities. It felt so wrong. I went and joined Bryan for the humbling rounds of bowing, amazed by the realisation that I actually seemed to care.

By the time we arrived back at the house, I was soaked, exhausted and starting to shake uncontrollably. Kazue gave me some painkillers and I rolled myself up in blankets. Almost immediately, I fell into a hypnogogic state of delirium. I lay on the floor, staring at Bryan and Kazue as they moved in a slow-motion haze around the room, talking in hushed, concerned tones. My sense of gravity twisted horizontally, making it appear as if everyone was stuck to the walls like spiders. I closed my eyes and gave in to the fever as a visual feast of monstrous images flashed through my dreams.

When I woke, it was still dark. The house was cold and quiet, and it took a long time for me to get my bearings. I lay listening to my breathing as sporadic gusts of wind blew softly underneath the *tatami*. A scuttling, beetle-like sound came from somewhere up in the roof, along with a gentle creaking as the wooden structure shivered. Across the room, the green LED light from the sampler blinked on and off, dimly illuminating Bryan, face-down, snoring away, with Kazue curled up next to him buried under a duvet. The fever had passed and the pain in my jaw had receded to a tolerable background ache. I felt light-headed, but calm. I lay still for a moment, enjoying a rare moment of peace and lucidity, and reflected on my situation. I'd come to Japan chasing after my dreams of achieving... What exactly? Kendo mastery? It was a joke; it would take a lifetime of study. I'd barely managed to attend classes regularly, let alone become a ninja warrior, so why did I find it so difficult to accept reality?

My clothes were soaked with perspiration, so I changed into a dry T-shirt, lit a candle and wobbled out to the bathroom to clear my head. Through the small, opaque windows, the night sky was changing to a deep navy blue. I pulled a jacket on, slid out of the back door and wandered among the dark, frozen vegetation. My steaming breath mingled with the frigid air and in the distance the dawn chorus was just beginning. It was that fleeting period just before sunrise, a subtle lightening of the sky, rarely appreciated with any twilight-esque wonder, more often than not barely noticed during a semi-conscious early scramble to work or a very late stagger into bed. I was wide awake now and, despite being jelly-legged and weak, my mind was clear. I actually felt good – inspired. I crept back inside and grabbed a *shinai*.

When I returned, the garden seemed to be bathed in an ethereal, wispy blue light. Everything was quiet and peaceful. Even the die-hard winter mosquitoes were sleeping. I tiptoed towards the ice-covered fruit trees. The *semi* were long gone and the rough, flaky bark looked black and poisonous. Brittle leaves crunched satisfyingly underfoot, the earthy sounds reverberating in the stillness.

I took a few practice swings and held the sword out in front of me, its tip quivering slightly as I relaxed my grip and projected my mind into the weapon. In the semi-darkness, my senses came alive and the sword fused into an extension of my body. I launched into some rapid improvised manoeuvres, spinning fast to defend myself from unseen assailants. I parried high and cut low; one, two, three attackers fell. My footwork was light and my breathing co-ordinated. Abruptly, I returned to an en-garde position, the sword hovering above my centre, totally calm, undisturbed, alert. Wait, that noise… A glint of steel to my left! I managed about ten minutes more practice, decimating a legion of attacking samurai, pounding the black, frozen ground with my feet, coiling and twisting around the trees, the sword whirling into a blur.

Finally, the cold forced me to down weapons and warm my hands in my pockets. For a long time, I stood perfectly still with my eyes shut, meditating, breathing rhythmically and listening to my heart pounding. My thoughts floated upwards, out of the frozen garden. I visualised looking down on the cold, black outline of the Ninja House, the train station, the red-and-white, Chernobyl-like chimney, the kendo school, Suzuki-san's home. Travelling faster and higher up towards the clouds, it felt as if all of Yoshiwara was lost in a deep, enchanted sleep. I pictured the factory, dark and still, the machines switched off, thousands of boxes unmade; the roads and motorways empty; the forests and rice fields cold and petrified – a wave of tranquillity wafting down from the mountains like a mist, permeating the towns and villages, swirling into the gardens and houses, creeping alongside the people I knew. Everyone safely tucked up in their beds, unaware of the fleeting but profound sense of peace that hangs in the air just before daybreak when the world stands still.

'Ahem, you okay?'

My eyes snapped open. Kazue was peeping out of the shutters with a concerned, drowsy look on her face.

'Oh, yeah, good, much better, thanks… Just been for my usual ten-mile run, y'know.'

'Uh. I went earlier… Did twenty miles. We thought maybe you really ill, possibly die. How is tooth?'

'It's stopped hurting, thanks. Yeah, that was *seriously* weird. I was really out there for a while.' I thought about some of the visions I'd experienced. It had been a bizarre trip – a distinctly Yoshiwaran nightmare.

'You were talking to yourself.'

'What was I saying?'

Bryan stuck his dishevelled, irate head out.

'Something about shutting the fuck up. Jesus, can you two go back to bed? It's the middle of the night, for God's sake.' With that he disappeared back inside. Kazue grinned and slid the shutters closed.

'No, really, I'm fine,' I called.

I turned and walked back towards the trees. The sun was just rising out of a spectacular winter horizon. Thin rays of light broke through the clouds, painting dancing golden patterns across the damp wooden planking of the house. I resumed my ramblings around the garden, swinging the sword melodramatically, and occasionally stopping to stare at things with that kind of born-again sense of wonder you sometimes get after recovering from an illness.

*

Only a warrior chooses pacifism; others are condemned to it.

Unknown

21

Kendo Dinner

The following week, we were invited to a special meal at the house of Takagi Sensei, the head of our *dojo*. It was an unexpected honour, and all the biggest kendo players from the local area were going to be there.

We dug out our smartest clothes and Kazue borrowed some clippers to cut my hair. As we got ready and Bryan attempted to iron a shirt with a heated saucepan, Kazue started on my crew cut. It seemed like a hilarious idea to begin by shaving a square out of the front of my head.[1] She held the mirror up and we fell about laughing – I looked ridiculous. Then, just as she was about to even it up, the clippers gave a splutter and died.

'Yeah, funny,' I said.

'Er, no. It's not me, really! They are broken.'

I picked the clippers up and tried the switch. Nothing. 'Oh – shit.'

'Hah,' said Bryan, looking up from his smoking shirt. 'What are the chances of accidentally getting a samurai haircut the night you have to go to dinner with a load of kendo masters?'

I cringed at the thought of sitting down at the banquet looking like I'd gone totally insane. I mean, sure, we were undeniably *henna gaijin* ('strange foreigners'), and people expected us to do weird shit, but there was a limit.

Thankfully, 20 tense minutes later, and after some very anxious servicing, the clippers buzzed back to life, and I evened up the rest of my hair in record time.

Takagi Sensei's house was discreetly tucked away behind thick hedges and spiky palm trees, the lights glowing softly in a damp silver haze. There was a definite air of anticipation as cars pulled up in the driveway and shadowy figures in suits emerged, bowed and shook hands. It felt a bit like a secret mobster gathering.

---

1. The style was popular among samurai – supposedly, it made wearing a helmet more comfortable; the fashion eventually spread beyond the samurai class.

We were welcomed into a hallway past some beautiful, shining lacquered screens. A line of knee-high tables cut through the middle of a long room with spotlessly clean *tatami* and smart flower arrangements in the corners. Takagi Sensei knelt patiently in front of a lethal-looking set of polished *katana*s set on a raised wooden plinth. He offered us a low bow and a warm smile. He was dressed in a smart grey suit and I was slightly taken aback that without his body armour he looked, well... normal. We returned the compliment and presented my last bottle of duty-free whisky, then took our places further down the line of tables, so as not to monopolise his time. A sliding door opened as his wife, dressed in an immaculate, deep-red kimono, stepped out, kneeled and bowed. It was the ultimate demonstration of a traditional Japanese household.

Other guests arrived. Suzuki-san and Nabi-chan appeared and took their places next to us. They were smart and well groomed, and I felt horribly under-dressed and inadequate. Immediately, they set about laying into the *sake*. There were many other faces I didn't recognise, and a few of the older guests and teachers from other *dojo*s looked surprised to see two Westerners. Set out on the tables was a veritable meat feast. I accepted a large drink from Nabi-chan, who located some flaccid pickled cucumbers and passed them over. I gagged. They were blisteringly hot and numbed my mouth, but I had no choice but to swallow, if I was to avoid insulting Takagi Sensei and making everyone else uncomfortable.

'Mmm, oh God, mmm, *oishi desu*,' I said, coughing and waving my chop-sticks about, as I tried to swallow. More were immediately passed down the line and my plate was piled high.

Once all the guests were seated and the welcoming speeches delivered, the usual *kampai*'ing and toasting began. The alcohol flowed and the room hummed in a familiar smoky haze. I made my best attempts to chat to my neighbours. Although my Japanese was still very basic, I was surprised by how much I could now communicate, albeit in a broken, clumsy way.

I spent a long time talking to a very composed, suited man kneeling next to me. He was interested to know what I thought of Japan and kendo. I told him about my life here and explained that although I found it hard, it was a unique experience and I wished I was a more worthy student.

'How do you support yourself?' he enquired.

I described working at the paper factory, how it was backbreaking and infuriating, but worth it to study kendo and be around the Yoshiwara teachers.

'But why don't you just teach English?'

'I don't have any qualifications.'

'Ah... So then, how did you get work visa?'

'I didn't. I just have a tourist visa. But it's okay, y'know. I keep it pretty quiet; no one seems to mind.'

'*So desu.*' ('I see.')

'How about you?' I asked. '*Anata wa shigoto desu ka?*' ('What work do you do?')

'I am… Chief of Police.' He refilled my glass and stared deep into my soul. His expression was unreadable. I held my breath.

'*Kampai,*' he said eventually, chinking my glass, smiling and changing the conversation. I breathed a sigh of relief.

The evening continued and, despite a slight creeping sense of paranoia, and possibly solely because we were Takagi Sensei's guests, a net-wielding immigration SWAT team failed to crash through the wall.

Conversation soon gravitated towards the shared passions of sword fighting and *bushido*. I did my best to listen respectfully, absorb what I could, keep my head together and fill people's glasses whenever possible.

A very old man came and knelt down next to me. He was thin and frail and appeared to be overflowing with emotion. '*Gaijin… braveu,*' ('Foreign people are brave') he suddenly blurted out in a husky voice. Someone whispered that he was steaming drunk and not to worry as I was the first Westerner he'd ever spoken to. A few people tried to persuade him to sit down and take it easy. I wondered if this was a prelude to an embarrassing incident. He poked at my biceps, wide-eyed, and said I was as big as Popeye. His accent was hard to follow, but I managed to get the gist of what he was saying. It turned out that he'd served in the Japanese navy during the Second World War. They'd torpedoed a foreign ship and, rather than surrender, the survivors had swum off and drowned or been eaten by sharks. Apparently, this was utterly fantastic.

'*GAIJIN BRAVEU!*' he reiterated, fiercely, in a manner that sounded alarmingly like 'Death to all Westerners!' Then he put his hand on my shoulder and I noticed an unyielding fire in his eyes. I didn't have the heart or the language skills to point out to him that the sailors had probably been justifiably terrified about being tortured or executed and were simply choosing the lesser of two evils. I very much doubted that they would have considered it heroic, but I guess one man's act of desperation is another man's glory. It was hard for foreigners to grasp this kind of mentality. At home, I rarely thought about 'honour' or 'dying a good death'; here though, it seemed to be an entirely normal preoccupation. The concept of self-sacrifice was ingrained so deeply into the Japanese psyche it had become a defining characteristic. During the war, *bushido* had been reinvented as a fanatically nationalistic fighting art. Brutality and unquestioning servitude were innate within military ranks, and the way of the warrior provided a convenient link between ancient samurai approaches to combat and death and the dreadful human cost of modern warfare – perhaps most famously encapsulated by the kamikaze[2] suicide dive-bombers. For the Allied forces, the shock of encountering an army that refused to surrender was something new. Arguably, the entire country may well have fought to the last man, woman and child, rather than accept defeat and dishonour. Only the threat of complete one-sided annihilation and the ordered surrender from the emperor brought an end to the conflict. It's often been argued that the appalling acts of nuclear war at Hiroshima and Nagasaki (thankfully, the only two to date) actually saved lives, as the casualties involved in a full-scale mainland invasion would have been unparalleled – something that always made me uncomfortable, having been raised as a CND-supporting, lefty liberal.

The twisted *bushido* of militarisation had proved to be too dangerous to be allowed to continue. After the Second World War, Japan was disarmed and martial arts were banned for almost a decade by the occupying American military command. The connection between *bushido* and the Japanese war effort was deeply conspicuous. Many *bushido* exponents had been killed; of those that survived, few had the will or resources to continue. Some teachers retired, sickened by the violence and loss of their students. For them, it spelt the end of a way of life. But for others, it was time for the martial arts to evolve and become more acceptable to the outside world. Some focused on competitions and sporting aspects, others took a more spiritual path; all of them emphasised the health benefits, and a few remained dedicated to fighting – or 'self-defence' as it became more respectably known.

I sat back and watched the laughing, chattering red faces across the tables. Suzuki-san was in hysterics about something and looked drunk out of his mind. He kept attempting to have a go with Takagi Sensei's razor-sharp *katana*s. It was quite dangerous, but everyone seemed to take it in a light-hearted manner. Takagi Sensei looked on playfully as people wrestled Suzuki-san to the ground. There was no harm done. As Takagi's protégé, Suzuki-san was awarded special privileges. It wasn't so long ago that he would have been forced to commit suicide for such impudence, but he probably would have just downed his drink, uttered a loud 'Ouchy' and died with a smile on his face. As ever, he had the uncanny ability to make everyone see the lighter side of life. It was hard to imagine the kendo teachers as a fanatical enemy; then again, it was even harder to imagine facing them in battle. Yoshiwaran kendo was different to ancient

---

2. 'Kamikaze', meaning 'Divine Wind' – a term first used to describe a typhoon that destroyed an invading fleet of Mongols in 1274.

budo, of course – no one would claim otherwise – but the warrior spirit was still present.

Everything we were taught in kendo was related back to traditional fighting spirit. Once, we had all gone to a kendo competition in a local stadium; it was a fairly rare occurrence and generally regarded by the Yoshiwara teachers as a bit of a detour from 'real' kendo. A few people from our class were fighting, including Bryan (much to his surprise). I took my seat with the teachers and gazed up at the large, exclusively Japanese crowd, glad that I didn't have to take part.

Bryan got kitted up. He was quieter than usual and looked distinctly pale.

'Do it, Bry,' I shouted, waving him on. 'Kick their fucking heads in.' (I figured no one could understand what I was saying.)

'*Bryan-san, fighto. Oss. Gambatte,*' came the shouts of support from Suzuki-san and the other teachers.

'I think I'm going to throw up,' he shouted back.

'Good, good, just do it in your helmet,' I called, nodding to Suzuki-san and the others confidently, as if Bryan had just announced, 'I've never felt so ready for something in my entire life!'

Judges stood in each corner of the fighting arena holding a red and white flag. Bryan was only identifiable by the red flag tied to his back. The combatants bowed and the match began. For the first few minutes, there was quite a bit of posturing and screaming. It looked like a draw – well, to me at least. I got the definite sense the crowd was watching Bryan expectantly to see what a Western kendo practitioner would be like. Both he and his opponent were quick. They prodded the tips of their swords together, searching for weakness. Bryan screamed and attacked forcefully. His opponent circled and feinted a few times. Then Bryan let off a few thundering blows. Crack. Smack. Suddenly, one of the judges stepped in and stopped Bryan. He conferred with a few of the other officials and, abruptly, the match was over. Bryan had been disqualified.

'*Nani desu ka?*' ('What's happening?') I asked Suzuki-san.

Suzuki-san and the others strained to find out what the problem was. They looked deeply concerned. Bryan came over to speak with us. He had hit his opponent so hard his sword had broken. He held his *shinai* up with a worried look on his face. The kendo teachers gave an audible sigh of relief; honour had been maintained, possibly even increased. They slapped him on the back and congratulated him. Short of him actually killing his opponent, it was a better result than anyone could possibly have hoped for. Bryan had done the Yoshiwara kendo school proud.

Afterwards, back at the *dojo*, Takagi Sensei had asked me what I thought about the competition.

'Many of the *kendoka* looked good,' I said in my broken Japanese. 'Very fast, but it's not like the kendo you teach here in Yoshiwara... It was different.'

'*Ah, sore wa sportsu kendo deshita.*' ('It was sports kendo.') He sighed and looked sad. Sports kendo – almost a dirty word; competition kendo might have looked good, people made a great deal of noise (well, more than usual) and scored lots of points, but most of the time it had no power or real quality of movement, the strikes being weak and lacking commitment. Many of the old-school teachers regarded it with disdain and adjusted their training accordingly. In contrast, I thought back to my first night at the *dojo*: the heat, the intensity, the masked screams and the rolling thunder – the total immersion in discipline. I could see straight away, even with untrained eyes, that real kendo wasn't about technique, and it certainly wasn't a competition – it was a matter of life and death.

After the war, Japanese martial arts evolved, re-emerged as a global phenomenon and, to a certain extent, became detached from the darker aspects of the samurai, but you could still find glimpses of it here and there. Real *budo* still exists in Japan, although it's generally a wiser beast than in the pre-war era. I wondered, not for the first time, what really lay in the hearts of the Japanese people. The posturing of the old man sitting next to me was proud and strong and contradicted his grey, shrunken frame. I smiled at him and he threw me a huge, toothless grin, but the cold light in his eyes didn't change. It came from a very different time, from a world that was almost gone.

The kendo dinner reminded me that my visa was running out. Bryan and I gratefully squeezed a day off and headed to Nagoya to renew it. I queued up in a dimly lit public building, wondering what I'd do if they ordered me to leave the country. Bryan was sorted with a heritage visa – he had another four years in Japan, which, as long as he continued studying kendo, meant he was free to come and go. I presented my passport to a bureaucrat and peeked over the desk as he sifted through the paperwork and began looking up some of the more unfamiliar characters in a dictionary.

'Uh, sorry there is problem,' he said abruptly. 'You have no return ticket to England.'

'No... that's right... Sorry,' I mumbled.

'Please, one moment,' he said, and then went to make a phone call. I waited patiently, imagining who he might be talking to. Was I about to be deported? Maybe he was speaking to my friend the police chief?

'Hi Chief, yeah. I've got the foreigner here. No, the other one. What do you want me to do with him? Is he training hard enough? Should we let him stay?'

'Hmm, how does he look? Have we broken him yet? Do you think he fully understands how young and naive he is?'

He resurfaced five minutes later looking worried and apologetic. 'I can give you six-month visa,' he began. 'But please... When finished, you must promise to leave. But first you must write here. Please say, "I promise to leave."'

He slid a blank sheet of paper towards me and, for a brief moment, I thought he might be taking the piss. He wasn't.

'No problem,' I said, wondering whether, if I defaulted on my contract, I would be brought back in and made to write lines.

For a long time, Bryan and Suzuki-san had been trying to persuade me to visit an *onsen* and I'd stubbornly refused. *Onsen*s were traditional (frequently unisex) baths, often built around natural hot springs, with elaborate plunge pools, hot tubs and saunas. The thought of getting completely butt naked with hundreds of Japanese was intimidating, to say the least. You rarely saw fat people in Japan (presumably due to the rice-and-fish diet) and, despite months of sweating in the factory, I was still on the chubby side and had a theory that once you reached a certain level of unfitness, you never got it back, however much you exercised.

One evening, after a few cans of Super Chu-hai (a kind of alcoholic lemonade), they announced that tonight was the night and began piling on the pressure.

'Look, it's all right,' said Bryan. 'The Japanese have all got small dicks too.'

'*Mini chimpo*,' agreed Suzuki-san.

'But... I don't have a small—'

'Okay, here's mine,' said Bryan, interrupting and suddenly pulling down his pants. 'See, we've all got one.'

Inside the foyer of the *onsen*, Suzuki-san and Bryan went to buy tickets, while I sat on a long, upholstered sofa and looked about. Everything was covered in pink tiles, like a gaudy leisure centre, and large potted ferns were dotted about between drinks-vending machines. It was around nine o'clock at night, but the place was still disconcertingly rammed. Next to me, families with towels wrapped around their heads milled about watching a big-screen TV and waiting for people to get changed. There was a programme on featuring some pop-ular Japanese comedians dressed as The Beatles. They were made up to have exaggerated Western features, with big round eyes and large bulbous noses; basically, the opposite of Asian stereotypes. It clearly wasn't malicious, and was actually the first really amusing thing I'd seen on Japanese TV.

As I looked on, I noticed the room had gone very still and quiet. People were staring at me. Hold up, I thought. I haven't even got my kit off yet! Then I realised – they were worried I'd find it racist. I laughed loudly and they breathed a collective sigh of relief. As much as the Japanese had never quite got their heads around foreigners, they were still terrified of causing offence.

We headed into the changing rooms and I began to peel my clothes off, deliberately taking my time, ensuring everything was neatly folded up and squared away. I stood by the lockers in my pants, feeling ridiculous.

Bryan and Suzuki-san were already naked, standing around striking lewd bodybuilding poses and pointing into the distance like catalogue models. Suzuki-san placed a *tenugui* (a tiny cotton headscarf used in kendo) around my shoulders, gave me an encouraging slap on the arse, then wandered off towards the baths.

'Yeah, thanks… That's much better,' I called after him. Then, with his laughing cries of '*mini chimpo*' echoing faintly back, I sucked in a couple of deep breaths and whipped my pants off.

'There, satisfied?'

'Yep,' said Bryan, looking up at the ceiling. We stood awkwardly in front of each other for a few seconds. I thought about whistling a tune.

'Good… Right then, come on,' I said and lumbered off after Suzuki-san, trying to hold my stomach in.

I passed through a foot wash and stepped into a dense cloud of water vapour. Dozens of silhouetted naked men and women of all ages were scrub-bing themselves under showers and relaxing in sunken pools, ranging in tem-perature from the freezing cold to the almost fatally boiling. I leapt into the nearest one and gave the other occupants as dignified a nod as I could muster. Everyone immediately stared down at me to see how I compared, then resumed their conversations. I guessed I must have measured up okay.

In the steaming haze, my muscles began to let go, as months of ingrained dirt loosened its grip. I quickly backtracked to a shower and washed myself for fear of turning one of the pools black with dissolving grime. It didn't take long for my previous bashfulness to be transformed into an almost exhibitionist kind of elated nudism. I tried out some of the finest power showers and Jacuzzis I'd ever experienced and strode about with my hands on my hips. I noticed a sauna through a side door and wandered inside. As my eyes became accustomed to the murky gloom, I became aware of a large group of people sat on raised benches behind me. I turned to see about 20 silent, naked, angry men staring at me. They were all tattooed from neck to waist – Yakuza style. Perhaps they were from the Kyoto chapter, come to finish the job. I nodded at them, cleared my throat, mentioned that it was a bit '*atsui*' and left the way I'd come.

I eventually spied Suzuki-san and Bryan through some glass doors, outside, soaking in a spot-lit hot tub. They were drinking beer and chatting beneath a freezing night sky. I padded over the frozen ground and slipped in next to them.

'*Onsen, suki desu ka?*' ('Do you like hot baths?') asked Suzuki-san with a grin.

I beamed back. It was the first time I'd felt truly clean and so supremely comfortable since I'd been in Japan. We soaked for a long time, turning wrinkly, till an irate attendant came and informed us that we had to leave. Someone had thrown up in one of the baths and the staff had agreed that since we were foreigners it must have been us. It was a shame. I did briefly think about suggesting it might have been one of the Yakuzas, but decided against it. Still, it didn't dampen our moods. We got dressed and headed home, laughing, feeling relaxed and glowing in the crisp, night air. I was liberated – high as a kite and wishing I'd lost my *onsen* virginity earlier.

*

The true science of martial arts means practising them in such a way that they will be useful at any time, and to teach them in such a way that they will be useful in all things.

Miyamoto Musashi, *The Book of Five Rings*

22

One Strike – One Kill

On a bright spring Sunday lunchtime, we were perched on thin, rickety metal stools in the parrot bar, sipping beer and having an intense conversation about martial arts with the kendo teachers. This had become such a frequent occurrence and was so predictable it was reminiscent of Chinese opera, with the actors following a time-honoured script and being judged on how well they performed their familiar roles. Everyone found comfort in routine. Nabi-chan took the straight-man role to offset Suzuki-san's clowning, Bryan got irate about Japanese rules and double standards and Aono Sensei sighed and shook his head, amazed by our sheer wrongness about everything. Takahashi Sensei interjected the occasional sane comment and I followed the dialogue with a constipated look of concentration, often failing to understand anything.

At some point in the banter, Nabi-chan turned to me and declared that I was 'not like Bryan-san' – like this would come as some kind of devastating revelation. He sounded tentative – as if he'd spent the entire time he'd known me preparing to break the bad news.

'*Hmm… hai, so desu,*' I cautiously agreed. I could sense a trap. It was usually Aono Sensei who dished out the ego-shattering remarks.

In many ways, Bryan and I were chalk and cheese. He was very… kendo; I was not. It had never bothered either of us before though. *Vive la différence!*

Then, 'Toby-san is like a Japanese old person,' Suzuki-san suggested.

Everyone leant in and carefully studied my reaction.

'Well, yeah, *so desu*. I guess you're right,' I said, sighing and shrinking a little. This wasn't fair; they were ganging up on me. I wondered if now would be a good time to prove myself by doing something really vigorous, but what? A one-handed press-up? Slam my balls in the fridge? Start a small business? What?

The group discussed it as though I wasn't actually in the room and everyone agreed. I was indeed like an old Japanese person. That was it – the jury had spoken! Now I was starting to feel really incensed. There was nothing like having your character assassinated to make you want to prove yourself.

Right, I thought, typically overreacting, First I'm young and naive, now

I'm past it. I've had it with this bullshit. I may not be quite as crazy as *some* people, but I'm certainly not an old man yet. I'll show them rock 'n' roll. They've no idea. I was born in a bassbin. As soon as I'm done here, I'm going bungee jumping and starting a fight. Maybe at the same time!

Bryan, who was pouring drinks, sauntered up laughing and patted me on the back.

'Look, it's okay, man. They don't literally mean you're old. They're just saying you're wise and thoughtful – like an old person. They're actually paying you a really massive compliment. It's me they're having a dig at.'

'Oh yeah, sure. I knew that – it's fine,' I said in a rather high-pitched, defensive tone.

It's probably a good thing, I thought to myself. Bungee jumping was bound to be expensive and overrated. Now, calligraphy and chess on the other hand…

'Toby-san, when you arrived we thought you would be just like Bryan,' explained Nabi-chan, 'but you weren't.'

'At first, we were disappointed,' added Aono Sensei, 'but now… we think maybe we like you better.'

I tried not to spit beer across the room, laughing as Bryan's expression abruptly changed. Such half-joking, half-testing exchanges were an everyday occurrence in Yoshiwara. The kendo teachers loved to get a rise out of us. When I'd first arrived, Bryan had been the 'Golden Child', and everyone just assumed another Westerner would be identical. It had taken several months for them to come to terms with the idea that I couldn't speak Japanese, let alone accept the fact that I might demonstrate a different kind of temperament or personality. Still, at least my lowly status had remained uncomplicated, 'young and naive' – a label that was maddeningly frustrating but occasionally a blessing in disguise. Bryan, on the other hand, was close to his second *dan* grade – certainly not a master yet, but no longer a total beginner. It was open season on giving him a hard time; now he was approaching the higher and far more punishing echelons of 'Ought to know better'.

The rest of the afternoon was spent at the Ninja House with the teachers, snoozing, eating crisps and chatting. I finally remembered to ask Aono Sensei about the Daruma doll on the shrine shelf.

'Ah, yes… *Daruma*,' he said, shutting his eyes and nodding sagely like Obi-Wan Kenobi. 'Daruma, hmm, Zen master, from China. Shorinji teacher.'

'Shorinji? You mean the Shaolin Temple, right? The Bodhidharma?'

'Bodhidharma, yes. You have heard of him?'

'Of course – I do kung fu. I *always* wanted to go to China,' I said, wistfully staring up at the shelf.

Aono Sensei began laughing so hard, I wondered if something had been lost in translation. The Bodhidharma was the original Zen patriarch, a sixth-century Indian priest who supposedly crossed the Himalayas, bringing Zen to China,[1] a secret teaching passed down directly from the Buddha. Legend has it that he founded the famous Shaolin Monastery and taught his students special techniques that were later developed into kung fu.[2] I once actually dreamt of the Bodhidharma crossing the snowy mountains in the dead of night; it left me with a strange and vivid image of an athletic Indian man in his fifties, climbing up a blue, rocky ravine, staring out from underneath a heavy cloak with mysterious, penetrating eyes. As a 16-year-old into martial arts, this was practically the equivalent of having Bruce Lee himself materialise in my bedroom and anoint me as his prodigy.

'Ahh, ha,' said Aono Sensei, wiping tears of mirth from his eyes and shaking his head. 'I have been to China, Tibet, India; I am priest, I speak many languages. I think you would find Shorinji *very* hard, hahahahaha.'

'I see,' I said, swallowing my rage and making a silent vow to go there just to prove him wrong.

'Daruma was very clever, eyes big from meditating, round like a ball. If you push him, he will always get back up. He is like *bushi*.'

'Daruma,' laughed Suzuki-san, curling himself into a ball and vigorously attempting to roll around the room wide-eyed. Bryan and I looked at each other with sudden comprehension – Suzuki-san's previous insane mimed explanations finally made perfect sense.

The history and evolution of martial arts were discussed late into the evening. It always amazed me how the teachers weren't exactly unfamiliar with the historical aspects of it all, but rather, just unconcerned. There was something pure and admirable about the way they stubbornly refused to comment on things they didn't know about. They were kendo teachers – that was their specialist subject. However, the subject of swords was a topic that sparked everyone's interest and generated an array of wild opinions and speculation. European fencing foils, Chinese broadswords, *shinai*, *tanto* (a Japanese knife),

---

1. This was 'a special transmission, outside the scriptures', not dependent on written words, directly pointing to the human heart/mind. Seeing into one's nature and becoming Buddha – traditionally attributed to Bodhidharma, but actually found in Tang Dynasty (618–907) writings, pre-dating his arrival.

2. Most academics agree that this is a largely fabricated story. Martial arts certainly predate the Shaolin Temple, as does Buddhism's appearance and development in China.

tsurugi (double-edged sword), *bokuto* and, of course, *katana*s – how they were made, used, stored and, particularly, how a live blade should be drawn from its scabbard – an art nowadays embodied by *iaido*.[3] The sword is the soul of Japanese martial arts; everyone is obsessed by it. Suzuki-san once bought a cheap *katana* online, and then nearly sliced his ear off when the handle broke in half. It is a sad fact that these days, most people use cheaper, substandard equipment. Real Japanese blades are so valuable that they go straight from the swordsmith to the bank vault.

When Takahashi Sensei mentioned that he had a friend who practised *iaido*, everyone expressed an interest in checking it out, and so it was that some weeks later the friend invited us for a private demonstration. Strings had been pulled and it was a rare honour.

On the appointed day, Suzuki-san suddenly appeared at the doors of the factory and shouted to Bryan that we should come with him. It felt like having your dad come to school and rescue you from an unfair detention.

The boss approached him, bowing and laughing nervously; he was aware of Suzuki-san's reputation as a kendo teacher and was obviously intimidated. Suzuki-san explained that we had to go – sorry, but it was a kendo matter. The boss accepted it without question.

As we drove off laughing, I surreptitiously flicked MC Squared the Vs, and wondered if Suzuki-san would pick us up like this every night.

The *iaido dojo* was tucked away in a large office complex, next to a busy main road. It had a dark, polished wooden floor and long, narrow windows covered by rattan blinds. We were introduced to several teachers dressed in black *keikogi* who were friendly and welcoming. Kneeling in a co-ordinated row of *seiza*, we were then treated to a magnificent demonstration of sword *kata*s.

The blades hissed and whipped satisfyingly as they sliced through the air. Just being in the same room with such dangerous weapons was a thrill; it occurred to me that Freud might have had something to say about that. Takahashi's friend executed a spectacular display of timing and control, as he performed a partner form, bringing his *katana* terrifyingly close to his opponent's head. There was no room for error; it was a meditation, pure and simple – total mindfulness! You could have heard a pin drop. The kendo teachers let out contented grunts and nodded admiringly, clearly impressed.

3. *Iaido* – the way of mental presence and reaction, but perhaps more widely understood in the West as the art of drawing the sword.

This was more than simple curiosity though; martial artists in Japan didn't tend to casually check out other styles. It was a meeting of disciplines where everyone's reputations lay on the line. To a certain extent, *iaido* appeared to be the antithesis of kendo. The moves were calm, exacting, clinical – sparring was clearly out of the question. One strike, one kill, a quick shake to flick the blood off the blade, then back for a nice comfortable *seiza* and perhaps a quick tea ceremony. All jolly civilised, really. Conversely, kendo dealt with the bruising blood, guts and pain of swordplay, the spirit of application – forget about how it looks and just do it. Never give up. Sweat till you collapse. *Fighto*.

It was the other side of the coin, but I guessed their aims were ultimately the same. Martial arts were a little like religion; the further down the line you went, the more they had in common and the closer you came to uncovering universal truths. It felt blasphemous to voice it to my friends and teachers, but I couldn't help thinking that I might have been a little more naturally suited to *iaido*.

Afterwards, we were given the opportunity to practise with *iaito* (blunt *katanas*). It was immensely satisfying to handle a real sword which, despite the lack of a live cutting edge, was still sharp. There was something deadly serious about it that suddenly made the severe discipline and focus of the samurai seem like a very practical necessity. As I practised the movements of slowly drawing the blade from the scabbard, intrusive thoughts arose – the sword slipping from my hands, slicing my fingers off, sailing across the room and coming to rest in the teacher's neck, a bright red fountain of blood spraying across the *dojo*.

Maybe I needed some time off…

Our lesson involved learning the correct way to bow to the sword, how to pick it up and wear it in our belts. I followed everyone else's lead as we went through a series of ritual moves, culminating in rising to a standing posture with the sword unsheathed, ready for action. As with everything in Japan, it was surprisingly difficult, while the *iaido* teachers made it look easy and natural. We practised a form that involved smashing an imaginary opponent in the face with the butt of our swords, then turning and cutting someone down behind us. It was ingenious; we drilled it repeatedly, the kendo teachers spilling over with enthusiasm, the *iaido* teachers happily sharing their art, as self-effacing as if they had turned up in the Yoshiwara *dojo*. Everyone conducted themselves with as much humility as any *dojo* novice I'd ever seen, concentrating hard and showing complete respect to one another. A perfect example of 'beginner's mind'[4] –

4. 'Beginner's mind' (*shoshu*) – the ability to conduct yourself with the lack of preconceptions and the

no ego, no attitude, nothing to prove. It was one of those evenings that made me appreciate why I had travelled halfway round the world.

One night, Suzuki-san arrived at the house looking serious and ashen-faced. He announced that Takahashi's wife had died. It had been unexpected and sudden – a brain tumour. I had never met her, but we drank a toast and expressed our shock and disbelief, then sat in silence for a long time. I'd never lost anyone close to me and couldn't imagine what Takahashi must be going through. It was rare to see Suzuki-san sad, and it made him seem older.

We walked to the *dojo* that evening full of melancholy. A wet March breeze gusted down from the mountains, quivering the grass and rattling shuttered windows and road signs.

The kendo hall was unnaturally quiet. A communal sense of hushed respect hung heavy in the air. As we went and bowed to Takagi Sensei, to my surprise I noticed that there, amazingly, at the edge of the class, was Takahashi Sensei with a wooden sword, practising a slow, solitary form. He had his back to us, and I had to look carefully for a while to confirm it was really him. There was an intensity to his movements that was tangible. When I really thought about it for a while, it began to make sense. Kendo was his rock, a coping mechanism, a lifelong companion that wouldn't desert him. This was simply his way of handling his grief. Other teachers approached him throughout the evening to exchange quiet words of condolence and sympathy, a gentle hand on the shoulder, solidarity, friendship and respect. Eventually, it was my turn. I walked up to him hesitantly, stopped and bowed, a proper bow, sincere – perhaps the only real bow I had ever really performed with all my heart.

'*Takahashi Sensei, watashi wa honto ni gomenasai.*' ('I'm really sorry.')

I don't remember his reply, but for me, the atmosphere that evening was charged and profound. I was drilled hard by Suzuki-san, repeatedly attacking horizontally held *shinai*, moving forward, projecting myself through the obstacles, not giving up and cultivating fighting spirit.

'Harder,' said Suzuki-san sternly. I struck harder.

'*Gambatte*,' he said.

I complied. I held nothing back. I screamed like a wild man and slammed the *shinai* forward with all my might.

'*Goodu*,' he said, raising an eyebrow and lowering his sword.

We stopped and just for a second, turned to watch Takahashi, alone in

openness of a novice; a Buddhist term popularised in the West by the Zen teacher Shunryū Suzuki (1904–71), author of the highly influential *Zen Mind, Beginner's Mind*.

the corner of the *dojo*, still going through his slow, immaculate sword forms. Suzuki-san gazed down at the floor for a moment and made a small noise that seemed to express all the troubles of the world. Then he looked up, raised the *shinai* again and urged me to continue.

*

I am not here to win, I am here to survive.

Hatsumi Sensei

23

All My Life's a Circle

As the last of the cold, wet weather gave way to warmer, blustery sunshine, something inside me was becoming restless. Days and months now seemed to pass by almost unnoticed. Gone was the wonder and novelty I'd had when I'd first arrived. Life had become routine. My mystical martial quest to the East now seemed like a deluded fantasy that had ceased to sustain me. Our depression and frustrations, which had peaked the previous autumn, were returning, but the feeling now was more akin to numbness, a nagging sense of indifference.

I knew that mastering kendo was going to be a missed opportunity, or at the very least, for the sake of my sanity, it was something that would have to wait. I wasn't even sure what I was trying to achieve here anyway, as the true mastery of kendo involved a lifetime of study, and I'd barely dipped my toe in the water.

At work, nothing had really improved throughout all this time, other than our ability to endure pain at the hands of the petty mini-bosses. The veiled insults and rude treatment of the MC and the Pug, which would once have had us pissing our pants with outrage and dancing up and down in fury, now, more often than not, were met with a tired shrug of indifference or a half-muttered swear word. I felt as though the paper factory had won.

I knew my time in Japan was running out. And the tipping point was an insignificant event that made me realise it was time to act.

An old Brazilian guy who'd worked at the factory a few years earlier had returned from setting up his own business at home – it failed miserably. He'd lost years of savings and was right back where he started again, penniless in the Factory of Dreams, making cardboard boxes and sending his pay cheques home to support his family in the hope of buying them a better life – a cycle of migrant poverty played out daily across the world. He talked fatalistically about the whole thing, as if it was no big deal, but everyone saw the dejected look on his face as he rejoined the packing line – head down, crushed, subservient, resigned to his fate. It was really tragic. However, it was only me who spied the boss, the MC and the Pug quietly leaning against a row of machines at the back of the factory, like biker thugs from a '50s B-movie, just standing there watching him, sporting wide, cruel smiles. Another returning drone come to make the boss rich. Their eyes looked full of contempt. It genuinely scared me.

I'd had enough; it was time to go home and face reality.

On a quiet May evening, I sat with the rest of the workers astride a low breeze-block wall outside the factory, swinging our legs like children, smoking and chatting as the shadows lengthened. It was a warm, balmy twilight and one of the machines had jammed, giving us an unexpected and merciful break. In the distance, a spectacular bank of dark-purple storm clouds slowly crept down from the peak of Fuji Yama. It looked totally unreal, like an airbrushed scene from a fantasy film.

Toni pointed it out for me. 'Fuji Yama,' he said, as if I might not have heard of it yet.

I smiled at him politely and tried to imagine what it might be like inside his head – television static came to mind.

'Fuji Yama is so big,' explained Shimizu-san. 'It makes its own weather system.'

I stared up at the volcano, trying to get my head around the scale of what I was looking at. Thin flashes of lightning preceded distant, rolling thunder. It was a magnificent sight. I would never forget working here at, er… um… I wiped my face on my T-shirt and turned to Bryan.

'Hey, what's this place called again?'

'Huh?'

'What's the actual name of the Factory of Dreams?'

'Oh, right. You mean IMS? I came up with the name. It stands for "International Material Supplies".'

'Ah… inspired.'

'Quite.'

'I'm thinking about going home.'

He nodded in a resigned kind of way and looked at me. 'Yeah, yeah. Me too.'

'Really?' I said, trying to imagine life with Bryan back in the UK.

'Well, home, as in I might go to Tokyo, stay with Kazue for a while.'

'What would you do?'

'I don't know, but anything's better than staying here.'

Later, as we rode home in a light drizzle, Fuji Yama rumbled and flashed on the horizon, and I wondered, not for the first time, if it might erupt.

It turned out that Kazue was also ready to make a move to something more permanent. She was an adventurous soul, but a Tokyo girl at heart. Yoshiwara had become too remote; we'd taken to calling it 'Yoshi-Sahara'. I figured that by the end of the month, I'd have just enough money for a return flight to London and maybe a few bottles of duty-free. I'd be leaving as penniless as when I'd first arrived.

We sat talking for a long time and all agreed that the Ninja House had had its day. It was hard to get too nostalgic about it though, and the cockroaches and mosquitoes would just have to fend for themselves. We'd all come to feel as though we were serving time in prison. The outside world had faded alarmingly into a distant memory. Would the UK have changed beyond recognition? What would I do? Where would I go? Just what were the employment prospects for a ninja box packer?

The next day at work, we were in for a nasty surprise. A new batch of paper had come in which required being spun on to much smaller, faster rolls. Now a single reel took about five minutes as opposed to the normal 15, which meant we all worked at the double (except, of course, the MC and the Pug). Everything had stepped up a gear and, by mid-morning, we were sweating buckets, desperately trying to keep up – no time for breaks. It was like being a novice packer all over again. I wondered: did the factory know I was trying to leave? The shimmering, Jedi-like apparition of the old lady appeared before me once more – 'Run, Toby-san, run!'

MC Squared was made jubilant by everyone scurrying around like ants, and began sounding a pressurised air hose like a siren every time the reels came to an end. The Puganought, on the other row of machines, quickly followed suit and, by the end of the day, Bryan and I had planned out their detailed and bloody murders in infinitesimal detail. I watched The MC's fat, buck-toothed, pock-marked face and wondered what I'd do without him. He really was a fucking twat, but – deep down – everyone needs a petty tyrant to rebel against to give their lives some meaning. And he was my fucking twat.

Actually, I almost felt sorry for him when I thought about it like that.

As I stood still at my packing station glaring, Bryan wandered past looking exhausted and aggrieved. 'You're a loser cause you're dead inside,' he cried above the drone of the spinning machines, quoting from *The Hustler*.

I nodded and stared back at him, fists clenched. 'I got ma mind straight Boss – please don't put me in the hole no more,' I shouted, quoting from *Cool Hand Luke*. (We'd recently brought a Paul Newman DVD box set)

We then performed an utterly unself-conscious rendition of the Dance of the Migrant Worker, locked arms and spun around a few times before striding off in different directions to our respective work stations, stony faced.

The run of smaller reels lasted for three cruel days. By the end of it, we were ruined. Evenings were spent sitting around the table at the Ninja House, heads lolling, listening to music, drinking and dreaming of better days ahead. Bryan became particularly fond of an old Harry Chapin tune: 'All My Life's a Circle'. It seemed very apt, and he'd play it over and over, singing along, dog-tired, with a broken look in his eyes. I kept my mind focused on escape and wondered how I would ever be able to explain the last year to people back home.

On payday, our money was presented in a plain white envelope amid much bowing and ritual. This time, I sat outside weighing it up. Something was wrong. It felt way under. I counted it several times and wondered if I was having the usual basic arithmetic problems. I showed it to Bryan and he was equally confused. I'd told the boss I was leaving. When we'd spoken about it, he hadn't really got his head around what I was trying to say:

'So you're going for a holiday.'

'No, I'm leaving.'

'You're going, then coming back?'

'Er, no. No, not really.'

The boss had smiled, as if I was joking. Why would anyone want to leave his paper factory? I was being young and naive again; I'd be back. They always came back.

Bryan went and spoke to him about my wages. When he returned, he was reticent and elusive.

'Hmm,' he said, looking awkward, 'I'm not sure if I understand this. I think he's saying you have to pay some kind of tax, but I reckon he might be screwing you over. I don't know yet – I need to speak to Kazue.'

Kazue rang the boss and had a long and heated conversation. She was sure he was screwing me over.

'He is saying it is because you haven't paid tax, but they don't pay tax for you because you are illegal. This is not Japanese way. He is being serious wankerist.'

Bryan was angry on my behalf, but I was surprised by my own reaction; instead of embarking on a deadly mission of assassination and revenge, I smiled weakly, lay back on the *tatami* and thought of home. We counted out the pennies and Kazue offered to lend me the shortfall to get my plane ticket.

The next day, I went to work at the factory for the last time. I had to, for my own peace of mind; I needed some kind of closure. The hours passed quickly and, by nightfall, I knew what I had to do. I walked around the factory saying good night to everyone. I hadn't told them I was going and, unsurprisingly, the boss was nowhere to be seen. It was the usual routine, but I performed it flawlessly and made sure I looked everyone in the eye. I left MC Squared till last. I took a deep breath, approached him calmly and bowed low.

'*Osaki ni shitsurei shimasu*,' ('Forgive my rudeness for leaving early') I said, with a clear and steady voice.

He looked up briefly from reading some kind of comic, cigarette dangling his mouth, regarding me with utter indifference.

'*Uh… Otsukaresama*,' ('We worked hard') he mumbled and went back to his reading.

Indeed we did, I thought to myself, as I walked slowly away, out through the sliding double doors for the last time. Indeed we did.

I turned to see the shimmering blue ghost of the old lady just visible in the half-light, her hand lightly resting on the parked forklift truck. She looked young and beautiful and was smiling at me.

Leaving Yoshiwara was a rushed blur. I barely remember saying goodbye to the kendo teachers. Everyone just assumed I'd return in a few weeks. Takagi Sensei told me to 'Please come back and train'. Suzuki-san reacted as though I had just said I was popping to the shop. He gave me a hug and said he'd see me soon. It was impossible not to admire his ability to make any difficult situation seem easy.

I rode the slow train down to Tokyo with Bryan. Halfway through the journey, I had a sudden change of heart about not punching everyone at the factory in the face, and I made Bryan promise he'd avenge me when he left.

Kazue very kindly drove us back to Narita Airport. I was weighed down with the boxed-up decks, but somehow managed to check them in without having to pay extra. As we stood by the entrance to the departure lounge waiting for my flight to board, Bryan produced a bottle of *shochu* and we spent half an hour doing shots, laughing and dancing the Migrant Worker for the last time. When I finally headed towards the gate, they walked alongside me behind an adjacent soundproof window. Kazue waved and Bryan pulled his T-shirt up and pressed his nipple against the glass, *Midnight Express* style. I could just make him out, shouting to send some Marmite and Earl Grey tea.

Before leaving Yoshiwara, Bryan had presented me with his trusty wooden sword. It was polished and worn from years of training. I'd always imagined that I would return with a full suit of samurai armour or at the very least a shining *katana*, but despite a lingering sense that I'd earnt the wooden spoon of martial awards, it had been a gift from the heart and, ultimately, that meant a whole lot more. I held the wrapped *bokuto* high in the air and shouted 'Freedom' at the top of my voice. A few departing tourists stopped and threw me some outraged looks. Bryan and Kazue smiled and I coughed, peered around and mouthed it at them again. They laughed.

I turned towards my gate and strode off, racked by a bizarre mixture of nostalgia and regret, relief and excitement. It was hard to leave my friends behind, and life without the kendo teachers was unquestionably going to be drabber, but I definitely wasn't going to miss the Factory of Dreams any time soon. Of course, I was disappointed that I wasn't returning home a martial-arts master, but, by God, I thought, if any fool ever challenges me to a cardboard-box-making competition, look out.

*

If you understand everything, you must be misinformed.

Japanese proverb

24

Fuji San

Time passed. I'd been back in England for about a year and often found myself nostalgically eating Super Noodles, reminiscing about Japan and boring anyone who was willing to listen to my stories of sword fighting and cardboard box making. Most people glazed over pretty quickly.

'So, how was Japan?'

'Yeah, good.'

'Bet you did loads of martial arts… Are you like, a *total* master now?'

It was at this point that the conversations tended to tail off in one of two directions (although nobody really listened either way). Either:

'Yes… pretty much.'

'Great, good to see you.'

'You too… Bye.'

Or:

'No, of course not. Actually, I just worked in a factory.'

'Oh wow, really, a factory? God, you're so modest. I bet you totally are a master now. Anyway, good to see you. Bye.'

It had taken time to readjust to a routine bereft of situations requiring blood, sweat and perseverance. I'd found myself heading in a new direction, having committed to setting up a record shop in Paris with a friend, and was biding my time till we opened. I'd spent six months doing odd jobs, failing to learn French (again), scratching and mixing a lot and taking a free business start-up course which had pretty much convinced me of two things: one – location was everything; and two – a record shop was an almost inconceivably bad business idea. I chatted to Bryan a lot over the phone; he suggested calling the shop 'Homage du Fromage'. I explained that I'd set my heart on a DJing career under the name 'Joe le Scratchy', but, unfortunately, only English people seemed to find this funny.

Bryan left the factory soon after me and moved to Tokyo to stay with Kazue and her parents. He'd blagged himself into a job teaching English; it had always been a matter of time. I was mildly disappointed to learn that he hadn't left an avenging bloodbath behind in the Factory of Dreams, but I totally understood that there came a point where you just wanted to slip away quietly and go and sit in an empty field and try to get the haunting sounds of 'Oi' and 'Sharey Sharey Lady' out of your mind. He'd passed his second *dan* kendo grading and had visited a few *dojo*s in the city, but despite their technical excellence, he found it just wasn't the same without the Yoshiwara kendo teachers. His new instructors lacked the classical *budo* mentality; some of them didn't even drink! Bryan wasn't going to waste his time with sports kendo and his practice had waned. Life had improved though, and one night he gave me a call.

So... me and Kazue have decided to get married.'

'No way. Congratulations.'

'And you're the best man.'

'Er, for real?'

'No arguments, it's already planned. This is Japan – remember!'

I was genuinely honoured and excited at the prospect of going back. The night before I was due to fly out, I was training at my local aikido *dojo*. It had been hard returning to martial-arts classes where people chatted a lot and had endless discussions about what *ki* was and how best it should be used – in a fight/for spiritual cultivation/making the tea, etc. I'd mentioned in passing to the instructor that I would be away for a while as I was returning to Japan, and at the end of the lesson, as we were lined up along the mats, he announced it to everyone and they gave me a hearty round of applause. I knelt there blushing, wondering if I should explain that I was actually just going to get drunk at a wedding. Instead, I bowed and tried to look resolute and hard. We were talking about Japan, after all, and even a wedding would probably require fighting spirit.

Kazue met me at the local subway station by leaping on to my back and clinging there like a limpet. As I staggered through the crowded platform, gasping in the thick summer heat, she filled me in on the situation. Bryan was staying at a secret location and I needed to be suited and booted with a hysterical yet moving speech ready by tomorrow night. It was going to be a traditional ceremony in a big hotel, all the kendo teachers were coming down and hundreds of people were going to be there. Oh... and how did I feel about doing the speech in Japanese? The jet lag was already kicking in and my body ached with fatigue. I stood in the crush of people and smoked a few cigarettes, lost for words.

Everything was so familiar: the people, the humidity, the passing conversations, the smell of Mild Seven – it was like I'd never left.

'It's good to see you,' I said to Kazue. 'You're getting married. Wow – congratulations.'

'Thanks. No big deal, really. Bryan needs visa... We want to be together too. But parents say, "Oi, married!"'

'So, are you nervous?'

'Yes,' she admitted.

'Hmm, I think you will... shit pants,' I said, laughing.

After sleeping for 12 hours, I sat alone on Kazue's bed with a pen and paper, trying to write my speech. My anxiety was steadily rising. It was slightly alarming that all my anecdotes either required that you'd been there at the time or had a deep cultural understanding of British humour and experience of getting expelled, drunk, high, lost, run over, hallucinating, hitchhiking, breakdancing, raving, or fighting – none of which I imagined made for good material in conservative Japan. I opted for a few weak jokes alluding to Bryan's previous life and a bit of slushy 'Seriously-folks-they're-made-for-each-other' stuff. Then I sat for a long time, trying to shake the mental image of hundreds of respectable Japanese people staring at me in silence with their mouths open.

On the day of the wedding, Tokyo was red-hot and clammy. I found myself loitering in the foyer of a massive five-star hotel, wearing an uncomfortable, itchy woollen suit, surrounded by guests and relatives. Bryan's dad, Andy, and his sister, Louise, hovered next to me in British solidarity. They'd arrived a few days earlier and were staying in the hotel with a cohort of helpers.

'Oh, all right, Toby,' said Andy, in a relaxed Devonshire accent, as if we had bumped into each other in the pub. Andy was a farmer and ran his own welding business; he was a cider-drinking, unflappable, old-school kind of a guy – not the sort of person you tended to run into in downtown Tokyo. I heard a familiar voice: 'TOBYSAAAAN.' It was Nabi-chan, beckoning me to follow him down a hallway. I ran after him into a side room, where I was bundled to the floor by the rest of the kendo teachers. They were shouting my name excitedly and hugging me. It was fantastic to see them all again and, in the time it took me to peel myself off the floor, a drink had been thrust into my hand and a round of *kampai*s begun. Suzuki-san and Takahashisan were looking legendary, dressed in ceremonial kendo regalia, holding shining *katana*s. They'd been putting the finishing touches to a sword demonstration that was due to happen after the ceremony.

Behind them stood a sweating, grinning personification of terror and anxiety – it took me a few seconds to recognise Bryan. He was kitted out in full traditional Japanese wedding robes, *hakama*, fan, etc., his head was shaved bald and he wore an exhausted expression.

It was really quite impressive that he was going through with this, as a wedding pretty much encapsulated every kind of social interaction he most dreaded.

'Jesus fucking Christ, Tobes,' he gasped, briefly interrupting his pacing to give me a hug.

'Yeah, look at you. Wow... I mean, it's great. *Seriously*, congratulations... Damn.'

I shook my head in proud disbelief. He looked amazing. Nervous, but amazing. We chatted at a million miles an hour and chain-smoked like expectant fathers. I did my best to try to calm him down, while the kendo teachers took photos of him and shouted words of encouragement.

A little later, Aono Sensei beckoned me into another adjoining room, where 20 or 30 high-ranking relatives were seated in stern rows as people were formally marched past and introduced. I stood to attention, bowed and presented myself. Aono Sensei gave them a quick résumé, then we stood to the side as the formalities continued. I wasn't sure what he'd said, but suspected it was something like: 'Toby-san is young and naive, a Christian and very wrong. Please forgive him.'

Then he turned, nudged me hard in the ribs and laughed. 'Kendo was too difficult for you, eh.'

I nodded and felt remorseful. He was right though. He really was. I *had* been young and naive. At least, my quest to master kendo had been. But instead, I'd had an experience unlike anything I could have imagined. It hadn't been like the martial-arts movies I loved so much; it had been real.

Aono-san then put his arm around me and gave me an unprecedented hug.

'But you are still one of us,' he said kindly, straightening my tie and smiling.

I was completely speechless. It was the nicest thing he'd ever said to me.

The wedding ceremony took place at a small Shinto shrine inside the hotel. Bryan and Kazue stood to attention in front of the altar, petrified but radiant. Kazue looked remarkable in her traditional *shiromaku*[1] kimono and headgear and, as ever, appeared as calm as a surgeon – no mistakes allowed. Her parents had laid down the law: if you're going through with this, then it's the traditional way or the highway.

---

1. *Shiromaku – shiro* meaning 'white' and *maku* meaning 'pure'.

The service lasted a long time and, as with most weddings, everyone breathed a sigh of relief when the formalities were over. Afterwards, we were escorted into a giant banqueting hall decked out with flowers, round tables, balloons and spotlights. I noted with interest that the table I was on was populated almost exclusively by young, attractive, eligible girls; someone was trying to tell me something. The place began to fill up, and soon hundreds of people were drinking and chatting like there was no tomorrow. The teachers were all seated at the front and loud bursts of '*Kampai*' rang out with a gusto that can only come from senior *kendoka* on the lash. Kazue's parents worked the room, checking on their guests and giving gifts. Bryan's dad followed, chatting away in English to an uncomprehending but receptive audience. He wandered past, stopped and attempted to pour me a pint of *sake*.

'This is a pretty good party, I reckon. Cheers, Tobe.'

A girl sidled up and announced that she was going to shadow my speech and help translate the bits I was struggling with – which was basically most of it. I showed her what I'd written and she froze in alarm before explaining that a certain word meant 'semen' if pronounced incorrectly. I sighed with the inevitability of it all and began practising over and over till she was satisfied. I felt my anxiety rising again: 'Ladies and gentlemen, hello and spunk!' Brilliant.

The lights went down and the opening chords of 'Bad Moon Rising' blared out over the PA system. Bryan strode into the room, spotlit, wearing a suit and trilby and looking sharp and focused, swiftly followed by Kazue, to the flowery melody of The Carpenters's 'Close to You'. The room erupted into an unrestrained frenzy of cheering and clapping, cameras flashed and glasses were raised. Once they were seated on stage, I was gobsmacked to hear the pounding, yet highly apt drum-and-bass classic, '*Ni Ten Ichi Ryu*',[2] which sampled traditional Japanese drums, woodblocks and sword slices. Suzuki-san and Takahashisan entered dramatically from opposite ends of the room and performed a dazzling *kata* in time to the music to rapturous ovations. It was a real spectacle and they couldn't have given a more fitting tribute. Then the speeches began. I don't remember who was up before me, but once my name was announced and the spotlight hit me, I stumbled to the stage on jellied legs and bowed in front of the packed room to an intimidating hush. I looked over at Bryan and Kazue and back to the expectant crowd.

'*Konbanwa!*' ('Good evening.')

---

2. Photek, '*Ni Ten Ichi Ryu*' ('Two-swords Technique'), Virgin (1997) – roughly, 'School of Two Heavens as One', referring to the double-sword style originated by the legendary Japanese master Miyamoto Musashi (1584–1645).

The kendo tables exploded into unrestrained applause. I waved and bowed back. (Phew, so far so good.)

'*Kazue wa cho kirei des.*' ('Kazue is very beautiful.')

(Thunderous applause.)

'*Hanayome kaizo hito wa cho kirei desu.*' ('Bridesmaids are very beautiful.')

(More thunderous applause.)

'*Bryan wa, lucky.*' ('Bryan is lucky.')

The crowd went wild: '*Hooray, kampai, fighto…*'

The next few minutes were a riot of cheering and laughter totally dispro-portionate to my speechmaking skills. I staggered back to my table, grateful for the anonymity of the darkness, shaking with relief. I don't think anybody really cared what I'd said; it was just the fact that I'd got up there and said it.

The wedding party dissolved into a series of half-remembered images and garbled conversations. We ended up in a basement club, where I managed to accidentally tell the Japanese girl I'd been attempting to chat up all evening that she was old, at which she angrily stormed off and ignored me for the rest of the evening. I'd been trying to say that she *wasn't* old, but Japanese grammar diffi-cult is. Meanwhile, everyone else was happy, singing and hugging each other, declaring their undying loyalty and cementing new friendships. The last thing I remember was leaning against a wall unable to speak, dripping in sweat as the room hummed around me. I didn't understand where I was or what was going on – it was just like old times in the Ninja House.

A few days later, I was back at Suzuki-san's house in Yoshiwara, kneeling at his living-room table with the kendo teachers, as the last rays of a glorious blood-red sunset shone through the mosquito screen of the back door. The long-eared 'wife-spy' cats purred their contentment and lounged next to us in the rapidly darkening room. An overhead fan cut through the clammy air as we sweated and talked in hushed tones. It felt as if everyone had played their part and hon-our had been done. Finally, we could relax and let off some steam. Bryan and Kazue were being newlyweds at the Ninja House and, as I sat alone with the teachers, it seemed as though a new chapter was unfolding. It was clear that they'd missed our company as much as Bryan and I had missed theirs. I lis-tened to their animated conversations about kendo, fighting spirit and life, and I understood more than ever.

In the early hours, as I slept among the teachers where we had fallen, Suzuki-san woke me with a soft shake of the shoulder. Bryan was standing next to him, grinning like a maniac.

'Wake up. We're going on an adventure,' said Bryan.

'What are you doing here? Aren't you meant to be with Kazue?'

Yeah, I was, but she's asleep. Plenty of time for being married later. Come on, let's go.'

'What? Where are we going?' My head was reeling from the previous night's drinking.

'Up Fuji Yama... Shhh... Ouchy. Japan *kibishi*,' whispered Suzuki-san.

'Oh God. Are you guys *serious*?'

'Kendo challenge, *fighto, ei goh!*' ('Let's go!')

It occurred to me that Suzuki-san possibly enjoyed pain. As we tiptoed out of the room, Nabi-chan stirred and whispered, 'Toby-san, up Fuji Yama. *Gambatte.*'

I motioned for him to come with us, but he just waved me away, rolled over and laughed himself back to sleep.

It was still dark when we reached the car park that signified the beginning of the ascent. I fell out of the van mildly drunk and giddy, already exhausted by the heavy toll of the previous few days. In fact, it would have been hard to have chosen a point in time when I was less prepared to climb a volcano. In contrast, Bryan seemed as fresh as a daisy.

Suzuki-san fumbled in the back of the van, gathering supplies. He presented us with sturdy, shoulder-height walking sticks with a few Fuji Yama stamps burnt on to them – mementoes awarded at the summit from previous expeditions. Then he brought his own out; it was covered with them all over, like old battle scars.

We set off along the path, winding up towards an unfathomable darkness. At first, the going was fairly moderate and I stumbled my way after them, trying to sober up and catch my breath. I stared at my feet and tried not to think about how far we had to go. But as the first blue haze of faint light revealed the upclose scale of the mountain, I began to get a sense of what lay before us. The path had widened and turned into tortuous, jagged, loose volcanic rock. It felt like one step forward, two steps back. This was about as intense a climb as was possible before training and equipment became necessary.

A few other early risers were out on the trail and we exchanged the odd greeting and words of encouragement. The route was broken up into several sections, each shorter than the last, but taking longer as the altitude increased. Soon, the sun burnt through the clouds and with it, the heat of the morning, warming the breeze and making us drip with sweat.

Fuji Yama was turning into my metaphorical nemesis. As I concentrated on putting one foot after the other, over and over, it occurred to me that the whole experience was distinctly Japanese – a challenge, a struggle, each stage requiring perseverance and stamina. You couldn't fight it; you just endured it – a lot like kendo training. Along the way, as we rose in altitude, the white bank of surrounding fog would tantalisingly reveal the vista momentarily, before concealing it again.

Occasionally, we would pass a drinks stall or teahouse, where a few weary-looking tourists were taking on fluids, determination and fatigue etched across their faces, but we mainly carried on. If I'd learnt anything during my time here, it was to take a certain amount of pain and trust in Suzuki-san's supernatural force of will that hardships were really no big deal, and we were actually having fun. For him, life was simple – everything that happened was either lucky or a challenge.

The last couple of stages were a sadistically slow-motion affair. I wasn't sure if the altitude was affecting me, but I felt high as a kite, and several times Suzuki-san and Bryan stopped to examine me with seriously concerned looks on their faces. The final stage was Everest-like in its intensity. I'd take a couple of steps, stop, pant, look up at the summit, curse, place my head against the staff and silently scream cheesy one-liners at myself: 'Come on man', 'Do it for honour', 'Think of the children', 'Fight, fight, fiiiiight' – repeat. At one point, an elderly chap who looked about a hundred years old overtook us. I watched him casually amble past and gasped a good morning with my mouth hanging open.

Yeah, that's it, you healthy old bastard. I bet you've just popped up here for a pint of milk. Jesus, what's wrong with these people? I thought, as I struggled along, panting like a dying fish.

As I finally staggered through the ancient, sun-bleached *torii*[3] gateway marking the summit, I was too numb with exhaustion to really feel triumphant. A steady gale blew across the pinnacle and a small collection of corrugated timber buildings weighed down by black rocks sheltered groups of shattered hikers and offered some respite from the cold. The inside of the volcano was an impressive black, smoking hole of massive, quarry-like boulders. It occurred to me that in all the time I'd spent gazing up at Fuji Yama, I'd never once imagined what it would actually be like up here or what lay inside the peak. Since that summer's morning when it had first revealed itself to me through the parting clouds, it had always been there, dominating the background, a Hokusai masterpiece, making it impossible for anyone to forget they were in Japan. Like

3. *Torii* – literally, 'bird perch': a traditional Japanese gate, seen as a metaphorical and actual entrance to a sacred site.

the distant horizon, it had existed in my mind more as a concept than a reality, but for anyone living in its shadow it was impossible not to fall under its iconic spell.

We collapsed on to some jutting rocks and, for the first time, I really looked down on the world below. We were high above the clouds, a vast panorama of brilliant sky and sunshine, so immense it was hard to look at. A few ripped Tibetan prayer flags fluttered and danced in the wind, and below us, tiny dots of determined hikers paused on the final stages of their climb, oblivious to everything but their pain and effort.

Suzuki-san rummaged in his backpack and pulled out a bottle of *sake*.

'You've got to be kidding,' I said.

'*Ie, ie.*' ('No, no.') He laughed, putting his hands together and doing a comedy chant. He poured a thin stream of alcohol into the wind as an offering, lit some incense, shut his eyes and said a prayer. Then he came and sat back down next to us and took a slug from the bottle.

'Now different,' he said, patting my chest and smiling. 'Toby-san, in Japan, up Fuji Yama, heart strongu – this is a pen.' He turned and placed his hand on Bryan's shoulder. '*Ichi-go ichi-e,*' he said dramatically.

Bryan nodded and Suzuki-san motioned for him to explain it to me. He toyed with the words for a moment, translating them in his head, then said, 'He means, one-time one-meeting,' with slow deliberation. 'It's a famous Japanese phrase referring to something that only ever happens once in a lifetime. He means we're lucky to be here, in this time and place; life is never going to happen quite like this again.'

I thought about what it had taken for me to get here: the craziness and ordeal of kendo and the unprecedented madness of the Factory of Dreams; in my mind, they'd almost become one and the same. I wasn't really sure if I'd walked the path of the warrior during my time in Japan. I suspected that I'd been stumbling about in some adjacent bushes, but it didn't seem to matter anymore. Either way, it had been a journey and, like all good journeys, it was the travelling and the company, not the destination that stayed with you. Bryan and Suzuki-san looked calm and regal, sitting chatting and smiling on top of Mount Fuji, confident, relaxed, samurai-like – as though they'd always belonged there. The scenery was sublime. We sat for a long time, supping the *sake* and gazing down at the ethereal white clouds. Finally, we began the equally arduous descent, urging each other on and laughing all the way.

Epilogue

In the cold hours of the early morning, as I departed Bristol bus station on the final leg of my return journey from Japan, I slung my heavy bags over my shoulder and began the long walk through the centre of town towards a friend's house. The streets were almost deserted apart from the occasional all-night taxi. Ahead of me, three suspicious figures crossed the road between the murky street lamps and began advancing towards me. There was something suspicious about the way they moved. I clocked it immediately – something threatening – but it was too late to alter my path. As they closed in, it became obvious they were looking for trouble.

'All right, mate, got any money?' It wasn't a request.

I was well and truly surrounded. Things were about to get serious. I clearly heard Suzukisan's voice echo in my mind: *Tobysan – fighto!*

'I said, you-got-any-money?' said the leader, pointing a finger aggressively towards me. In the time between him finishing his sentence and taking his next in-breath, I struck him directly in the windpipe – hard and fast. Before his body hit the ground, I was already behind the second guy and had him crying out in pain as I took control of his balance and half crippled him with a twisting nerve lock on his arm. Instinctively, I used his immobilised body as a barrier between myself and the third guy, who was staring down at his friend on the floor, watching him writhing and gasping for air. The colour drained from his face – he took one look at me and ran for it. Then it was a simple manoeuvre to flip the second guy on to his back on top of his choking friend. I slid a wooden *bokken* from my bag and swung it round my head a few times. The two guys picked themselves up and limped off as fast as they could. I turned and winked at the group of attractive girls watching me from a distance…

'*I said, you got any money, mate?*'

I snapped back to reality. Carefully and very calmly, I put my bag down on the ground and looked him dead in the eye. I was resigned and ready for whatever was about to happen. The other two stood either side of me, looking jittery and unsure of themselves, peering into the distance, shifting their weight nervously from side to side.

'No,' I said in a calm but absolutely confident, matter-of-fact way.

I saw them take in the body armour and swords protruding from my bag. They glanced back at each other hesitantly; it was obvious they were reconsidering me as an easy late-night target. I was probably a dangerous escaped lunatic and almost certainly going to be a hell of a lot more trouble than I was worth. Besides, I was probably skint anyway.

'Sorry, guys,' I said in an upbeat, friendly way, giving them a genuine smile. 'I've really gotta go. See you later.'

With that, I picked up my bag and began walking away. I didn't look back, but carefully monitored their movements by the reflections in the windows of parked cars. Quietly, they watched me go and didn't follow. I hadn't backed down. I hadn't panicked. And I sure as hell wasn't scared. As I walked on down the road, I heard Suzukisan's kendo wisdom in my head one more time.

'Lucky.'

Author's Note

Lost in Translation

I never did quite master Japanese (along with kendo), therefore any mistakes in translation, inaccurate Romanisation of Japanese characters or attempts to explain "Jinglish" (Japanese English) are entirely my own and I beg the reader's indulgence.

Acknowledgments

Paper Tigers has been a long and emotional journey, which only came to fruition because of friends, family and patrons who believed this was a story worth telling. A heartfelt thank you to everyone who pledged to turn this book into a reality. Your generous support and enthusiasm have been humbling.

I am hugely grateful to the entire Unbound team, particularly Xander Cansell and Annabel Wright, and my superb and patient editors, Sadie Mayne, Emma Brady, Molly Powell and Anne Newman. The very talented Mark Ecob at Mecob Design Ltd. And a special thanks to Rory Mitchinson for his expert help with the Japanese.

Love and appreciation to everyone who read my early drafts and gave me feedback: my mother, Hannah, Molly, Sarah, Lucy, Toby, Matt, Dom & Caroline. Your encouragement was invaluable.

Finally, I owe a sincere and deep debt of gratitude to Suzuki Sensei and the Yoshiwara kendo teachers all those years ago for inspiring a couple of Western dropouts, and to Kazue Sakata and family for their warmth and hospitality. And most of all, to my friend Bryan, who lived his life like a dragon and was never a paper tiger.

Patrons

Stella Ayles-Evans
Jess Barlow
Paulina Batiste
Paul Botterell
Orlando Buckland
Phineas Cheshire
Carianne Clarke
Viv Curley
Elizabeth Ely
Hannah Ely
Louise Endacott
Dan Fenwick
Mike Fitzgerald
Geoff Fox
Kaley Gorman
Amber Hale
Imogen Harding
Toby Hatchett
Matthew Henderson
Alison Hynd
Jeffrey Inwood
Dan Jamieson
Jim Karthauser
Josef Karthauser
Akane Kawatake
Letty Lightfoot
William McCarthy
Simon Mogridge
Brian Moss
Amy Oliver
Gregory Olver
Vanessa Pilny
Madeleine Pittaway
Michelle Pluck
Luce Poynter

Naomi Puddefoot
Alix Riley
Jo Robertson
Simon Ryder
Lydia Samuel
Saori Shimada
Joe Short
Robin Smith
Jessica Stickland
Gabor Szokol
Gavyn Upham
Sean Wheeler
Rush Wickramasinghe
Alice Wood